Ethnic Lobbies
and US Foreign Policy

ETHNIC LOBBIES

AND

US FOREIGN

POLICY

David M. Paul
Rachel Anderson Paul

LYNNE
RIENNER
PUBLISHERS

BOULDER
LONDON

Published in the United States of America in 2009 by
Lynne Rienner Publishers, Inc.
1800 30th Street, Boulder, Colorado 80301
www.rienner.com

and in the United Kingdom by
Lynne Rienner Publishers, Inc.
3 Henrietta Street, Covent Garden, London WC2E 8LU

Library of Congress Cataloging-in-Publication Data
Paul, David M.
  Ethnic lobbies and US foreign policy / David M. Paul
and Rachel Anderson Paul.
        p. cm.
  Includes bibliographical references and index.
  ISBN 978-1-58826-609-5 (hardcover : alk. paper)
  1. United States—Foreign relations—1989—Citizen participation.
2. Minorities—United States—Political activity. 3. Lobbying—United States.
I. Title.
  JZ1480.P483 2008
  327.73—dc22

                                                            2008023386

British Cataloguing in Publication Data
A Cataloguing in Publication record for this book
is available from the British Library.

Printed and bound in the United States of America

    Printed on 30% postconsumer recycled paper

    The paper used in this publication meets the requirements
    of the American National Standard for Permanence of
    Paper for Printed Library Materials Z39.48-1992.

    5 4 3 2 1

To our parents

Contents

Tables and Figures

▓ Figures

Acknowledgments

A number of scholars graciously provided valuable advice over the course of this project, including Paul Allen Beck, Clyde Brown, Stacey Pelika, Ken Wald, Herb Weisberg, and Jack Wright. In addition, Tom Ambrosio, Rick Herrmann, Ric Uslaner, and Hillel Weinberg provided very helpful feedback, including reading various drafts of the manuscript.

Arnold Dashefsky, Ron Miller, and Ira M. Sheskin graciously provided data for estimating Jewish populations in a number of key metropolitan areas. Angela Brittingham of the US Census Bureau and Sofia Mariona of the Center for Responsive Politics supplied us with information about the research methods of their respective organizations. Kay Lehman Schlozman allowed us to use the survey that she and John T. Tierney developed as the basis for our survey of ethnic group leaders.

At Ohio State University–Newark, Tauni Graham was very helpful in securing library resources. A number of students at the university provided research assistance, including Nick Bendure, Kate Bowman, Matt Brown, Ashley Caggiano, Michael Logan, Leonard "Bud" McManaway, Alex Nixon, Emily Perry, Leslie Piatt, Erin Richardson, Jennifer Richie, and Kirill Zelin. Nick Bendure's help was especially valuable over the final year of the project (and Nick received the 2008 Newark Campus Student Employee of the Year award for his efforts with this project).

A number of policymakers provided generous assistance, either in terms of reviewing the in-depth survey in the pretesting phase, participating in the study itself, or elucidating issues that arose during the study. They include Gregory Adams, Ted Brennan, Bruce Brown, Kevin Fitzpatrick, Adam Francis, Tiffany Guarascio, Dennis Halpin, Robert King, Deborah Malac, Bob Ney, Walter North, Frank Pallone, Leonard Scensny, Pat Tiberi, and Hillel Weinberg. In addition, a number of ethnic group leaders graciously lent their time to this project, including Tom Albert, Karl Altau, Bill Fletcher, Aram

Hamparian, Stephan Kline, Sean McManus, Floyd Mori, Stella O'Leary, Helen Samhan, and Kani Xulam. Other policymakers and ethnic group leaders also were very generous with their time, but declined to be acknowledged. In an era when many policymakers refuse academic interviews, these policymakers and ethnic group leaders deserve special thanks for providing scholars and citizens alike a better understanding of the foreign policy–making process.

Finally, we thank everyone at Lynne Rienner Publishers for their support of this book, and in particular Leanne Anderson, Shena Redmond, Sonia Smith, and Claire Vlcek for their help in ensuring that the book was published.

— David M. Paul,
Rachel Anderson Paul

1

Introduction

In March 1999, the North Atlantic Treaty Organization (NATO) expanded to include three new members: Poland, Hungary, and the Czech Republic. While US president Bill Clinton and US secretary of state Madeleine Albright were jubilant, not all world leaders shared their enthusiasm, and many groused that the US-led effort to expand NATO had less to do with national and geopolitical security, and more to do with domestic, ethnic group politics. In 1997, Canadian prime minister Jean Chrétien complained to Belgian prime minister Jean-Luc Dehaene and Luxembourg prime minister Jean-Claude Juncker (and inadvertently into an open microphone) that NATO expansion was occurring because "ethnic voting blocks in the United States are pushing their cause" (Harris 1997, A24). Chrétien went on to object that NATO expansion "has nothing to do with world security. It's because in Chicago, Mayor [Richard] Daley controls lots of votes for the [Democratic] nomination" (as quoted in Harris 1997, A24). Even Casimir Lenard, the director of the Polish American Congress and a key supporter of NATO expansion, seemed to agree that President Clinton had electoral reasons for spearheading the NATO expansion: "He needed votes. . . . That's how it happened" (as quoted in Longworth 1998).

NATO expansion of these three states and the eventual expansion to include more Central European, Eastern European, and Baltic states would seem to be a clear example of ethnic American groups driving US foreign policy. Over the past several decades, the ability and power of ethnic interest groups to influence US foreign policy have become accepted as fact by scholars, journalists, and analysts. For example, Samuel Huntington argues that, in addition to commercial interests, "transnational and nonnational ethnic interests have come to dominate foreign policy" (1997). Likewise, the late George F. Kennan asserted that there have been numerous instances since World War II where "ethnic minorities have brought pressures with a

1

view to influencing foreign policy on behalf of what they perceive as the interests of their former mother country" (1977, 6). Tony Smith claims that "ethnic groups play a larger role in the making of U.S. foreign policy than is widely recognized" (2000, 1), while Eric Uslaner contends, "foreign policy decisions increasingly reflect ethnic interests rather than some overarching sense of national interest" (2002, 356). In a similar fashion, numerous journalists report that ethnic lobbies influence significantly the formulation of US foreign policy (see Felton 1984b; Doherty 1995a, 1996b; Longworth 1998).

Yet others contend that foreign policy decisions are determined by other actors, and these scholars give little attention to the influence of ethnic lobbies and other interest groups. Although he acknowledges that ethnic groups are the "most noticeable" of the organizations active in foreign affairs and defense policy, John Tierney asserts that "generally speaking . . . the record of ethnic group lobbying success is far less imposing, to the point that most analysts seem to agree that the impact of such groups on American foreign policy is minimal" (1994, 118). Peter Haas emphasizes that knowledge-based experts play a key role in affecting foreign policy because they articulate "the cause-and-effect relationship of complex problems, helping states identify their interests, framing the issues for collective debate, proposing specific policies, and identifying salient points for negotiation" (1992, 2). Still other scholars prescribe to the median-voter model, contending that elected officials strive to gauge public opinion and develop policies that are similar to the policy preferences of most voters (see Jacobs and Page 2005 for review). If the median-voter model is correct, ethnic groups should have little sway over elected officials unless they comprise a sizable portion of a politician's district.

So, which perspective is most correct? Are US policymakers, and hence foreign policy, beholden to ethnic groups? Or do ethnic groups play a relatively modest role in the formulation of US policies? This study aims to help scholars, analysts, and citizens understand better the role that ethnic interest groups play in formulating foreign policy. While business, labor, and public interest groups are widely studied, there is a relative dearth of research on ethnic lobbies. Historically, many scholars ignored ethnic interest groups in part because of the perception that interest groups, in general, have a modest impact on US foreign policy (Paul 1999). While domestic politics have long been characterized as a competition among contending interests, foreign policy remained relatively insulated from group pressures for much of the history of the United States. Yet, globalization has increased the influence of foreign dynamics on traditional domestic realms, such as trade, labor, and the environment. This, combined with the end of the Cold War, has resulted in an environment in which ethnic groups are more likely to deem lobbying as advantageous and necessary.

A major question addressed by this project is: Which ethnic lobbies are most powerful, and why? Although the power of ethnic interest groups has come under increasing scrutiny over the past several decades, little systematic research has been completed that examines a cross section of ethnic groups and lobbies.[1] The Israeli, Armenian, Greek, Irish, and Cuban lobbies are routinely cited by policy analysts as having a disproportionate amount of political sway. For example, Uslaner (2002) states that the Israeli lobby is the most powerful ethnic lobby, followed by the Cuban and Greek lobbies. David Ottaway and Dan Morgan stated in 1999 that the Jewish American and Armenian American lobbies are "two of the best organized and financed Washington lobbies" (A15). Elyse Semerdjian reported in 1997 that the three most effective ethnic lobbies were the Israeli, Greek, and Armenian lobbies. However, no quantitative data exist that measure the ordinal influence of these and other ethnic lobbies, and the lack of data inhibits the systematic study of why some ethnic groups are more powerful than others. For example, in the absence of a ranking of the most powerful ethnic lobbies, it is impossible to use quantitative methods to determine which factors help explain the relative influence of these lobbies. Even if the conclusion is that ethnic groups exercise less influence than their critics charge, we may gain a better understanding of the role ethnic groups do play in the policymaking process. Even scholars who caution that ethnic groups are not as powerful as their detractors claim still assert that "ethnicity has become an essential ingredient in the domestic politics" of the United States and other states (Goldberg 1990, 3). A more rigorous analysis of ethnic groups will also allow us to evaluate the applicability of broad interest group theories to different kinds of interest groups. For example, we can examine if ethnic interest groups behave like other grassroots or mass-membership organizations.

A second question asked in this book is: How does the power of ethnic lobbies compare to business, labor, elites, and public opinion? If scholars are to understand the nature of the foreign and intermestic[2] policy choruses, and determine if they sing in a pluralistic, elitist, or majoritarian key, it is important to examine all sections of the choir. For example, the analysis by Jacobs and Page (2005) largely excludes ethnic groups, while the study by Powlick (1995) does not distinguish between business, labor, and ethnic groups. We hope to contribute to understanding the pluralistic puzzle better by determining what role ethnic groups and other actors actually play in the policymaking process.

Further, this study contributes to our understanding of democratic governance, by seeking to answer the question of who gets to influence foreign policy, and ascertaining the degree to which the public can affect the foreign policy–making process. If ethnic American groups are *too* powerful, then democratic governance may be held hostage by a small minority of

Americans. On the other hand, if ethnic American groups have very little influence, then democratic governance may also suffer, since the policy-making process is unresponsive to citizens.

In addition, it is hoped that this study enriches the interest group literature by better conceptualizing and measuring influence, and we contend that the context of the group's goals and activities is critical to understanding the relative power of the group. Specifically, we assert that groups that are defending the status quo have a strategic advantage and, hence, will be perceived as being more powerful than groups attempting to alter the status quo. Further, like Smith (2000), we believe that the political and social context affects the ability of ethnic interest groups to influence the policymaking process. The terrorist acts of September 11, 2001, and the subsequent war on terrorism may have reduced the ability of some or all ethnic groups to influence foreign policy.

Finally, like Smith and DeConde, we hope to make a contribution to the normative debate on the implications of ethnic group activity. The power of ethnic lobbies to influence policymaking is an issue of substantive importance to both scholars and practitioners. Although there may be benefits of ethnic group involvement in foreign policy formulation, such as bringing new ideas to the policymaking process generated by previously marginalized groups, many contend that "the negative consequences of ethnic involvement may well outweigh the undoubted benefits this activism at times confers on America in world affairs" (Smith 2000, 2). For example, John Mearsheimer and Stephen Walt created a firestorm of controversy by asserting that the policies advocated by many Jewish Americans and the wider Israeli lobby actually "jeopardize U.S. national security" (2007, 8). Moreover, eyeing the success of ethnic groups such as Jewish Americans and Armenian Americans, other ethnic groups (such as Indian Americans and Pakistani Americans) are trying to increase their impact on US foreign policy making (see Pomper and Chatterjee 2000; Morgan and Merida 1997; McIntire 2006). In the words of George Kemp: "As different ethnic groups achieve new prominence in the United States, the diversity of foreign policy concerns will increase, and so too will the overlap between foreign policy and domestic issues" (1999, 163). In short, critics are concerned that as these new ethnic American groups enter the policymaking arena, their voices will further impair and cloud the formulation of American foreign policy.

The findings presented in this book may counterbalance some of these apprehensions. We do not disagree with Smith's assertion that ethnic lobbies have greater access in foreign and intermestic policy making today than, say, in 1940. However, we are not convinced that this increased access is detrimental, or that ethnic groups as a whole have too much influence in the policymaking process. Indeed, there is evidence that ethnic groups can pose an important countervailing force to business interests and the lobbies of foreign governments. For example, ethnic lobbies have brought increased attention to human rights abuses, and efforts by ethnic Americans have made US immigration policy more equitable by easing restrictions on non-European immigrants. The findings also confirm that new ethnic American groups are entering the policymaking process, but the study found little evidence that their efforts have an overwhelming influence on US foreign policy. The hope is that this study will enable scholars and practitioners to better judge the relative and contextual influence of ethnic groups when developing normative judgments of that influence.

■ The Contemporary Foreign Policy–Making Environment, Ethnic Groups, and Pluralism

Although contemporary scholars acknowledge that ethnic groups have long sought to influence foreign policy, many scholars who studied foreign policy during the twentieth century virtually ignored ethnic groups and other domestic actors, considering them to be irrelevant to foreign policy making. This was due in part to the Cold War, which helped establish a foreign policy consensus that featured "a layer of political leadership that in large measure agreed on the ends and means of U.S. foreign policy, an attentive public that followed this leadership, and a mostly inert, mass public generally uninterested and uninvolved in foreign affairs, but nevertheless hostile to communism" (Melanson 2005).[3] Often, the strength of this consensus left little room for domestic actors to influence the foreign policy process. However, the Vietnam War and the end of the Cold War eroded the consensus, yielding a splintered range of opinions regarding US foreign affairs that required presidents to form coalitions in an attempt to construct a new foreign policy consensus (Melanson 2005). Likewise, Robert Entman (2004) asserts that the ability of presidents to successfully influence public opinion has declined since the end of the Cold War because the media are providing greater independent coverage of foreign policy issues.

The lack of a post–Cold War consensus and changes in the geopolitical environment created new opportunities for ethnic groups to affect the foreign policy–making process since there is no longer a singular "national interest" driving US policymaking. For example, Smith posits that, since the collapse of the Soviet Union and the end of the Cold War, ethnic Americans are more interested in being active in world affairs than the general public, and the opening of the political system at home has allowed greater ethnic group influence in foreign affairs. Likewise, Michael Clough argues that "the regionalization of global policy making, the impact of ethnicity on American foreign policy and the rise of powerful global issue groups" have fundamentally changed the foreign policy–making process (2001, 2). Walt (2005) contends that even the war on Al Qaida and terror does not provide the overarching objective to limit the ability of domestic forces—such as ethnic diasporas—from setting foreign policy priorities.

Further, as distinctions between the foreign and domestic policy spheres became increasingly interconnected and nebulous, many foreign policy issues began affecting Americans economically, leading to an increase in domestic groups seeking to influence foreign policy (Uslaner 1991). Manning (1977) describes this blurred distinction between domestic and foreign policy as "intermestic," and many analysts believe frameworks that exclude domestic actors are not valid depictions of the foreign policy process (see, for example, Adler and Haas 1992, 367).

In addition, institutional changes in the legislative branch may be an important component to the changing nature of foreign policy making. While Congress yielded much of its foreign policy authority to the president during the 1950s and 1960s, Congress became much more active in foreign affairs in the 1970s in large part because of the unpopular Vietnam War (Lindsay 1994). Further, congressional reforms implemented in the 1970s weakened the power of committee chairs, relaxed the jurisdictional boundaries of committees, and allowed individual members of Congress greater ability to shape legislation through offering floor amendments. In addition, Congress increased its institutional capacity to conduct research by creating entities such as the Congressional Research Service and dramatically increasing the size of Capitol Hill staffs (Melanson 2005). These institutional changes and reforms afford members of Congress much greater opportunities to become foreign policy entrepreneurs, even if they do not sit on the relevant standing committees or possess seniority (Tierney 1994; Melanson 2005). As a result, "Congress today involves itself in a dizzying array of foreign policy issues . . . [and] congressional activism on foreign policy promises to continue in the coming years" (Lindsay 1994, 1). These institutional changes also provide greater incentives for external actors—such as interest groups, think tanks, and even foreign governments—to lobby Congress in an attempt to shape US foreign policy.

Scholars offer diverging judgments, however, on the extent to which Congress does, in fact, determine foreign policy. Some assert that Congress's effect is minimal, as the legislative branch is apt to acquiesce to executive initiatives (Koh 1988; Hinkley 1994). Others disagree, positing that "while Congress enjoys greater success in influencing domestic policy, it remains an important force in the making of foreign policy" (Lindsay 1994, 141). However, James Lindsay contends that the influence of Congress varies greatly depending on the nature of the foreign policy issue. For example, Congress has little influence on foreign policy crises: instead, the president has far greater sway and members of Congress have "little choice but to follow the president's lead" (Lindsay 1994, 147). Nonetheless, Congress can affect strategic policies that outline basic objectives and tactics of foreign policy, such as many diplomatic and defense matters, because the Senate must consent to treaties, Congress has substantial power in terms of regulating commerce, and Congress establishes defense appropriations (Lindsay 1994, 153). Congress enjoys even greater influence with structural policies, such as foreign aid, immigration, and military procurements.

While ethnic groups target Congress because it is often easier to access, the executive branch is not immune from interest group pressures either. For example, Kemp (1999) asserts that concerns of ethnic groups and other domestic groups, such as environmental groups, influence the staff of the National Security Council (NSC). "U.S. foreign policy toward Cuba, South Africa, Israel, or Eastern Europe has to take into account the important domestic constituencies with special interests in these areas" (Kemp 1999, 163).

Ethnic interest groups can affect policymaking for the same reasons that domestic interest groups can influence legislative and bureaucratic decisionmaking: while Americans have long been suspicious of interest groups, the American political system was designed to allow interest groups access to the policymaking process. James Madison, the chief architect of the US Constitution, warned of the "mischief of faction," arguing that factions were a threat to the public good and to personal liberties. Madison (1787) defined a faction as "a number of citizens . . . a majority or a minority . . . adverse to the rights of other citizens," a broad definition that could entail virtually all interest groups today, as well as political parties. Some leaders and members of interest groups may cringe at the phrase "adverse to the rights of other citizens," but the observation is astute: politics involves trade-offs, and championing one issue or right often comes at the expense of another. Few, if any, groups are championing issues that do not infringe on others in at least some capacity: for example, land preservation comes at the expense of property rights. Madison warned that, at their extreme, factions posed two dangers to the nation: they could threaten the public good by promoting the selfish interests of the faction at the expense of the broader public, or they could jeopardize the stability of the political system by encouraging divisiveness within the nation.

Despite these concerns, Madison did not believe factions should be banished, for then "the cure is worse than the disease." Instead, he reasoned that the political process should be designed to control the effects of factions, and he crafted a political system with multiple access points that allow interested parties to affect policymaking in two legislative chambers and the executive branch.[4] Madison hoped that the political system would allow any interested parties to join the political fray, thus ensuring that no one faction could or would dominate the governing process. Political scientists call this competition among interests and groups in policymaking *pluralism,* and many argue that US policymaking is the result of pluralism and not majoritarianism. That is, policymaking does not reflect the majority will of the population: instead, it is a reflection of the political struggle between competing interests.

A criticism of pluralism is that, at times, there is very little competition among interests as some groups and organizations dominate the policymaking process. In such cases, those with power often argue there is nothing disturbing about their influence, since other groups are free to form and attempt to alter policy outcomes. Some even justify their influence on normative grounds, stating that those with power *ought* to dominate the policymaking process. For example, in defending the influence of the Israel lobby, Mitchell Bard contends that "pluralism does not assume that all interests are equal. In fact, most interests are unequal and it is the most powerful, that is, the one that enjoys the balance of lobbying power, which should dominate the market of political ideas" (1991, 5). Not everyone agrees with Bard's assessment. For example, Mearsheimer and Walt argue that while the Israel lobby is simply a collection of powerful interest groups—and not "some sort of cabal or conspiracy"—the lobby has pursued policies that "make little sense on either strategic or moral grounds" (2007, 111–112). As such, they dispute Bard's belief that the strong necessarily should dominate the foreign policy–making process.

▓ Explaining Interest Group Formation

Pluralism is a major paradigm in political science, and political scientists spent much of the twentieth century developing and critiquing the concept. For example, David Truman (1951) argued that as society changes and becomes more complex, new interests form and new groups organize as a result. Nonetheless, not all new interests will translate into new groups: in the case of some causes, interests will remain latent and groups will remain unfounded. However, if a latent interest is threatened by a disturbance, then the interest is likely to organize itself in order to mobilize other like-minded individuals and protect the interest. Truman's *disturbance theory* hypothesizes that interest groups are created in response to social or economic crises in order to make demands of government. In addition, disturbances can help organizations gain new members, often quickly, as the success of a perceived enemy can motivate individuals to join a group and fight the enemy. For example, membership in environmental groups increased during the Ronald Reagan administration, as latent environmentalists became active environmentalists in the face of a perceived threat (Ainsworth 2002). Truman believed the competition among interest groups and the mobilization of new groups would eventually result in an equilibrium in the policymaking process to the extent that new groups respond to crises and balance the demands of other groups. Truman's work provided the core foundation of modern pluralist theory: pluralist politics involves the mobilization of interest groups, with these groups representing different interests and blocs in society; and organized interests and policymakers will engage in bargaining and compromise, thereby ensuring that public policy reflects the preferences of society as a whole.

However, other political scientists posited that group formation and maintenance are by no means guaranteed. Mancur Olson argued that groups often work to obtain collective or public goods, which he defined as "any good such that, if any person . . . in a group . . . consumes it, it cannot be feasibly withheld from others in that group" (1965, 14). For Olson, *individual rationality* trumps the likelihood of individuals working together for collective good and thus prevents some groups from forming: an individual understands that if the good is acquired by the group, then the person will be able to consume the good regardless of whether he or she contributed to its attainment. Many individuals, knowing that they will be able to enjoy the good regardless of their efforts, will choose not to work toward achieving the common good. As a result, the common good is often not achieved because too few individuals contribute to its realization. Clean air is often cited as a classic example of the collective action problem. Individuals may desire clean air, but believe that their actions alone will not determine if the air is clean or not. Individuals also understand they will not be denied the cleaner air if it is achieved. As a result, when faced with the added inconvenience of carpooling or riding a bus, they choose not to change their behavior, and the public good is not achieved. Olson contended that groups must use selective material benefits, benefits that will be given to members and withheld from nonmembers, to induce individuals to join the group.

Others have argued that the Olsonian view, while powerful, does not take into account the full spectrum of benefits that interest groups can offer members. Robert Salisbury (1969) extended Olson's theory by asserting that groups use material, solidarity, and purposive rewards to attract and retain members. For example, the AARP (formerly the American Association of Retired People) uses material rewards such as discounted health insurance to entice Americans over the age of 50 to join their group. Unions provide individuals with social, solidarity, and fraternal rewards that are noticeably absent for nonmembers: indeed, workers who do not join a union may be subject to social stigma, a kind of negative social reward. Many groups use purposive rewards, a recognition that an individual's efforts are critical to the success of the group, to encourage membership and donations. Ideological groups like the Christian Coalition and public interest groups like Amnesty International often appeal to individuals to "make a difference" by joining their cause. Of course, groups often use a mix of rewards (Salisbury 1969; Moe 1980, 1981). For example, the Sierra Club, in addition to providing purposive rewards, may give members material rewards like an attractive calendar, and unions often provide a combination of all three rewards. Research by Terry Moe (1980) provides evidence that purposive incentives are the most important inducement for noneconomically based political groups (like ethnic groups), while selective material benefits are most important for business and labor groups, although purposive incentives are also important for these organizations.

Like all interest groups, ethnic groups face the same problems as they attempt to achieve their own collective goods, from securing foreign aid, to changing immigration policy, to promoting human rights. Most individuals believe their actions alone will not help the group achieve its goals, so they choose not to join the group and work to achieve the collective good. Because of this, ethnic organizations are likely to develop selective incentives to build and maintain membership, and groups that develop such rewards are likely to have a greater and more active membership base. For example, many ethnic groups are not overtly political, instead acting as fraternal organizations (and, thus, providing social rewards to members). However, ethnic groups may provide material benefits (such as calendars, newsletters, and discounted insurance) to members, as well as purposive benefits. Many ethnic groups, like the American Israel Public Affairs Committee (AIPAC) or the Armenian National Committee of America, use purposive rewards to encourage brethren to fight on behalf of their ancestral homeland, donate to a political action committee, and/or contact their members of Congress. However, ethnonational groups face a particularly difficult burden, since they often are attempting to capitalize on a sense of unity with a homeland that many or most members of the ethnic group have never visited or seen.

Entrepreneurs can be critical to group formation and maintenance, since they can provide the initial capital needed to overcome the collective action problem (Salisbury 1969). Salisbury notes that while crises may be important in providing an environment for mobilization, entrepreneurial leadership provides the catalyst for group formation and maintenance. Entrepreneurs can develop the selective incentives to attract and retain members, helping ensure that the group does not wither. An individual (or group of individuals) may form a group for the same reasons that people join groups: for purposive (such as a desire to affect foreign policy), for social (such as a desire to promote community), or for material reasons (such as being paid to be the organization's president).

Part of the power of ethnicity is that it relies on deep attachment to a collective identity, so much so that individual and collective identities can become fused: "when the community is threatened, so is the individual, while the success of a community enhances its members' sense of self-worth" (Esman 1994, 15). But the relationships among individuals, their ethnicity, and ethnic groups are complex and dynamic. Ethnic groups and ethnic leaders may have an exogenous effect on ethnic communities and these collective identities: both groups and elites can boost an ethnic community's pride, and groups and elites can draw on (some might say exploit) potential threats to the ethnic community to mobilize ethnic brethren.[5] In addition, ethnic groups may provide incentives for individuals to maintain ties to the greater community, thereby strengthening communal ties among ethnic individuals. For example, a Greek American group may use tensions between Greece and Turkey to encourage Greek Americans to join and remain active in the Hellenic organization. The Greek group may send action alerts to Greek Americans urging them to help protect ancestral Greece by contacting their members of Congress to enact an arms embargo against Turkey, and to encourage Congress to continue giving military and foreign aid to Greece. The Greek organization may remind members and potential members that their letters to Congress make a difference, as do their donations to a Greek American political action committee, which allows the organization to reward its friends and punish its enemies in Congress. Through its activities, the Greek organization helps to provide a purposive benefit to Greek Americans, one which may help unite the ethnic community beyond the independent effect of the tensions between Greece and Turkey. Because of this, the Greek organization may have an exogenous impact on the Greek American ethnic community.

Maintaining Interest Groups

Interest groups can take many different forms, from small and elite organizations to large mass-based entities. Salisbury (1984) distinguishes between "membership" and "institutional" groups, asserting that these two types of groups have different motivations and differing levels of resources available to them. *Membership or grassroots organizations* are composed of individuals who share a similar policy goal. These groups are often latent, and an organization will not form unless someone takes action to overcome the collective action problem. Pamela Oliver (1984) contends that leaders are especially important to the formation of grassroots organizations, and these leaders are often motivated by the belief that no one else will strive to solve the group's problems. Because of this, leaders must act because no one else will. The main political power of grassroots organizations derives from their main resource: people, or more specifically, people who vote (Gerber 1999). In contrast, *institutional organizations*—such as the US Chamber of Commerce, the American Association of Universities, and the National Governors Association—do not focus on developing a grassroots base, instead inviting a select few to join the organization. Often, members have a financial incentive to join. Olson argued such groups are privileged: they will form naturally, because individuals recognize they will achieve more by working together. The main resource these groups enjoy is financial. Unions are grassroots organizations, while business groups are institutional groups. Ethnic interest groups can fall into either category, although it is expected that ethnic organizations will be more grassroots in nature than institutional since grassroots mobilization plays such a key component in ethnic group influence.

Retaining membership is often a challenge for grassroots groups. While some individuals will join a group and remain a member for decades, others will join once and never renew their membership. Preserving the membership base can be a costly endeavor for groups, and they rely upon marketing techniques such as direct mail to attract new members needed to replace lapsed memberships. Some groups, even groups that view and promote themselves as grassroots organizations, overcome the collective action problem via a patron and client relationship in which a few resource-rich individuals or organizations provide economic and political sponsorship to the organization (McCarthy and Zald 1977; Walker 1983). This strategy mitigates or even negates the need for amassing a large membership in order to finance a successful interest group. Instead, entrepreneurs rely more heavily upon patronage for funding than on amassing membership. Often rewarded with a title (such as a "Gold Member" or part of the "President's Circle") and given recognition in the organization's literature and on its website, patrons can provide significant amounts of funding that subsidize the organization's activity and take pressure off the organization to use its resources to find new members. An analogy is that grassroots organizations are like a sieve and its members are grains of sand poured into the sieve: while new members join, there are always existing members falling out of the group (Johnson 1997). Patrons are akin to stones that help to fill the sieve, thereby reducing (but not eliminating) the need to find new sand to add to the sieve.[6] In doing so, patrons help organizations focus their energies elsewhere. Smith hypothesizes that the threshold for an ethnic interest group to gain access to, and thus have an opportunity to affect, the policymaking process is a budget of "perhaps" $1 million and 250,000 voters across a few congressional districts (2000). Patrons can help make achieving that monetary threshold relatively easy, allowing the organization to devote its resources to mobilizing its membership.

Like patrons, government grants and support can also be critical to the survival of groups, because grants often help offset the overhead costs for organizations, as well as subsidize the salaries of group staffers. Several ethnic organizations, including the Cuban American National Foundation (CANF) and the Armenian Assembly of America, have received millions of dollars from the federal government, either in terms of grants or as payments for services (Newhouse 1992; Dobbs 2001). In addition to helping subsidize groups, the government has played a role in the formation of organizations. For example, according to Smith (2000), in 1953 the State Department asked the president of the World Jewish Conference to "oversee the founding of a single representative institution. The result was the creation of the Conference of Presidents of Major Jewish Organizations, expected to articulate general policy and to be in contact with the President, and the upgrading of AIPAC . . . to operationalize policy and deal with the Congress" (111). Likewise, Patrick Haney and Walt Vanderbush (1999) contend that CANF was formed, in part, at the suggestion of Richard V. Allen, Reagan's national security advisor from 1981 to 1982.

In sum, the study of ethnic political movements is driven by questions concerning ethnic identity maintenance, social and ethnic mobilization, and interest group and social movement participation. To explain the existence and success of ethnic interest groups, it is necessary to develop an understanding of how these groups maintain support given expectations that ethnicity should become less politically important as the world modernizes. Maintaining ethnic identity and convincing ethnic brethren that political participation is important and relevant are necessary to ethnic interest group survival. Understanding the ways that leaders activate ethnic masses over time helps elucidate the reasons for ethnic identity persistence and ethnic interest group success. The above discussion of the interest group literature provides several insights that may explain the formation of ethnic interest groups. First, disturbances may impel ethnic political mobilization, but elites and entrepreneurs may also play a critical role in facilitating collective action by an ethnoracial community. Second, selective incentives, especially purposive and solidarity incentives, are likely to play a role in explaining ethnic mobilization.

Power, Influence, and the Status Quo

Many of the charges leveled against ethnic interest groups are also directed at pluralism more broadly: critics of pluralism often assert that interest groups have become too powerful in the policymaking process, and, as a result, governance suffers (see Lowi 1969; Rauch 1994). In order to assess this claim, the term "power" must be defined more precisely. Traditionally, power is conceptualized as the ability of person A to get person B to do something that B would not otherwise do, and some scholars contend that the study of power is best operationalized by examining conflicts between actors and groups over important issues (see Bachrach and Baratz 1962 and Lukes 1974 for reviews and critiques). However, others assert that this conceptualization of power is unnecessarily limited. For example, in what they label as the second face of power, Peter Bachrach and Morton Baratz contend that "power is also exercised when A devotes his energies to creating or reinforcing social and political values and institutional practices that limit the scope of the political process to public consideration of only those issues which are comparatively innocuous to A" (1962, 918). That is, A has the ability to suppress debate and conflict over certain issues. In a similar manner, E. E. Schattschneider (1960) argues that the powerful will attempt to limit the scope of conflict and thus keep certain issues out of the policymaking process.

While this project examines visible conflicts over agenda control and policymaking, the study of power is nonetheless fraught with difficulties. For example, a member of Congress may not want to admit that an interest group has power over the congressperson. Indeed, the only way to truly test the power of the interest group is to remove the group and see if the behavior of the member of Congress is any different in the group's absence. Political scientists do not have this luxury and must develop other methods of measuring power. Power is an abstract, and tangible measures must be identified.

A central proposition to this research is that some groups have a strategic advantage because they wish to protect existing policies or the status quo. One of the truisms of the US policymaking process is that it is easier for groups to protect existing policies than it is for groups to secure new policies. The openness of the policymaking process creates multiple points at which groups can veto new policies, thus making it easier for groups to protect the status quo than to change it (Hayes 1992). As a result, policymaking tends to be incremental in nature, with few fundamental changes from year to year. Like a military unit perched on top of a hill, groups that seek to protect the status quo possess a tactical advantage and find it easier to defend their position than groups that are attempting to alter existing policies. As such, it is expected a priori that those groups that work to protect the status quo are in a more powerful position, and these groups will be perceived as more influential than those groups that desire to change the status quo.

But is the perception of power a reality? For example, the American Israel Public Affairs Committee (AIPAC) is often cited as the most powerful ethnic interest group in the United States. Indeed, in a 2001 survey conducted by *Fortune* magazine, AIPAC was ranked as the fourth most powerful lobbying group in Washington, trailing only the National Rifle Association, AARP, and the National Federation of Independent Business (Birnbaum 2001). Likewise, Uslaner asserts: "American Jews are distinctive in their ability to affect foreign policy. They have established the most prominent and best-endowed [ethnic] lobby in Washington" (2002, 358). It is clear that the United States has long supported Israel: President Harry S Truman backed the partition plan in 1947, and the United States recognized Israel immediately upon its declaration of independence in 1948 (DeConde 1992; Mearsheimer and Walt 2007). What is less clear is why this relationship has remained so strong. In the words of Mearsheimer and Walt, "With the partial exception of Soviet support for Cuba, it is hard to think of another instance where one country has provided another with a similar level of material aid over such an extended period. . . . the sheer magnitude of U.S. aid [to Israel] is remarkable" (2007, 36). Is this strong relationship between the United States and Israel due to the power of AIPAC, or is it due to other considerations, such as the strategic importance of Israel in the volatile Middle East? Would US policy toward Israel be the same if there was not a single "Jew in America"?[7] Scholars disagree on whether US policy toward Israel is driven by the Jewish American lobby or by strategic interests, and the possibility remains that AIPAC may or may not be as influential as some might think. Since we cannot reverse time, remove AIPAC from the policymaking process, and see if US policy toward Israel is the same, we cannot tell the true power of AIPAC. However, we do know that AIPAC does have a strategic advantage in the current policymaking environment, at least in comparison to groups that may oppose strong US relations with Israel, because it is protecting the status quo. This advantage helps increase the perceived and real influence of the group.

The fact that groups have different goals in terms of protecting or changing the status quo likely means that groups have different strategies. It may also mean that groups may have different types of influence. A strategy of maintaining the status quo requires the ability to influence at least one veto point. Such veto points may be quite small: perhaps a sympathetic committee chair is all that is needed to block changes to existing policy. More likely, maintaining groups wish to have access to several key actors across several institutions in order to influence policy. Ideally, these policymakers would control access to the policymaking agenda, so that proposals to change the status quo can be prevented from even making it to a vote.

In contrast, a strategy for changing the status quo requires the ability to build and marshal enough support to overcome veto points across a number of institutions. Amendments to laws or changes in appropriations require legislative approval, and the legislative process is arduous to navigate. As well as the constitutional veto points of legislation requiring the approval of both chambers of Congress and of the president, "the internal rules and procedures of Congress provide additional veto points where minorities may block or amend threatening proposals" (Hayes 1992, 35). Successful legislation requires the approval of successive majorities at the subcommittee, committee, and floor levels of both the House and the Senate. If the Senate and House versions of the bill are not identical, then the bills must be reconciled and the resulting legislation must be approved by both chambers. Failure at any one of these points kills the measure, and opponents will concentrate their resources on the locations they believe are most hostile to the legislation and thus most likely to obstruct its passage. Groups that desire to change the status quo must secure the support of majorities of both chambers of Congress, as well as majorities in the relevant subcommittees and committees in both the House and the Senate, a harder task than for those seeking status quo goals.

Groups may also be required to implement a mixed strategy: one that attempts to both secure the support of successive majorities and protect the status quo. For example, Jewish Americans who wish to promote US relations with Israel have a strategic advantage: strong US-Israeli relations currently exist, so these ethnic groups are promoting the status quo. Nonetheless, the appropriations process is an annual endeavor, and American groups that support Israel must work to ensure that the United States maintains its monetary and military commitment to the state of Israel. This is a different task than, say, an Armenian American organization that is attempting to block a change in US policy toward Azerbaijan or a Cuban American organization that is attempting to protect the US trade embargo of Cuba. Unless those policies have sunset clauses, they remain the status quo indefinitely.

To date, scholars who examine ethnic interest groups have analyzed more traditional predictors of group influence, such as the size of the ethnic community, the financial resources of the community and its groups, and the degree to which these groups are well organized and institutionalized. However, a better appreciation for the role that the status quo plays in ethnic group politics can aid in our understanding of why some ethnic interest groups appear quite powerful, while others do not.

■ Exploring Numerous Issue Realms

A unique feature of this study is the examination of numerous foreign and intermestic issue realms in which ethnic groups participate and attempt to influence policymaking. By doing so, we can better understand if ethnic groups have influence in some realms more than others, and better address if ethnic groups have influence at all in a specific policy area. After all, simply because an organization, lobby, or lobbying sector is interested in swaying policies does not mean that any influence is achieved. This is, in part, because ethnic communities and organizations are only one set of actors interested in these policy realms.

Many ethnic American communities are interested in influencing foreign policy, and lobbies attempt to affect relations between the United States and the ethnic ancestral homeland. For example, Irish Americans are credited with pushing the Clinton administration to become engaged in the Northern Ireland peace process, and the African American community is credited with influencing the Clinton administration's decision to intervene in Haiti (Glastris et al. 1997; Schlesinger 1997). In some cases, ethnic communities try to strengthen ties between the United States and the ancestral homeland, encouraging the United States to develop stronger relations with the ancestral state. For example, during the Balkan conflict in the 1990s, Serb Americans chided the United States for being pro-Muslim and pro-Croat during the Balkan War, and Serb American groups such as the Serbian Unity Congress pushed for stronger US relations with Serbia (Paul 1999; Doherty 1995b). Jewish, Greek, and Indian American organizations desire for the United States to maintain strong relations with Israel, Greece, and India, respectively. In other cases, ethnic lobbies encourage the United States to isolate, pressure, or punish enemies of the ancestral state. For example, Armenian Americans helped enact an embargo against Azerbaijan in the 1990s, and the Greek and Armenian lobbies have long attempted to weaken US relations with Turkey (Watanabe 1984; Doherty 1995a; Smith 2000). In 2000, Eritrean Americans rallied for the United States to push Ethiopia to accept the peace plan developed by the Organization of African Unity to end the border conflict between Ethiopia and Eritrea (Melvin and Graham 2000). Taiwanese American groups worry that US relations with China have grown too strong. In 1999, Indian Americans were credited with mounting a successful grassroots campaign that pushed Congress and the Clinton administration to urge Pakistan to stop its incursion into the disputed Kashmir province (Lancaster 2000). During the Cold War, Central and Eastern European groups regarded the leaders of their ancestral homelands as puppet regimes, and the communities encouraged the United States to take a hard line against the Communist states (Shain 1994). The same is true today with most Cuban groups.

In addition to analyzing foreign policy per se, we surveyed policymakers about the influence of ethnic groups regarding six other policy realms: foreign aid, human rights, immigration, military and security, oil and energy, and trade policy. *Foreign aid* is central to foreign policy because aid is used as a carrot to reward foreign states, and ethnic groups are frequently advocates for increasing or maintaining aid to their ancestral homelands. Foreign aid can also be an intensely political issue since it involves distributing a finite amount of dollars, and increasing aid to some countries or regions often results in cuts in aid to other regions (Dobbs 2001). Jewish American and other pro-Israeli groups are credited by scholars and journalists with helping to maintain high levels of US aid to Israel, and Israel is by far the largest recipient of US foreign aid (Frankel 2006). Armenian American groups are also very interested in foreign aid, and Tony Smith asserts that "it is widely agreed that the high levels of U.S. aid to Armenia (the second highest per capita in the world, after Israel) . . . would be inconceivable" were it not for the Armenian American lobby (2000, 69–70; see also Dobbs 2001). Greek groups have lobbied for years for foreign aid to Cyprus and that aid to Greece should be proportional to US aid to Turkey by a 7:10 ratio

(Felton 1984b; Doherty 1995a). In the wake of the collapse of the Soviet Union, Central and Eastern European groups advocated for greater foreign aid to nations formally under Soviet influence to help build their democratic institutions.

Ethnic groups and other actors in the foreign policy–making process often attempt to link foreign aid to *human rights* policies. For example, in the mid-1990s the Greek and Armenian American lobbies, humanitarian groups, and key members of Congress attempted to restrict aid to Turkey unless Ankara dropped its blockade of humanitarian aid to Armenia. In addition, two other human rights issues were cited as eroding support for aid to Turkey: Turkey's counterinsurgency campaign against the Kurds, and Ankara's refusal to recognize the Armenian genocide (Doherty 1995a, 1996b). In the 1990s, Indian Americans fought attempts by Representative Dan Burton (R-IN) to limit foreign aid to India because of its human rights record in Kashmir and toward India's Sikh minority (Doherty 1996b; Pomper and Chatterjee 2000). Irish American groups worked for more than a decade to prevent job discrimination against Catholics in Northern Ireland by linking the MacBride Principles to the foreign aid authorization bill (Kenworthy 1990; Doherty 1996a). Many Cuban American groups argue that the embargo against the Castro regime should be continued because of its record on civil liberties and human rights (Gugliotta 1998). Human rights concerns are not always linked to foreign aid, and ethnic groups can encourage the United States to pressure foreign regimes to curb human rights abuses. For example, Eritrean Americans and Ethiopian Americans have lobbied the United States to take a tougher stance against their former homelands after civil liberties and civil rights have been curtailed by ruling regimes (Bahrampour 2006; Snyder 2006). Both African American and Jewish American organizations worked to raise awareness of the humanitarian crisis in Darfur, in hopes of pressing the United States and UN to take action to halt the ethnic genocide being carried out in the region (Banerjee 2006).

While defense policies are often viewed as distinct from foreign policy, the two are very much entangled (Lindsay 1994), and *military and security* policies are not immune from the pressures of ethnic (and other domestic) groups. Since the birth of Israel, the Israeli American lobby has advocated for the United States to support Israel with large amounts of military assistance and equipment, and Jewish and Arab American groups have wrangled for decades over US arms sales to Israel, Egypt, Jordan, Saudi Arabia, and other countries in the region (DeConde 1992; Boustany 1990; Mearsheimer and Walt 2007). Greek Americans lobbied successfully for an arms embargo against Turkey after the latter invaded Cyprus in 1974. Before the embargo was rescinded in 1978, Turkey closed several dozen US bases and listening posts in retaliation. In 1995 during the Balkan wars, a coalition of Muslim, Jewish, and Arab American groups advocated for an end to the arms embargo against Bosnia, while Serb American organizations charged the American media with being biased against the Serb side of the conflict (Doherty 1995b; Curtiss 1999). Pakistani Americans opposed the halt of military aid to Pakistan in 1990 because of the country's growing nuclear program, and Pakistani Americans targeted the chief architect of the measure, Senator Larry Pressler (R-SD), for defeat in 1996. The result was an election proxy war between Pressler and Democratic challenger Tim Johnson, with Indian Americans pouring at least $150,000 into Pressler's reelection campaign, and Pakistani Americans giving at least that amount to Johnson (Morgan and Merida 1997). Indian Americans seek stronger military ties between the United States and India, and some Indian Americans even advocated for the United States to resume military sales to both India and Pakistan in the late 1990s in order to begin building military ties between the United States and India (USINPAC 2007a; Lancaster 1999).

Like foreign aid, *trade* and trading sanctions can be used as tools of foreign policy. Although punitive trading measures are not usually welcomed by the executive branch, sanctions are often sought by ethnic groups and members of Congress (Doherty 1997). Cuban Americans successfully lobbied for the passage of the Cuban Liberty and Democratic Solidarity (Libertad) Act of 1996, which expanded sanctions against the Castro regime. Also in 1996, the Israeli lobby helped win sanctions against Iran, although the lobby lost in its bid to keep sanctions against Libya out of the bill, and human rights activists were also successful in imposing sanctions against new investment in Myanmar (Doherty 1997). Other ethnic groups have encouraged trade with their ancestral homeland. For example, Mexican American groups and members of Congress provided critical support for the passage of the North American Free Trade Agreement (NAFTA) in 1993, although Mexican American members of Congress were credited with forcing changes to the agreement, including programmatic funding benefiting US residents who live close to the US-Mexico border (Glastris et al. 1997; Shain 1999). At times, ethnic-based groups can be split over trade. For example, although Vietnamese Americans traditionally took a hard line against opening relations with Vietnam, it appears that the Vietnamese American community was split in 1994 over whether President Clinton should lift the US embargo against Vietnam (Burress 1994; Scroggins 1994; Sylvester 1994; Wisby 1994).[8] In 2005, Hispanic groups were divided over the Central American Free Trade Agreement (CAFTA), with some Hispanic organizations such as the League of United Latin American Citizens opposing the free trade pact, and business-based groups, such as the United States Hispanic Chamber of Commerce, supporting the agreement (Holzer 2005).

As with trade policies, policymaking toward *oil and energy* is of keen interest to business organizations. Nonetheless, ethnic groups can and do weigh in on these policies. For example, by promoting economic sanctions against Iran, the Israeli lobby affected oil and energy policy, since Iran is a large exporter of petroleum. The 1996 sanctions against Iran were amended to include Libya, another exporter of petroleum. Frequently cited as a classic example of an ethnic entanglement into foreign policy, Armenian groups opposed the Clinton administration attempts to give US assistance to Azerbaijan, a nation that controls expansive oil reserves in the Caspian region (Doherty 1995a; Longworth 1998; Dobbs 2001).

Finally, as has been the case throughout much of the history of the United States, *immigration* is an important issue that bridges domestic and foreign policymaking. Nathan Glazer and Daniel Moynihan argue that "without too much exaggeration it could be stated that the immigration process is the single most important determinant of American foreign policy. This process regulates the ethnic composition of the American electorate. Foreign policy responds to that ethnic composition" (1975, 23). There is little doubt that, since immigration holds the promise of bringing family members to the United States, it is a highly salient and weighty issue for many ethnic groups. Even ethnic communities that exhibit little interest in foreign affairs and policies related to their ancestral homeland may try to influence immigration policy. For example, with the exception of recent trade pacts, Mexican Americans generally ignore US-Mexican relations and focus their energies on domestic issues (Jones-Correa 2002). However, Mexican American organizations have been, and still are, very active in immigration policy. Smith states that "observers agree that Mexican Americans were active in shaping the Immigration Reform and Control Act of 1986 and the Immigration Act of 1990" (2000, 75), and Mexican and Hispanic groups are very active today regarding immigration reform. They are not alone, and numerous ethnic groups oppose cuts to (and support increases of) legal immigration of family members of recent immigrants to the United States, while other ethnic groups lobby for a greater number of work visas for high-skilled workers coming from countries such as India (Idelson 1996). Irish Americans successfully included a provision in the Immigration Act of 1990 requiring that 40 percent of the 40,000 visas distributed by contest in 1991 be given to Irish applicants (Kamen 1991). Immigration is also a politically charged issue that can disrupt traditional voting patterns. For example, Cuban Americans, Korean Americans, and Vietnamese Americans, three ethnic groups that traditionally lean Republican, all displayed hostility toward a 1996 plan by Republican leaders to reduce the number of family visas granted (Idelson 1996).

In summary, many ethnic interest groups are interested in affecting not just foreign policy and foreign aid allocations, but a host of other connected realms, including immigration, military and security, trade, and oil and energy policy. But what effects do ethnic groups have on these policies? The next section details how this project examined the scope and nature of ethnic group influence in the policymaking process.

■ **Research Design: Exploring the Comparative Role of Ethnic Groups**

There is little doubt that ethnic American groups try to influence the policy-making process regarding the above foreign and intermestic policy realms. What is much less apparent is the degree to which ethnic groups do, in fact, enjoy influence over these policies. We used a number of techniques to examine the comparative role of ethnic groups in policymaking, including surveys and in-depth interviews of policymakers and examining journalistic accounts and analysis of the foreign policy–making process. Both quantitative and qualitative research methods were employed to explore why some ethnic groups have greater influence in the foreign policy–making process.

One of the main arguments of this book is that ethnic groups are not the only voices that attempt to sway foreign policy. Another interest group sector, that of business and trade organizations, is often characterized as having a disproportionate amount of sway in US policymaking and is also very interested in US foreign policy. For example, Robert Keohane (1984) demonstrates that domestic oil producers and business groups greatly influenced postwar foreign policy and trade agreements. Jeffry Frieden (1996) argues that peak business associations and business groups are able to influence trade policy through the legislative branch. In his 1997 polemic, Samuel Huntington argues: "In case after case, country after country, the dictates of commercialism have prevailed over other purposes including human rights, democracy, alliance relationships, maintaining the balance of power, technology export controls, and other strategic and political considerations." Business interests and ethnic lobbies are at times very much opposed to one another. As expected, business groups do not support trade restrictions, and often business organizations are at odds with ethnic and humanitarian groups over trade sanctions and embargos (Sammon 1995; Doherty 1997). Yet, business groups and ethnic lobbies can be allies when their interests coincide: business groups have worked with Indian American organizations to increase trade with India and expand the number of visas for high-tech workers (Pomper and Chatterjee 2000; Idelson 1996). Likewise, business groups and companies like Boeing coordinated with the Central and Eastern European American lobby to support the expansion of the North Atlantic Treaty Organization (NATO), since the enlargement could lead to more sales of US-made arms and technology (Longworth 1998).

In addition, foreign governments and other foreign principals attempt to influence US policies by penetrating the American domestic political process (Walt 2005). Although these actors are forbidden from making campaign contributions, foreign lobbies conduct expensive lobbying and public relations campaigns, some of which are headed by former members of Congress (Albert 2001; Rothstein 2006). For example, since 2000 the government of

Turkey hired former chair of the House Appropriations Committee Bob Livingston (R-LA), former chair of the House Rules Committee Gerald Solomon (R-NY), and former Democratic leader Dick Gephardt (D-MO) to fight bills that call for the recognition of the Armenian genocide (Schmitt 2000; O'Brien 2007). Some scholars assert that foreign entities can influence US foreign policy substantially in their own right (Hrebenar and Thomas 1995; Hula 1995). However, Walt (2005) contends that foreign states are much more likely to sway US policies if "they join forces with sympathetic domestic interest groups—and especially ethnic diasporas—in order to encourage closer ties than might otherwise occur" (195). Indeed, Walt contends the US political system is "especially receptive to foreign manipulation" because there are "a wide range of media outlets, a tradition of free speech and interest-group politics, and a divided system of government offering multiple channels of influence" (2005, 197). Foreign states, especially those that share cultural and political similarities with the United States, can mobilize a sympathetic diaspora within the United States and "exploit the basic dynamics of interest-group politics": interest groups comprised of enthusiastic supporters are likely to be accommodated by policymakers in the absence of strong, countervailing opposition groups (198). Walt contends that Israel has been the most successful in mobilizing Jewish Americans and other social groups on its behalf, but other prominent examples of transnational penetration include Greek, Armenian, Taiwanese, Korean, and Indian efforts.

Further complicating analysis is the fact that ethnic lobbies, organizations, and citizens are not just trying to influence elected leaders: there is ample evidence of elected officials working to mobilize and influence ethnic communities. Both Democrats and Republicans court recent immigrant groups in hopes of convincing new citizens to support their candidates. While mobilizing ethnic communities has a long history in the United States, the growth of immigration over the past several decades, coupled with the competitiveness of the last several election cycles, has led both parties to step up their efforts to register, court, and mobilize new citizens (Tillotson 2004). Elected officials also court ethnic groups to support and mobilize grassroots support for legislation. For example, President George W. Bush wooed Hispanic groups in his effort to pass CAFTA in 2005, and Bush administration officials mobilized Indian American organizations the following year to win congressional approval of the US-India Nuclear Civilian Agreement (Weisman 2005).

It is important to remember that an ethnic lobby that desires to influence foreign policy is likely to be only one voice in the decisionmaking process, as business groups, ideological organizations, human rights groups, unions, and even other ethnic lobbies may try to influence policy outcomes. Further, ethnic lobbies face a significant disadvantage compared to business organizations: there are far more business groups, they tend to be very organized and engaged in policymaking, and these organizations have far greater financial resources than other types of lobbying and advocacy groups (Schlozman and Tierney 1986; Berry 1997). Because of this, some scholars argue that while business interests may not get everything they want, "they get a great deal" (Lindblom 1977, 187).

Like other mass-based organizations, ethnic groups do have one resource that many business organizations lack—an ability to tap a grassroots network of concerned voters (see Gerber 1999). Additionally, if a policy is salient to an ethnic community, then the issue may mobilize ethnic members to participate more in the electoral and policymaking process; not only can these individuals affect electoral outcomes, but they may be mobilized to participate in a grassroots lobbying campaign to influence the legislative process. Indeed, the issue may be so important that it drives individuals to behave like "single-issue voters," who will ignore partisanship and other issues and make a vote decision based on the candidate stances on a lone, important issue (see Congleton 1991; Abramowitz 1995).

However, despite institutional and policymaking shifts that increase the influence of individual legislators in the foreign policy–making process, foreign policy making is still very much centered in the executive branch (Weissman 1995), a branch that, while not immune from domestic pressure groups, is nonetheless far more difficult to access than Congress. Furthermore, American ethnic groups are minority groups, usually lacking significant representation within this policymaking process. Even scholars concerned with the ability of ethnic lobbies to influence foreign policy unduly acknowledge that ethnic minorities are usually underrepresented in the foreign policy–making process, which has long featured an "overwhelming predominance of Euro Americans" (Smith 2000, 9; see also DeConde 1992). Indeed, when ethnic minorities do ascend to the highest levels of the foreign policy–making process, it is newsworthy: take, for instance, Colin Powell's appointment to secretary of state in 2001, or the elections of Mel Martinez (R-FL), Barack Obama (D-IL), and Ken Salazar (D-CO) to the US Senate in 2004.[9]

For these reasons, it is hypothesized that ethnic groups, as a class of interest groups, do not dominate the foreign policy process or enjoy greater influence than other domestic actors, like business groups. That is not to say that ethnic lobbies can have no influence, but that as a category of special interest groups, the influence of ethnic groups does not exceed the influence of other domestic actors in the foreign policy–making process.

Identifying Ethnic Organizations

In order to address the objectives of this project, we examined ethnic American interest groups and their effect on the policymaking process from a number of different angles. As a first step, ethnic American groups that exhibited some interest in the foreign or intermestic policymaking realms, such as trade, immigration, or foreign policy, were identified. Specifically, we searched for ethnic-based membership organizations that met one of two institutional criteria: (1) the group representing the ethnicity was using a Washington lobbyist, or (2) the self-identified ethnic group made campaign contributions to a federal office seeker since 1998. Our logic is that to influence the policymaking process effectively, an ethnic community will need some degree of presence in Washington, DC. A federal political action committee (PAC) or a representative who is registered to lobby helps to meet that threshold.

To identify organizations that employed a Washington lobbyist, electronic searches were conducted in 2004 and 2006 of *Washington Representatives* for ethnic-based organizations using multiple keywords to ensure that all relevant groups were identified. For example, we searched for the terms *Greek, Greece,* and *Hellenic* to find organizations that serve Greek Americans. Business organizations and trade groups, like the United States–New Zealand Council and the Egyptian Exporters Association, were not included in the population since they are not grassroots organizations. Likewise, non-US groups, such as the Pakistan Human Development Fund and Cameroonian National Congress, were not included, since they are not membership organizations that cater to Americans.

To identify campaign contributions to federal candidates, we searched Federal Election Commission archives in 2004 and 2006 for reports filed by ethnic-based PACs since 1998. As with the earlier search, we used a multiple keyword search to ensure that all relevant groups were identified. We also searched the website for the Center for Responsive Politics (www.opensecrets.org), which tracks PACs, other campaign contributions, and lobbying expenditures using the same criteria.

Combined, the searches identified over eighty-five groups or organizations representing thirty-eight ethnicities. Undoubtedly, our search conditions excluded some ethnicities that are truly grassroots in nature, such as Sri Lankan Americans or Estonian Americans, both of which were identified by a few policymakers interviewed for this project as ethnic groups that had contacted them. Nonetheless, we believe the criteria yielded a valid inventory of the most active ethnic lobbies in US foreign policy. We then collected data on these groups and lobbies, including PAC contributions, lobbying expenditures, and their efforts to mount grassroots campaigns to influence policymakers.

Policymaker Survey

A central component to this project is an in-depth survey of policymakers. Before the in-depth survey was implemented, we conducted a pilot study in

2004, and questionnaires were mailed to members of Congress, key congressional staffers, and ethnic interest group leaders and lobbyists (see Paul and Paul 2005). The questionnaire measured broad perceptions regarding the ability of ethnic groups to influence US policymaking in general and in several specific areas, including immigration, energy and oil policy, trade policy, domestic and foreign aid, military and security policy, civil rights, and human rights. The survey also asked respondents to rate the influence on a scale of 0–100 of each of the ethnic lobbies we identified as being active in foreign or intermestic policymaking processes.

In order to better understand the degree to which ethnic groups can influence the policymaking process, as well as appreciate which groups enjoy more influence than others, we then conducted an in-depth survey of policymakers and ethnic group leaders. Between August 2005 and March 2007, fifty-four members of Congress, congressional staffers, officials at cabinet agencies, interest group leaders, and other foreign policy actors were interviewed to examine the influence of ethnic groups on foreign policy making. We believe the survey provides insight into the role ethnic groups play in the foreign policy–making process during this time period. For the survey, we randomly selected twenty-five members of Congress and we also asked to interview fifteen members of Congress who are cited as champions of ethnic interest groups, critics of ethnic interest group involvement in foreign or trade policies, or who are especially interested in foreign affairs. In addition, we selected fifty congressional offices and asked to interview the staffer assigned to foreign affairs, the legislative director, or the chief of staff; and we interviewed committee staffers who are assigned to the House Committee on International Relations and the Senate Committee on Foreign Relations and their subcommittees. Our sample of twenty-eight Capitol Hill policymakers included fifteen Democrats and thirteen Republicans, representing urban, suburban, rural, and mixed districts in ten states.[10] We also identified thirty-five career professionals in the Department of State and two other federal agencies and asked to interview these bureaucrats.[11] Finally, we identified several nonelected elites involved in foreign policy and interviewed one of these elites. In all, forty-one policymakers were interviewed (Table 1.1) for a response rate of 27 percent.[12] Collectively, we believe these members of Congress, congressional staffers, committee staffers, and career professionals represent a very good sample of policymakers[13] involved in foreign and intermestic policies: on average, the respondents had 12.9 years of experience with their current employers and possessed 14.2 years of foreign policy experience.[14] Respondents were given the option of receiving the interview questions ahead of the interview, and the interviews lasted anywhere from 20 to 60 minutes, with the modal interview taking 30 minutes. Interviews were not recorded, and our notes were transcribed immediately following the interview. Most staffers and bureaucrats requested to remain completely anonymous for the project, and several respondents

Table 1.1 Position and Ideology of In-Depth Interview Participants

Position of Respondent	Number Interviewed
Member of Congress	4
Legislative director or chief of staff	7
Senior legislative assistant or legislative assistant	7
Committee staffer	10
Agency careerist	11
Agency appointee	1
Nonelected elite	1
Ethnic group leader	13
Total number of respondents	54

Ideological Perspective of Policymakers	Number Interviewed
Extremely liberal	0
Somewhat liberal	13
Slightly liberal	7
Moderate	7
Slightly conservative	4
Somewhat conservative	6
Extremely conservative	2
Refused	2
Total number of policymakers	41

Note: Ideological data on ethnic group leaders were not collected.

stated that the answers given were more candid because their anonymity was guaranteed.

The policymakers who participated in our study provided thoughtful, and in many cases quite detailed, answers to our questions. Many of the policymakers spoke of life experiences that prompted their interest in, and helped to shape their perspectives regarding, foreign affairs. Several spoke of an interest in their own ethnicity or becoming interested in foreign affairs because one of their parents was an immigrant. Others cited work overseas, internships with the State Department, or educational opportunities overseas as prompting an interest in foreign policy. Several policymakers cited service in the military as influencing their interest in, and perspectives of, foreign affairs.

In addition, we interviewed thirteen leaders of major ethnic American groups. Like the interviews of policymakers, the interviews of ethnic leaders were conducted either face-to-face or by phone, and the sessions were not recorded. These interviews lasted about an hour, and our notes were transcribed immediately following the interview. Many of those interviewed had twenty or more years of advocacy or policymaking experience.

In addition to analyzing the comparative role of ethnic groups in the policymaking process, we explored the factors that help explain the influence of different ethnic lobbies. We focused on five main factors that may affect the power of ethnic lobbies: population, resources, assimilation, saliency, and goals. After collecting data from a number of sources, we conducted ordinary least squares (OLS) regression analysis to determine which factors best help explain why some ethnic groups are more influential than others. Qualitative data were collected on each of the thirty-eight ethnic lobbies by examining their literature and websites, and by analyzing journalistic accounts.[15]

■ Outline of the Book

Chapter 2 examines the importance of ethnicity, race, and nationalism—phenomena that can have tremendous effects on the behavior of individuals. One of the effects of ethnicity is that it helps create communities of individuals, who may then form groups that attempt to influence the political process. The chapter analyzes the major ethnic groups and organizations that are engaged in the foreign policy–making process, including models of how ethnic groups are organized.

Chapter 3 focuses on the strategies and the tactics ethnic groups use to influence the policymaking process, including electioneering, direct lobbying, and grassroots lobbying. One of the charges leveled against interest groups involves their prowess in the electoral arena, specifically regarding campaign finance. Much has been made of PACs over the past several decades, and some scholars have concluded that "PACs are probably the primary source of cynicism and distrust of politics in the United States today" (Wright 2003, 115). PACs are federally regulated organizations that are formed to collect and distribute monetary and in-kind contributions to federal candidates. This chapter examines PAC contributions by ethnic interest groups from 1998 to 2006, in terms of both how much money is contributed by ethnic-based PACs and contribution patterns exhibited by ethnic PACs. We find, in general, that ethnic interest groups play a surprisingly small role in the PAC universe, accounting for about 1 percent of all PAC contributions. We also find that ethnic groups spend relatively little on direct lobbying.

Chapter 4 develops a theory for understanding the factors that contribute to the influence of ethnic groups. Five broad factors are examined, including the size and dispersion of their population, their resources (such as wealth and organizational assets), the saliency of foreign policy issues to the ethnic groups, their assimilation into US society, and the degree to which their goals are an attempt to alter the status quo.

Chapter 5 examines which ethnic groups are the most influential. The Jewish American and Cuban American lobbies are found to have the most influence in foreign policy making, and seven others (the Irish American, Armenian American, Hispanic American, Taiwanese American, African American, Greek American, and Indian American lobbies) were judged to have a moderate degree of influence. This chapter also presents the multivariate analysis that examines what factors are most important for determining the influence of ethnic groups.

Chapter 6 presents the results of the survey and interviews of policymakers regarding the comparative influence of ethnic groups, which yielded many interesting findings. For example, we found little evidence that policymakers believe that ethnic interest groups, in general, have too much power. While most respondents cited examples of one or two lobbies having influence, respondents generally believed other actors have much greater influence than ethnic groups. Of the thirty-eight ethnic groups studied, only three ethnic lobbies were judged as having too much influence by a majority of policymakers: the Israeli (or Jewish American) lobby, the Cuban American lobby, and the Armenian American lobby.

Chapter 7 concludes the book, and we offer our final thoughts and analysis on the scope and influence of American ethnic groups.

Conclusion

We agree with Milton Esman that ethnic solidarity is a reality, as is the competition that exists between ethnic communities for political values and resources. In many political systems, ethnic communities vie for "relative political power, control over territory, access to and participation in the decision-making institutions of the state, or, alternatively, autonomy within the polity or complete separation. They include terms of access to education and employment . . . and the symbolic issues of recognition and respect for a community and its culture" (Esman 1994, 23). While ethnic communities within the United States do not contend for territory like, say, Nebraska, these ethnic communities do compete for *resources,* like foreign aid allocations, control over governmental programs (like Radio and TV Martí), immigration quotas, strategic and defense allocations, and trade policies. Increasingly, ethnic tensions surface in electoral races, with House, Senate, and gubernatorial contests serving as proxy battlegrounds for antagonistic ethno-racial groups and communities. In addition, ethnic politics affect party politics as well, as groups compete for relative political power within a party (a very real possibility for African Americans and Hispanic Americans within the Democratic Party), or tensions between groups threaten party cohesion (which has been the case between African Americans and Jewish Americans within the Democratic Party at times), or electoral considerations threaten to cause or widen rifts within a party (such as efforts by some Republicans to appeal more to Hispanic Americans by easing immigration restrictions, which angers more nativist elements of the party). For all of these reasons, there is no doubt that ethnic politics are a reality. We hope that the analysis presented here can better determine the extent to which this reality may or may not be a normative concern for Americans.

Notes

1. Notable exceptions include Alexander DeConde's 1992 examination of the impact of ethnicity on US foreign policy and the historical roots of Anglo dominance on such policy, and Tony Smith's 2000 analysis of ethnic influence on foreign policy and the normative implications of such influence.

2. Intermestic policies are realms that link relations with other states to domestic economic concerns. Prominent examples include trade, immigration, and energy policies (Manning 1977; Barilleaux 1985).

3. It is important to note that consensus during this period did not "just happen," as "Cold War presidents worked diligently to achieve domestic legitimacy for their foreign policies" (Melanson 2005, 37).

4. Although not necessarily predicted by Madison, interested parties have a fourth access point as well: the courts. For at least half a century, interest groups have used the courts to initiate new policies, such as desegregation through *Brown v. Board of Education* (1954).

5. Herbert Hirsch (1995) notes that elites may manipulate historical memories for the purpose of mobilizing groups to commit genocide.

6. Patrons do not eliminate the need for members, since members are critical for grassroots mobilization. Further, if the organization can convince an individual to join the group and pay dues, the individual may feel more vested in the organization and participate at higher levels.

7. According to his letters, President Dwight D. Eisenhower gave "strict orders to the State Department that they should inform Israel that we would handle our affairs exactly as though we didn't have a Jew in America" (as quoted in DeConde 1992, 136).

8. A dozen years later, most Vietnamese Americans appeared to support efforts to permanently normalize trade relations between the United States and Vietnam, although some Vietnamese Americans and humanitarian groups opposed the efforts (Iritani 2006).

9. Obama was only the third African American elected to the US Senate since Reconstruction, while Martinez and Salazar were only the fourth and fifth Hispanic Americans in the Senate. At the time of their elections in 2004, there were no blacks or Hispanics serving in the Senate (Adelman 2000; Coile and Salladay 2000; Toner and Seelye 2004).

10. We interviewed respondents representing districts from every region of the United States, and the inclusion of committee staffers expanded the geographic representation of our research. In some cases, committee staffers began as personal staffers for the chairperson or ranking member of committee or subcommittee and moved later to committee staff. Many of these staffers remained associated with their district offices and retained ties to the district.

11. From the executive realm, we interviewed directors and deputy directors in six bureaus of the Department of State, one agency appointee, and a few desk officers. We also spoke with one high-ranking official in one other federal agency.

12. Nearly all of the interviews were done in person or by phone, and two respondents provided written answers instead of an interview.

13. There was no evidence that the sample was skewed to favor ethnic interest groups. While a few Capitol Hill respondents were cited by others as being champions of ethnic interest groups, other respondents hailed from districts that have no significant ethnic communities.

14. About half of respondents had some significant foreign policy–making experience prior to current work (such as a bureaucrat who worked previously for another agency, a staffer who had served in the executive branch, or a bureaucrat who had experience on Capitol Hill).

15. See Appendix A, questions 27–64, for a list of all thirty-eight ethnic groups studied.

2

Ethnic Groups in the United States

Two major concepts central to this study are *ethnicity* and *race*. Both can have powerful effects on individuals and groups, and both concepts are important to understanding the role of ethnic politics in the United States. Despite agreement regarding the importance of the concepts, a consensus does not exist regarding the precise definitions of ethnicity and race. Smith (2000) defines "*ethnicity* as a voluntary organization of people with a collective identity based on an intellectually formulated and emotionally felt assertion of their distinctiveness from other peoples" (21). This collective identity or sense of togetherness may be based on a common history, culture, language, religion, and/or race. Although often interchanged with ethnicity, *race* refers to a group of people who are more or less distinct based upon physical characteristics which are genetically transmitted. Nonetheless, race has a cultural basis as well, since an individual can be of multiple races, but the individual may only feel that she is a member of one race. Because the terms *ethnicity* and *race* are related, are often used interchangeably, and often have similar effects on political behavior, some scholars have adopted the term *ethnoracial*. For example, Smith argues that an ethnoracial group "which can also be distinguished by a racial or religious distinctiveness (or by both) . . . [is] likely to demonstrate a greater sense of its separation from the rest of society and correspondingly a higher degree of political solidarity" (2000, 22). This project is more concerned with the political ramifications of these phenomena than the sociological distinctiveness of the concepts. As such, the terms *ethnicity, race,* and *ethnoracial* will be used interchangeably.

Part of the power of ethnicity is that it "normally taps deeper layers of socialization, experience, emotion, and pride than collective identities that are more instrumental to the individual" so that individual and collective identities can become fused: "when the community is threatened, so is the

31

individual, while the success of a community enhances its members' sense of self-worth" (Esman 1994, 15). Ethnicity may remain dormant within an individual until a perception of threat, such as challenges to the status quo and existing power and political structures, resurrects the efficacy of ethnicity to community members. For example, Esman posits that the "need for ethnic solidarity arises only when strange, threatening, competitive outsiders must be confronted" (1994, 13). An obvious example is the influx of a new immigrant group might be perceived as a threat to native groups. Nonetheless, ethnic solidarity is not just important to the native population, it is equally (perhaps more) important to the immigrant group, which must confront a new environment and possible harsh treatment.

Ethnicity is also tied to the most important political ideology to emerge over the past 300 years, *nationalism.* Nationalism calls on "people to identify with the interests of the national group and to support the creation of a state . . . to support those interests" (Baradat 2000, 47). Nationalism is often based upon ethnicity. For example, Smith contends that nationalism "is a politically more demanding variant of ethnic consciousness, one that calls for the existence of a state on a designated territory to give sovereign political form to the collective life of an ethnically described people" (2000, 21). The importance of nationalism is difficult to overstate: while only some nation-states prescribe to an ideology such as democracy, communism, fascism, or capitalism, *all* modern nation-states use nationalism to motivate their citizens.

A prominent concern regarding the power of ethnoracial identities is that they may conflict or compete with national identities. As a result, some nation-states may try to repress ethnicities that they view as a challenge to the dominant national identity. For example, Kurds are not allowed to be schooled in the Kurdish language in Turkey because Ankara fears that promoting the Kurdish identity might precipitate Kurdish nationalism and threaten Turkish sovereignty. Within the United States, concerns of divided loyalties have existed since colonial times, with individuals fearing that members of ethnic communities would favor their mother country over the United States in a conflict between the two nation-states (DeConde 1992). This anxiety emerged during both world wars, ultimately leading to a repugnant policy of forcing Americans of Japanese descent into detention camps for the duration of World War II.

There is no doubt that the politicization of ethnicity, race, and nationalism can have profound and, at times, terrible political consequences. The twentieth century proved to be the bloodiest period in all of history, and nearly 110 million people died in nationalist wars (Kegley and Wittkopf 1999). Many of these deaths were triggered by ethnic hatred, and as a result

the twentieth century . . . witnessed perhaps the worst mass murders in all of history. While government persecution and murder of minorities is not a modern phenomenon, the development of systematic methods for destroying entire [ethnic or racial] populations led to the genocide of millions. The Holocaust of six million Jews in Nazi Germany resulted in international efforts to prevent genocide, yet systematic murder has continued, resulting in the deaths of millions in Cambodia, Rwanda and Yugoslavia. In addition, the violence of the twentieth century has also resulted in the displacement of millions of people. Ethnic and religious groups have been forced from their homelands due to government policies and persecution (as in the case of Armenians in 1915) or have fled as the result of economic or political chaos (as in the case of Irish immigrants). (Paul 1999, 1)

These events have prompted many scholars to question why ethnic identity has increased as a basis for political power and influence. Some scholars predicted that modernization and urbanization would lead to a decline in salience of ethnicity, as individuals of all ethnicities would strive to achieve the same material and social ends (see especially Deutsch 1961). Ironically, the opposite has occurred, and since World War II there has been an increase in ethnic-based political action in the United States and elsewhere (Esman 1994, Smith 2000). More recent scholars have refuted the idea that ethnic mobilization dissipates with modernity. For example, Rothschild (1981) argues that the politicization of ethnicity occurs as "reaction against modernity" (256), while Enloe (1986) contends that modernization actually stimulates ethnic awareness. "The existence of ethnic political organizations and the increasing demands of ethnic groups in modernized countries such as the United States, Great Britain and France exemplify the fact that modernization may not, necessarily, lead to the demise of ethnicity as a form of collective identity, nor the demise of ethnic centered mobilization" (Paul 1999, 23).

The scholarly debate has now shifted from *if* ethnicity will remain salient to the political identity of individuals to a discussion of the *consequences* of this increase in ethnic-based politics. For example, although he prefers the term *"conflicted* rather than *divided* loyalties," Tony Smith asserts that "ethnic and national identities can clash . . . or find themselves in circumstances, that rally ethnic groups in the United States in a way the greater national community may be slow to endorse or may actually oppose" (2000, 24). It is this concern, that ethnoracial and ethnonational loyalties can and at times do conflict with the national interest, that drives much of the trepidation about ethnic group politics in the United States.

Perhaps adding to the concern of Smith and others, foreign leaders often recognize the potential value of encouraging American immigrants to lobby the US government for policies that benefit the foreign state. As noted in Chapter 1, Stephen Walt (2005) asserts there are numerous examples of foreign governments partnering with ethnic diaspora to influence US policies. For example, Israeli leaders and American Israel Public Affairs Committee (AIPAC) officials have periodically coordinated efforts to sway US policymakers (Frankel 2006; Mearsheimer and Walt 2007). Over the past decade, Mexican leaders have reached out to Mexican Americans, encouraging the latter to lobby their elected representatives to support NAFTA. Polish, Czech, and Hungarian ambassadors encouraged ethnic Americans to lobby Congress in support of the enlargement of NATO, and James Goldgeier argues that "in terms of broad-based, grassroots organizational efforts, the most important single figure in the central and eastern European lobbying community was Polish Ambassador to the United States Jerzy Kozminski" (1999, 138). Deposed Haitian president Jean-Bertrand Aristide "energized the diaspora through radio broadcasts and public appearances," in a campaign to convince US leaders to restore the Haitian democracy (Shain 1994). Occasionally, foreign leaders have also attempted to entice members of the diaspora to return. For example, Ireland has encouraged Irish Americans to emigrate to Ireland, now that the country is experiencing strong economic growth. After the collapse of the Soviet Union, leaders of Poland, Czechoslovakia, Lithuania, and Albania "made direct patriotic appeals to their respective diasporas, offering them citizenship and encouraging their economic and political support" (Shain 1994, 834).

However, there can be significant obstacles impeding the ability of foreign leaders to influence their American brethren. First and foremost, ethnic Americans may have little interest in appeasing the leaders of the ancestral homeland. For example, Yossi Shain describes the relationship between Mexican leaders and Mexican Americans as "ambivalent" (1999, 670). Shain also notes that other immigrant communities, such as Chinese Americans and Iranian Americans, fled their homelands, and these ethnic groups have no desire to support the leaders of their ancestral homeland. Other ethnic groups that do desire to strengthen US relations with their ancestral homeland may seek policies that are not supported by foreign leaders. For example, some Indian Americans lobbied for the United States to resume military sales to both India and Pakistan in the late 1990s, despite opposition by the Indian embassy to arms sales to Pakistan (Lancaster 1999). Indeed, journalists reported that some Indian Americans chafed at efforts by the Indian government to manipulate the Indian American community, with one ethnic leader stating: "We have to look at what is good for the United States. . . . We are not agents of the Indian government" (Lancaster 1999).

Given the ethnic diversity of the US political community, coupled with the pluralist and open nature of its policymaking process, it is not surprising that ethnicity can and does affect US policymaking. The next section examines the scope of ethnic lobbies that try to influence the foreign and intermestic policy realms.

■ The Scope and Nature of Ethnic Lobbies in America

To better address the extent to which ethnic American groups organize and mobilize around foreign and intermestic policy concerns, we identified and examined hundreds of ethnic-based groups. Many of these groups are cultural organizations or community groups focusing on local concerns, such as housing, education, and health care. Many organizations are founded to help new immigrants, especially ethnic brethren, adjust to life in the United States by explaining basic American law and teaching English (Trejos 2005). As immigrants become citizens, some groups also register members to vote, promote civic engagement, and encourage political parties and candidates to court the ethnic vote (Williams 2006). Indeed, most ethnic groups are not involved in foreign policy, although some of these organizations do promote immigration rights. In 2004 and 2005, we identified more than eighty-five ethnic-based organizations with some interest in foreign or intermestic policy. Many, but not all, of these organizations are based in Washington, DC, or have offices located in the nation's capital. Given the scope of ethnic organizations that exist in the United States, this is not an exhaustive census of ethnic lobbies, but it does provide a more comprehensive view of the ethnic lobby universe than other studies of ethnic American lobbies.

There is likely no one best way to organize a discussion of ethnic lobbies in the United States. Because most lobbies are geographically based—that is, they represent ethnicities that hail from a specific geographic region—the following discussion is structured by continent.

African American Lobbies

In terms of influencing foreign policy, African American groups focus on both the continent of Africa and the Caribbean. Although at times overlooked, the pan-African lobby has sought to influence foreign policy for nearly a century, when William E. B. Du Bois and Marcus Garvey founded separate pan-African organizations in the 1910s (Smith 2000). In 1935, the African American community rallied to oppose Italy's invasion of Ethiopia, and some leaders in Washington encouraged African American organizations to press for greater sanctions against Italy in an attempt to counter the well-organized Italian American lobby. The Ethiopian mobilization efforts "stimulated among blacks a desire for further participation in the formulation of foreign policy," which led to the founding of the Council on African Affairs in 1937 (DeConde 1992 108). The civil rights movement further galvanized African Americans' awareness of foreign policy issues, and the African American lobby pressed for the end of European colonial rule in Africa and elsewhere in the 1950s. Efforts by blacks to elevate African foreign policy concerns led to the establishment of a separate bureau of African affairs in the State Department in 1958 (DeConde 1992).

In the 1960s African Americans gained influence in part because of the Voting Rights Act of 1965 and the Civil Rights Act of 1964, which helped increase the size of the black electorate (DeConde 1992). Beginning in late

1963, African Americans worked to isolate South Africa, first supporting an arms embargo against the South African government. The African American lobby worked to affect US policies toward Africa throughout the 1960s and 1970s, although US policies were more often influenced by the desire to contain communism than by African Americans (Smith 2000; Scott and Osman 2002). Nonetheless, African Americans were "strikingly successful" in working with the Carter administration to influence US policy toward Rhodesia/Zimbabwe (Smith 2000, 62). The African American lobby achieved its greatest success with the 1986 US sanctions against South Africa because of its apartheid policy; scholars have described efforts by African Americans to end apartheid as "one of the most effective diasporic efforts to alter world politics in recent years" (Shain 1994, 834).[1] In addition, the African American lobby was successful in influencing US policy toward Haiti and restoring Aristide to power in 1994. Shain describes the Haitian intervention as a "dramatic demonstration" of the power of a newly mobilized ethnic lobby: President Clinton acted "more in response to the organized elements of the African American electorate, primarily the Congressional Black Caucus and the African American international lobby TransAfrica, than to a broader national consensus" that restoring Aristide was necessary (Shain 1995, 72).

More recently, the lobby has focused on bringing attention to the humanitarian crisis of Darfur and the African AIDS epidemic. However, in terms of influencing foreign aid policies toward Africa recently, it would appear that the African American lobby has struggled: some policymakers we interviewed who focus on Africa reported never hearing from African American groups about US policies toward Africa. While numerous African American organizations exist that focus on domestic issues and civil rights, only a few African American groups concentrate solely on foreign policy concerns.[2] Perhaps the most influential African American organization dedicated to foreign policy is the TransAfrica Forum. The organization was founded in 1978 as "the first mass-based African-American lobby" that aspired to influence policy toward Africa and the Caribbean (DeConde 1992). Within a year, it had 10,000 members and would eventually "establish itself as the foremost channel for the expression of African-American attitudes on foreign policy" (DeConde 1992, 179). The TransAfrica Forum is a 501(c)(3) organization and, because of its nonprofit status, is careful not to formally lobby.[3] However, the organization does attempt to educate the public and policymakers about issues related to Africa, Haiti, and the Caribbean, and the organization encourages its members to talk with their congressional representatives about these issues. TransAfrica was involved in opening the debate on US assistance to National Union for the Total Independence of Angola (UNITA) in Angola's civil war, and the organization spearheaded the Free South Africa movement, which helped pressure Congress to impose sanctions against South Africa (Weissman 1995).

Only a few ethnic lobbies and organizations that focus on a particular nation or state in Africa were identified in researching this project, a finding supported by some policymakers who specialize in Africa: several stated that individuals will contact them and advocate for policies aimed at specific African nations, but these policymakers reported they are seldom or never contacted by organized ethnic lobbies. An exception to this is groups representing ethnicities from the Horn of Africa, including Eritreans, Somalis, and Ethiopians, and these ethnicities are increasingly attempting to influence US foreign policy (Snyder 2006). However, it appears that the vast majority of Eritrean, Ethiopian, and Somali American organizations are community groups focusing on local concerns, such as helping new immigrants adjust to life in the United States, fighting discrimination, voter registration, and domestic issues like education and health care (Williams 2006; Trejos 2005). Nonetheless, there is an Eritrean-based political action committee, some Somali Americans are working to develop a PAC (Williams 2006), and several policymakers reported being contacted by all three ethnicities about foreign policy concerns.[4]

Asian American Lobbies

Many policymakers interviewed for this project asserted strongly that there is no pan-Asian lobby, only lobbies that focus on specific Asian nations or homelands. Perhaps this should not be a surprising finding: just as one wouldn't necessarily expect the existence of a pan-European lobby, a pan-Asian lobby would be difficult to achieve. In part, this is due to historic tensions between the ancestral homelands of many Asian American groups. According to Yen Le Espiritu, "The Chinese, Filipino, Korean, Asian Indian, and Vietnamese American communities continue to be divided among themselves over the politics of their countries of origin. Some of these political differences have sparked violence" (1992, 60). Nonetheless, Espiritu does contend that, over time, Asian Americans may be able to bridge these historic divides and conflicts. Time in the United States has allowed "centripetal forces to emerge," and as groups interacted, they have "become aware of common problems and goals that transcended parochial interests and historical antagonisms" (Espiritu 1992, 30). There are umbrella Asian American organizations, such as the National Council of Asian Pacific Americans (NCAPA), but these federations tend to focus on domestic concerns. For example, the NCAPA's 2004 *Call to Action: Platform for Asian Pacific National Policy Priorities* lists a host of domestic concerns and only a few intermestic issues, such as immigration reform, equity for Filipino veterans of World War II, and an extension of the Hmong Veteran's Naturalization Act (NCAPA 2004). Other organizations focused on US-Asian relations, like the US-Asia Institute, are think tanks or nongovernmental organizations (NGOs), and they do not exhibit any evidence of using ethnicity to mobilize Asian Americans to influence foreign policymaking.

In addition, as was the case with other immigrant groups, "Asian-American efforts to influence foreign policy have not always been welcomed and at times have met with determined resistance. Without too much exaggeration, it can be said that foreign policy activism by Asian Americans on balance has been more discouraged than encouraged, more derided than applauded" (Watanabe 2002, 135). However, in many respects, Asian Americans have faced an even harsher political environment than European immigrants who faced discrimination. According to Paul Watanabe:

> Asian-Americans, who have been consistently racialized as disguised foreigners, have been especially discouraged from foreign policy–related interests and activities, and they have been forced to confront a double-barreled assault. . . . Everything possible has been done to treat them as outsiders regardless of whether they wished to assimilate. Simultaneously, these Asian immigrants and their successors have also been condemned for "behaving foreign" and displaying any inkling of interest in the politics of and U.S. policy toward their nation of origin. (2002, 135–136)

Despite these impediments, there exist numerous interest groups representing different Asian ethnicities that have some interest in foreign and intermestic policies, from institutionalized groups such as the Korean American Coalition, the Japanese American Citizens League, and the Pakistani American Congress to smaller, grassroots organizations that represent Hmong Americans and Filipino Americans. Historically, "Asian-American activism on foreign policy considerations has been irregular, but far from non-existent" (Watanabe 2002, 134). For example, Filipino, Indian, Korean, Cambodian, Vietnamese, and Bangladeshi Americans have lobbied about policies related to their ancestral homelands, and Pakistanis and Sikhs have become more active in policymaking out of the concern that the War on Terror will lead to discrimination against their ethnicities (Watanabe 2002; see also Geron et al. 2001).

In many cases, policymakers interviewed for this study reported that the Asian American ethnic lobbies focus on fairly narrow issues and often have little influence in foreign affairs. For example, several respondents stated that the Japanese American lobby focuses much more on the civil rights of Americans of Japanese and Asian descent, rather than concentrating on relations between the United States and Japan. Three Asian ethnicities stood out from the interviews of policymakers as being especially active in foreign policy making: Indian Americans and, to a lesser extent, Korean Americans were identified by several respondents as ethnic lobbies that are increasing their political influence, while Taiwanese Americans were identified as an influential lobby that, according to a few respondents, may be declining in power.

According to Walt, "the Indian-American diaspora has become an increasingly powerful force in shaping U.S. foreign policy in South Asia," and a number of factors have contributed to the rise of the Indian American lobby (2005, 210). First, the Indian American community is fairly large and wealthy, and it has become increasingly politically active since the 1980s. In addition, India has emerged as the world's largest democracy, which is not only a source of pride for many Indian Americans, but also an argument used in support for stronger US-Indian relations. Further, the Indian government has recognized the importance of mobilizing the Indian American community on its behalf. Finally, just as India and Israel have developed a strategic partnership, the Indian American lobby has begun teaming with the pro-Israel lobby in Washington.

Nonetheless, there are impediments to the ability of the ethnicity to influence the policymaking process effectively. Perhaps most important, the community is very diverse: India is made up of different languages, states, religions, and sects, resulting in an Indian diaspora that is much more varied than most other immigrant groups. Perhaps as a result, according to one Indian American policymaker interviewed for this project, "We don't have an overarching issue that unifies us." A number of Indian American organizations exist, but many focus on business sector issues primarily and not foreign policy issues. An exception is the US India Political Action Committee (USINPAC),[5] a PAC founded in 2002 to provide electoral support for candidates who "support the issues that are important to the Indian American community," including US-India relations, immigration, and domestic issues such as civil rights, protection from hate crimes, and entrepreneurial support (USINPAC 2007b). In addition to campaign contributions, USINPAC lobbies policymakers and organizes grassroots campaigns. As Indian Americans assimilate into the political process, some hope to establish other, more foreign policy–specific organizations. For example, at the 2006 Indian American Friendship Council meetings, a roundtable of Indian American policymakers discussed Indian American political participation, and how such participation could be increased. One policymaker, answering a question of how Indian Americans could promote the US-India Civilian Nuclear Cooperation Agreement better, stated that the community needs to create an organization to study and promote US-India affairs.

> The organizational structure of the Indian American community is not set up to promote the platform. Having a central organization like AIPAC is critical. We need ex-congressional staff doing the lobbying. Why are we having Indian-American doctors, businessmen, and hotel owners talk about the India non-proliferation treaty? We need a central organization, funded by the Indian American groups, to address their issues in a serious

way. What does a doctor know about this? We need a Ph.D. in Asian security studies (to lobby on the issue). A central organization could provide that.

Still, journalists report that the Indian American community is increasingly active in foreign policy issues, and some speculated the community played a central role in the 2006 ratification of the Henry J. Hyde US-India Peaceful Atomic Energy Cooperation Act (Pomper and Chatterjee 2000; McIntire 2006; Anderson 2006).

Korean American organizations are not as focused on foreign affairs as Indian American groups. Although there is evidence that Korean American organizations began "to show some constituency influence for the Korean cause" by the mid-1980s, the primary goal of these groups was to "enhance the ethnic interest of Koreans in the United States" (Moon 1988, 79). The same is almost certainly true today. The Korean American Coalition's mission statement promotes engagement by Korean Americans in civic, community, and legislative affairs; protecting civil rights; encouraging Korean Americans to become community and civic leaders; and establishing ties between the ethnic community and government leaders (Korean American Coalition 2007b). There is no mention of foreign affairs on the organization's mission statement at all, although the Federation of Korean Associations USA does set a goal "to construct the foundation for a developed relation with Korea and peace" (Federation of Korean Associations USA 2007). Still, some policymakers reported that the Korean American community is becoming increasingly organized in foreign affairs, and the Korean American Coalition did mount a grassroots effort in 2006 and 2007 to lobby the House of Representatives to pass House Resolution 759, commonly known as the Comfort Women Resolution (Korean American Coalition 2007a). The issue is important to Korean Americans because "during its occupation of Asia and the Pacific Islands between the 1930s and World War II, Japan used as many as 200,000 young women from Korea, China, the Philippines and in some cases Western Europe for sexual servitude in a program designed to increase the efficiency and morale of Japanese soldiers" (Tiron 2007). The resolution called on the government of Japan to "formally acknowledge, apologize and accept historical responsibility in a clear and unequivocal manner for its Imperial Armed Forces' coercion of young women into sexual slavery, known to the world as 'comfort women.'" Journalists and scholars also stated that "some critical behind-the-scenes support for the bill stems from the growing importance of the Chinese-American and Korean-American lobbies" (Dudden 2006; see also Tiron 2007).[6]

The term *Taiwanese American lobby* may be a misnomer in a way: some policymakers interviewed for this study asserted that ethnic constituents interested in policy toward Taiwan considered themselves to be Chinese Americans. Chinese Americans had limited activism prior to 1950, including opposing the sale of US scrap steel to Japan in the 1930s and some lobbying to end discriminatory immigration policies (DeConde 1992). After communist forces drove the nationalist Chinese government from mainland China, much of the domestic support on behalf of nationalist China was based on ideological forces and not ethnicity. For example, one of the main organizations that formed to oppose US recognition of the People's Republic of China and to support the nationalist Chinese government was the Committee of One Million (Bachrack 1976). The Committee of One Million was dedicated to fighting communism, and it was not ethnic-based; instead, it was organized by business leaders,[7] and members of Congress were involved heavily in its work (Bachrack 1976). Alexander DeConde describes the "China lobby" at this time as mainly consisting of "Nationalist Chinese officials around whom worked other Chinese, former American military leaders, publicists, and Republican politicians" (1992, 149). While the China lobby of the 1950s was not "a true ethnic pressure group . . . individuals connected with it did attempt to exploit ethnoracial consciousness with various tactics" (DeConde 1992, 150).

Eventually, the Taiwanese American community became politically active and enjoyed considerable sway, as Chinese Americans who supported the Kuomingtang (KMT) or Nationalist party developed a sophisticated grassroots organization and gained substantial access to Congress and some members of the executive branch (Omestad 1988). However, as the Taiwanese American community has both grown and diversified, the "KMT supporters in America can no longer monopolize debate over Chinese affairs" (Omestad 1988, 195). Some more recent immigrants from Taiwan support independence, and groups such as the Formosan Association for Public Affairs "publicized human rights abuses in Taiwan and lobbied for congressional resolutions urging democracy" in the 1980s (Omestad 1988, 196). According to Thomas Omestad, the "community of Taiwanese-Americans has changed the way Congress views Taiwan" (1988, 195). Although policymakers interviewed for this project acknowledged that splits do exist in the ethnic community, many policymakers reported that Taiwanese Americans are active in the political process, and the Taiwanese lobby helps publicize travel restrictions placed by the executive branch on Taiwanese leaders when they visit the United States.

European Lobbies

Given America's history of immigration, it is not surprising that so many ethnic American groups serve European-based ethnicities. European Americans, especially Anglo Americans, have dominated the foreign policy–making process from the founding of the United States (DeConde 1992). Many policymakers we interviewed disputed the idea that a true Anglo

American lobby exists—that is, an ethnic-based lobby that seeks to affect US-British relations. Even if such an organized lobby does not exist, some scholars argue that Anglo ethnic ties do influence foreign policy making. For example, DeConde criticizes studies of the influence of ethnicity on foreign policy that ignore Anglo Americans and instead focus primarily on "new immigrants" who arrived in the late nineteenth century and later. DeConde asserts that Anglo Americans embedded in the foreign policy–making process were as conscious of their ethnic bond to the mother country as other immigrant groups. Even when the number of Americans of British stock declined to about half of the population in the twentieth century, Anglo Americans "remained essentially in control of the foreign-policy establishment" (DeConde 1992, 154). Elites helped to maintain the idea that the United States and Great Britain share a common ethnic heritage. For example, Winston Churchill spoke of a "common citizenship" between Americans and British in his famous Iron Curtain speech in 1946. In 1956, the British believed the Americans would never oppose British actions against Egypt. By 1970, "British-American relations on their own had lost some of their old importance in American foreign policy. Yet the old Anglo-American elite and its allies, even if occasionally forced to share power, still kept the relationship with Britain more 'special' than that with any other country. As always, one of its key ingredients remained the ethnic bond" (DeConde 1992, 156). Still, we found little evidence that an organized ethnic lobby exists to serve this traditionally powerful ethnic group, although a new congressional caucus has formed to strengthen ties between the United States and Great Britain.[8]

One ethnicity that has fought to countervail the Anglo presence in US foreign policy making is the large Irish American community. For a population so large, and for a lobby that is perceived by many as being influential, there are relatively few Irish American organizations engaged in the foreign policy process. One of the oldest national Irish organizations focused on foreign policy is the Irish National Caucus (INC), founded in 1974 in part because no other Irish American organization existed to lobby Congress. The organization is expressly bipartisan, and the INC achieved its greatest success in the 1998 enactment of the MacBride Principles.[9] The Irish American Unity Conference was founded in 1983, and the organization "advocates the end of British colonial occupation and the peaceful reunification of Ireland." Although there are several Irish American PACs registered with the Federal Election Commission (FEC), only the Irish American Democrats (IAD) are active. The PAC was founded in 1996 in order to help support Bill Clinton's reelection effort and ensure that his efforts toward the negotiations that eventually led to the 1998 Good Friday Accord would continue. Both the INC and IAD also champion aid to Ireland, and policymakers reported that Irish American groups lobby for visa waivers. Irish American leaders reported that the influence of the Irish American lobby is a bit of a conundrum: while there is widespread sympathy in the United States toward Ireland, a large Irish American population, and numerous political leaders of Irish descent, the Irish American lobby has found it difficult to get Irish Americans and the US government to focus on the issue of Northern Ireland. Some scholars argue that Irish Americans have become so assimilated that the community no longer finds foreign policy or even Northern Ireland salient. However, DeConde argues that "this assessment underrates the ability of the activist Irish-Americans to involve, if not influence, the foreign-policy establishment on Anglo-Irish problems" (1992, 176).

Many ethnic groups that hailed from south and southeastern Europe have a strong tradition of influencing foreign policy in the twentieth century. According to DeConde, "the descendants of southeastern European immigrants . . . [became] bolder and more effective in challenging the traditional managers of foreign policy. At the same time, much more often than in the past, the governing elite sought support from these minorities in attaining strategic international goals" (1992, 138). For example, in 1948, the United States turned to Italian Americans to help influence Italian elections (DeConde 1992). Indeed, the Italian American lobby once enjoyed the distinction of being one of the three powerful "I" lobbies (joining the Irish and Israeli American lobbies). However, policymakers interviewed for this study argued that the Italian American lobby is almost certainly losing influence in foreign policy, in part because Italian Americans are assimilated, and in part because the United States and Italy enjoy strong relations and a lack of salient foreign policy issues. Indeed, Italian American groups appear much more focused on domestic policies, including negative portrayals of Italian Americans in the entertainment industry, than on foreign policy concerns.

For much of the past three decades, the Greek (or Hellenic) American lobby was very active in foreign affairs and, by many accounts, an influential player. The Hellenic lobby achieved its greatest success after the 1974 Turkish invasion of Cyprus, when the US Congress ratified an arms embargo against Turkey despite opposition by President Richard Nixon and Secretary of State Henry Kissinger. According to DeConde, "All parties concerned with the issue recognized the Greek lobby as the primary force in the passage of the legislation" (1992, 173), although Watanabe (1984) contends that resentment among members of Congress with Kissinger's leadership style (and his ignoring of Congress) led to a marriage between the Greek American lobby and congressional activists on the embargo. The embargo was lifted in 1978, and since then some analysts have "viewed . . . Greek ethnic politics as ineffective," although most others believe the "Turks might have slaughtered" many Greek Cypriots if the Greek American lobby had not pressured the United States to intervene on the issue of Cyprus (DeConde 1992, 174). For years, Greek American groups "have lobbied almost exclusively on two issues—an earmark of $15 million for the government of Cyprus and continuation of the 7-to-10 ratio, which requires the United States to provide $7 in military aid for Greece for each $10 provided to Turkey" (Doherty 1995a). More recently, the Greek American lobby was also active regarding the aftermath of the disintegration of Yugoslavia, the Balkan conflict, and the creation of the Republic of Macedonia.

There are several Greek American organizations. One of the most prominent, the American Hellenic Institute (AHI), is composed of three entities: the parent company; a foundation, which generates publications and hosts conferences; and a public affairs committee, which handles the lobbying. The AHI does not organize a PAC, in part because it does not wish to deal with FEC regulations. The organization is focused primarily on foreign policy, and it strives to reach across the Greek community. For example, the AHI has developed a business network in an effort to bring members in the Greek American community together. AHI leaders acknowledge it can be difficult to bring Greek Americans into the organization on just the issue of foreign policy. However, AHI leaders reason that if they can get Greek Americans involved in the organization for other reasons, they may be able to make them understand the importance of foreign policy.

Other ethnic lobbies that represent Americans who trace their heritage to southeast Europe include the Albanian, Croat, and Serb lobbies. All three lobbies were active after the end of the Cold War and during the Balkan wars of the 1990s. While the Croat lobby appears to have faded since the end of the Balkan conflict, the Serbian and Albanian lobbies are both still active in the policymaking process. The main Serb organization is the Serbian Unity Congress, which states part of its mission is to help rehabilitate the image of Serbia. The Serbian Unity Congress has concentrated its recent efforts on opposing independence for Kosovo, and the organization has worked to encourage members of Congress to join the Serbian congressional caucus. Two main Albanian American organizations exist. The National Albanian American Council (NAAC) asserts that it "provides timely information and analysis of Albanian issues to policy and opinion makers in Washington. . . . NAAC members also provide expert testimony at hearings before the United States Congress and commentary for leading television news programs and at academic forums" (National Albanian American Council 2007). The organization also encourages political participation on the part of Albanian Americans and collects humanitarian aid for the people of Albania. The Albanian American Civic League, formed in 1989 by former congressman Joseph DioGuardi (R-NY), touts that it is the "only registered lobby in Washington, DC, representing the concerns and interests of the Albanian people" (Albanian American Civil League 2007). The organization also operates a fairly large PAC.

There exist numerous organizations that represent ethnicities whose ancestral states were under Soviet control. During the Cold War, a host of ethnic groups representing Czech, Estonian, Hungarian, Lithuanian, Latvian, and Polish Americans lobbied the United States to take a hard line against the Soviet Union. After the Cold War, many of these groups lobbied for a greater US embassy presence in the ancestral homelands, as well as greater US aid to promote democratization. In addition, the debate surrounding the enlargement of NATO prompted activism on the part of many of these ethnicities.

Now, according to some policymakers interviewed for this project, some of these organizations appear to be fading and there are fewer salient foreign policy issues for which the groups can mobilize their ethnic communities. For example, one Capitol Hill policymaker remarked, "I've heard the Polish lobby was very strong during the Cold War, but now they seem rudderless." Other lobbies and organizations have worked specifically to develop new foci for foreign policy engagement. For example, the Joint Baltic American National Committee developed a white paper in 2004 to help guide the organization's foreign policy mission after the expansion of NATO (Joint Baltic American National Committee 2004). Likewise, the National Conference on Soviet Jewry, which advocated free emigration of Soviet Jews, refocused its efforts after the fall of the Soviet Union. Groups representing Polish Americans, Baltic Americans, Ukrainian Americans, Czech Americans, and Hungarian Americans continue to work on foreign policy issues. Some ethnic leaders of these organizations complained that the US focus on the Middle East has led to reductions in programs that focus on other areas of the world, such as Radio Free Europe and Voice of America.

Latin American Lobbies

Much has been made of the increasingly large Hispanic population in the United States: Hispanic Americans are now the largest minority group in the United States, and the Hispanic population is growing rapidly. "As the Hispanic population in the United States expands, Latinos are likely to become more active players in foreign policy debates, particularly on U.S. relations with Latin America" (Jones-Correa 2002, 115). However, as is the case with the Asian American lobby, the Latin American lobby is hindered by the fact that Hispanic Americans hail from numerous nations. In addition, there may also be a generational divide that limits the pan-Latin lobby. Recent Hispanic immigrants to the United States tend to engage in "constant, informal contact with their countries of origin" regarding a number of issues, including remittances and dual citizenship (Jones-Correa 2002, 115). Hispanic immigrants to the United States, because of the substantial amount of remittances sent back to the birth countries,[10] are an important source of economic development, and some leaders of Latin American countries also raise campaign contributions and court votes from these immigrants (Shain 1999; Jones-Correa 2002).

Michael Jones-Correa argues that as Latino immigrants assimilate, their interest in their mother countries dissipates, further reducing the likelihood of a pan-Latin lobby: "It may be that a united Latino foreign policy is a chimera—tantalizingly tempting in the distance, it will always slip away just as it lies within reach" (2002, 126). Indeed, Hispanic American elites, most of whom were born in the United States, largely ignore foreign policy issues and instead focus on domestic issues. For example, a 1997 survey of Hispanic American leaders showed that a host of domestic concerns, such as education, race relations, and economic growth in the United States, outranked foreign policy priorities (Jones-Correa 2002). Only with the issue of immigration do recent immigrants and Hispanic elites work together organizationally and substantively (Jones-Correa 2002).

Two Latino ethnicities, Cuban Americans and Mexican Americans, stand out in their interest in foreign policy. According to Jones-Correa:

> In practice, the only consistent and sustained foreign policy involvement by Latinos in the United States has been Cuban-American lobbying for sanctions against Castro-led Cuba. Here, however, Cuban Americans may be the exception that proves the rule. Unlike most other Latino residents of the United States, Cuban-Americans arrived as political asylees, fleeing a newly established communist regime in Cuba. As a result, many Cuban migrants felt their decision to come to the United States as one of coercion rather than choice, and their stay in this country as one of exile rather than permanent settlement. (2002, 119)

The desire by Cuban Americans to influence US policy toward Cuba and bring an end to the Castro regime is legendary, and Cuban Americans have founded numerous organizations dedicated to influencing US foreign policy, such as Citizens for Liberty in Cuba, CubaLibertad, and the Cuban American National Foundation (CANF). Among ethnic lobbies, only CANF approaches AIPAC's status: indeed, CANF was explicitly structured after AIPAC (see Haney and Vanderbush 1999; Brenner and Landau 1990). Patrick Haney and Walt Vanderbush assert that CANF played the role of "near co-executor" of US policy toward Cuba for years (1999, 341), and the organization played a significant role in establishing funding for, and subsequent management of, Radio and TV Martí. Tony Smith contends that "CANF demonstrated real power over American foreign policy" in the ratification of the 1996 Helms-Burton Bill and other legislation related to Cuba (2000, 69). John Newhouse argues that CANF became "one of the country's most powerful political-action groups," and the group assumed a great deal of control over Radio Martí and processing Cuban immigrants from third countries (1992, 76–77). CANF's influence was not just limited to the Caribbean: the group also promoted US assistance to UNITA in the Angolan civil war, because Cuban troops were aiding the Popular Movement for the Liberation of Angola–Party of Labour (MPLA) government (Weissman 1995).

For much of their history in the United States, Mexican Americans have focused much more on domestic concerns than on foreign policy, in part because "the relationship between Mexicans on either side of the border can be best characterized as ambivalent. Although the two groups share strong connections based on family ties, history, and culture, Mexico's domestic upheavals and the experiences of Mexicans in the United States have had a distancing effect" (Shain 1999, 670–671). Like other ethnic groups, Mexican Americans "have often found themselves entangled by the question of their allegiance" (Shain 1999, 676); so many have embraced Mexican culture but eschewed political participation related to Mexico, instead focusing on domestic issues such as civil rights, education, political opportunities, and employment. As the Mexican American community has grown and assimilated, and as more Mexican Americans have become voters, more Mexican Americans have become elected officials and policymakers. Some Mexican Americans, especially those born in the United States, "have discovered the political and economic power of the Latino community inside the United States and its potential for doing business with Mexico" (Shain 1999, 681). According to Shain, Mexican American elites have realized they can engage in the foreign policy–making process, and attempt to influence US-Mexican relations, without compromising their American identity. Much of their foreign policy efforts has focused on free trade and immigration, and Mexican American leaders played a role in helping to ratify NAFTA. Indeed, some scholars asserted that NAFTA was a pivotal issue for the Mexican American community, because it helped fulfill "a dream they've had for a long time . . . to be like the Jewish lobby in the U.S. for Israel" (as quoted in Solis 1993, 10).

A decade after the trade pact was ratified, it does not appear that NAFTA fulfilled that dream: most Mexican American groups and elites focus on domestic issues, such as civil rights and advocacy, and many organizations founded by Mexican Americans, such as the League of United Latin American Citizens, serve the broader Hispanic community. These organizations do, however, address the intermestic issue of immigration. For example, the Mexican American Legal Defense and Education Fund (MALDEF) states that it concentrates its efforts on the issues of employment, education, immigration, political access, language, and public resource equity (Mexican American Legal Defense and Education Fund 2007).

■ Middle East and Eurasian Lobbies

No ethnicity has a stronger institutional presence in the foreign policy–making process than the Jewish lobby, and there is no shortage of Jewish-based organizations that are engaged in foreign or intermestic policies, such as the American Jewish Congress, Jewish Institute for National Security Affairs, Jewish Peace Lobby, and NCSJ (formerly the National Conference on Soviet Jewry). Two organizations are especially important for providing an institutional presence for Jewish Americans in the foreign policy–making process. First, although it is technically a pro-Israeli group,[11] AIPAC provides the Jewish community with an organization dedicated to strengthening and maintaining strong ties between the United States and Israel. AIPAC's organizational prowess is legendary, and it was rated as the fourth most influential lobbying organization in the country in 2001, behind only the National Rifle Association, AARP, and the National Federation of Independent Business (Birnbaum 2001). To most observers, and the consensus of those interviewed for this study, AIPAC is the gold standard of an effective lobbying organization. According to some observers, AIPAC's greatest asset has been the "several thousand affluent grass-roots members for whom Israel was not just a cause but a sacred mission" (Frankel 2006, 16), a statement echoed by some policymakers interviewed for this study. Others note AIPAC's extensive lobbying efforts on Capitol Hill. For example, John Mearsheimer and Stephen Walt assert that AIPAC has achieved "an almost unchallenged hold on Congress" by channeling financial support to members of Congress and congressional candidates, supplying information and rhetoric to congressional offices, and providing free congressional trips to Congress (2007, 162). In an effort to emulate the successes associated with AIPAC, other ethnicities have founded organizations built upon the AIPAC model.

The second major coordinating body for Jewish Americans is the Conference of Presidents of Major American Jewish Organizations, which is composed of the leaders of fifty-one Jewish organizations. The mission of the conference is to formulate and articulate "the 'Jewish position' on most foreign policy matters" (Bard 1991, 13), and the first two goals listed on the conference's website are to "strengthen and foster the special U.S.-Israel relationship" and to "ensure that Israel's interests are heard and understood by policy makers, opinion molders and the American public." According to Bard, the "conference is the main contact between the Jewish community and the executive branch, while AIPAC tends to be the conduit with the legislative branch" (1991, 13).

Despite the wide consensus of the influence of the Jewish American lobby today, Mearsheimer and Walt contend "there was nothing inevitable or predetermined about the current special relationship between the United

States and Israel" or, for that matter, the eventual power of the Jewish American lobby (2007, 7). Clearly, ethnic political considerations played at least some role in US policies toward the Middle East since the 1940s. For example, scholars attribute President Harry Truman's 1946 decision to reverse his earlier position and endorse the establishment of a Jewish state in Palestine to support for such a state among Jewish Americans, who made up a large percentage of his donors (Weil 1974; DeConde 1992).[12] Likewise, President John F. Kennedy's decision to authorize the first major sale of US weaponry to Israel in 1963 was based on strategic factors, but also was affected by "skillful Israeli diplomacy, the influence of several pro-Israel advisers, and Kennedy's understandable desire to maintain support from Jewish voters" (Mearsheimer and Walt 2007, 25).

Many scholars assert that it was not until the Six Day War of 1967 that the Jewish American lobby began to exercise tremendous influence in the policymaking process. However, since 1967, many contend that the "overall thrust" of US policy in the Middle East is especially influenced by the "activities of the 'Israel Lobby'" (Mearsheimer and Walt 2006, 1; see also Smith 2000, 58; DeConde 1992). Mearsheimer and Walt assert that the lobby is especially effective in lobbying both Congress and the executive branch, funding think tanks, and silencing critics by labeling them as being anti-Semites. They also argue that the Israel lobby is extremely effective at shaping public opinion. They conclude that "while other special interest groups—including ethnic lobbies representing Cuban Americans, Irish Americans, Armenian Americans, and Indian Americans—have managed to skew U.S. foreign policy in directions that they favored, no ethnic lobby has diverted that policy as far from what the American national interest would otherwise suggest. The Israel lobby has successfully convinced many Americans that American and Israeli interests are essentially identical" (Mearsheimer and Walt 2007, 8).

Others note that pro-Israeli PACs make several million dollars in campaign contributions to federal office seekers every election cycle, a figure that does not include individual contributions made by Jewish or pro-Israeli Americans to campaigns (McMahon 2004). "When combined with individual contributions to particular candidates and donations given to the national party organizations themselves, pro-Israel forces wield considerable electoral clout" (Mearsheimer and Walt 2007, 156). Some have argued that such contributions have defeated members of Congress who were not supportive of Israel: "Pro-Israel money helped defeat Republican Reps. Paul Findley of Illinois and Pete McCloskey of California and Sen. Charles Percy of Illinois, all of whom were deemed too sympathetic to Arab causes and too critical of Israel" (Frankel 2006, 17). Mearsheimer and Walt agree with this assessment, stating that the Israel lobby will target "politicians who appear reluctant to follow its lead" (2007, 159). One senior policymaker interviewed for this project, who does not believe that ethnic groups have too much influence in congressional elections, did state that Jewish groups targeted Earl Hilliard (D-AL) and Cynthia McKinney (D-GA), both of whom were defeated by primary opponents in 2002. Others argue that members of Congress (especially those with presidential ambitions) have strong incentives to be pro-Israel, since "89 percent [of Jews] live in twelve key electoral states" and "there are no benefits to candidates taking an openly anti-Israel stance and considerable costs in both loss of campaign contributions and votes from Jews and non-Jews alike" (Bard 1991, 8).

As we would expect, defenders of the Israel lobby do not believe it has too much influence, arguing the foreign policy–making process is pluralistic and there are limits to the lobby's sway. For example, Bard asserts that "pluralistic forces, specifically, the Israeli lobby, shape U.S. Middle East policy. [However], the lobby's influence is not unlimited as its critics suggest" (1991, 5). He notes that the president has the single greatest influence on national security issues, and the Israel lobby has been unable to overcome "the president's opposition to its position" at times (1991, 290).

Jewish Americans are not the only ethnic group that strives to influence US foreign policy in the Middle East. Arab Americans emerged as a political force in the latter half of the twentieth century, in part because of an influx of Arab immigrants after World War II. However, according to DeConde, the lobby remained largely ineffective for the next several decades because "public sentiment, the press, television, and the movies all remained against them. . . . to effect any change in foreign policy, the Arab-Americans had to battle ethnic prejudice and a hostile socio-political environment" (DeConde 1992, 138). Two major Arab American organizations formed in the 1980s, in part to change the social and political environment. The Arab American Institute (AAI) was founded in 1985 to "nurture and encourage the direct participation of Arab Americans in political and civic life in the United States" (Arab American Institute 2006). The AAI focuses much of its attention on two main areas: campaigns and elections and research and policy. The organization also has a 501(c)(3) foundation that promotes "Arab American heritage, ethnic cooperation, demographic research and international exchange." The Arab American Leadership Council Political Action Committee is affiliated with AAI, and there is a link for the PAC on the AAI website.[13] Another organization, the American-Arab Anti-Discrimination Committee (ADC), was founded in 1980 in response to the Abscam scandal (a public-corruption sting operation involving a fictional shaikh) and the negative stereotyping of Arab Americans. Like the AAI, the ADC works to incorporate Arab Americans into the political process, and the organization has worked with executive agencies to place Arab Americans in the bureaucracy. Although it focuses a great deal on domestic issues facing Arab Americans, like discrimination in the United States based on both race and religion, the organization does try to influence foreign policy.[14] Like the Greek and Armenian groups, both AAI's and ADC's websites are designed to pull individuals into the political system, and AAI sponsors internships to help promote political activism among young Arab Americans.

Perhaps in part because of the founding of these two organizations, Arab American groups seemed to gain influence in the 1980s and 1990s (Pressman 1985; Stanfield 1991), and according to some interviewed for this project, there was increased optimism among Arab American leaders that Palestine would become an independent state. However, an already difficult sociopolitical environment became very harsh for Arab Americans after September 11, 2001, an environment that one ethnic leader described as "miserable." Because of this, although Arab American organizations have a desire to influence foreign policy, much of their efforts are focused on discrimination against Americans of Arab descent instead. One Arab American leader interviewed for this project discussed the organization's efforts to be proactive in policymaking, a strategy that became impossible after September 11 as the organization scrambled to respond to the Patriot Act and racial profiling. Some policymakers agreed that Arab American groups spend much of their energies responding to events and policies rather than setting policies. In addition to the ramifications of September 11, the current Bush administration is decidedly more pro-Israel than previous administrations (Stolberg 2006), and this created a difficult political environment for groups that support Palestinian independence. Several policymakers and other ethnic leaders we interviewed expressed empathy for Arab American organizations, arguing that the groups couldn't seem to "catch a break." For example, many Arab Americans found the uproar over the Dubai port deal to smack of racism: after all, the American ports in question were already managed by a foreign (British) firm. However, some Arab American leaders we interviewed also stated that, generally speaking, Democrats were more likely to assist Arab American organizations. Since Democratic members of Congress were leading much of the furor over the Bush administration proposal, some Arab Americans felt caught between fighting racism and not condemning their friends within the Democratic Party who were criticizing the deal.

Compounding the difficulties associated with the political and social environment, another reality impedes the Arab American lobby: in reality, it is a "pan" lobby, like the African American and Hispanic American lobbies. Arab Americans are a diffuse community, and the Arab diaspora includes individuals of different ethnicities and religions. Even relatively geographically concentrated Arab American communities, like the one located in Dearborn, Michigan, include large segments of Lebanese, Iraqis, and Yemenis (MacFarquhar 2007). As a result, the Arab American lobby is "unlikely to speak with a unified voice on Middle East issues" (Mearsheimer and Walt 2007, 142; Bard 1991). Because of the varied and diverse nature of Arab

Americans as a whole, the Arab American lobby suffers in comparison to other lobbies that support a single ethnicity (Longworth 1998).

Within the Arab American universe, Lebanese Americans appear to be the most organized subgroup. The most prominent Lebanese American organization is the American Task Force for Lebanon (ATFL), which is composed "primarily of prominent and dedicated Americans of Lebanese heritage who share a common interest in Lebanon and the goals of the organization. The unifying goal is to work towards reestablishing a secure, stable, independent, and sovereign Lebanon with full control over all its territory" (American Task Force for Lebanon 2006). According to policy-makers, the organization is active in the policymaking process, and a fairly active PAC is associated with the group.

Shifting to Eurasian lobbies, one of the most active ethnic lobbies is the Armenian American community; for this study, in terms of examples given by policymakers of how ethnic American communities attempt to influence policymaking, only the Jewish and Cuban American lobbies were mentioned more than the Armenian lobby. The Armenian American community is often cited by observers as one of the most influential ethnic communities in the foreign policy process (Doherty 1995c; Greve 1995; Walt 2005). According to Smith, "It is widely agreed that the high levels of U.S. aid to Armenia (the second highest per capita in the world, after Israel) and the embargo of official assistance to Azerbaijan . . . would be inconceivable American policy were it not for this ethnic American community" (2000, 69–70). Since Armenia gained independence from the Soviet Union, the Armenian community has focused on a number of foreign policy issues, including US relations with Armenia and Azerbaijan; US aid to Armenia, Azerbaijan, and Turkey; and US recognition of the 1915 genocide of Armenians living in the Ottoman Empire. There are two main Armenian American organizations: the Armenian Assembly of America (AAA) and the Armenian National Committee of America (ANCA). The ANCA is affiliated with a broader, worldwide Armenian diaspora network, although the organization's leadership and membership are composed of Armenian Americans. Both the AAA and ANCA have permanent headquarters in Washington, DC, and have in-house governmental affairs professionals, allowing the organizations easier access to policymakers on Capitol Hill and elsewhere in the nation's capital. Both organizations have a strong presence on Capitol Hill: several staffers we interviewed reported working with governmental affairs professionals from both organizations. Both organizations have sophisticated websites, which encourage political participation by providing links to write members of Congress, read position papers, and otherwise become active in the organizations. Leaders of these organizations argue that sizeable Armenian communities exist in perhaps 250 congressional districts, and active Armenian Americans are engaged in an additional 50 congressional districts. Many of the same leaders of the ANCA also organize the Armenian National Committee PAC, although there is no link from the ANCA website to this PAC. A second major Armenian PAC, ARMENPAC, is not affiliated with either the AAA or the ANCA.

Turkish and Kurdish Americans also try to influence the political process. Several respondents stated that the Turkish embassy is more active than Turkish American organizations in attempting to influence US policies toward Turkey and the Middle East. Much of the focus of Turkish American lobbying efforts involves greater foreign aid for Turkey. While Turkey is seen by many as a valuable and dependable NATO ally, Turkey has also been criticized by members of Congress for its "harsh counterinsurgency campaign against the Kurds" (Doherty 1996b). Because of this, Kurdish Americans join Greek and Armenian Americans in efforts to reduce US aid for Turkey.

Other Middle Eastern ethnicities have become more active in foreign affairs recently. For example, Assyrian Americans have rallied in support of the 2003 US invasion of Iraq (Stern 2004), and several Assyrian American PACs have been organized (although none has contributed to federal candidates to date). Iranian Americans have become more involved in the policymaking process, but the community is fairly divided and does not speak with one voice (MacFarquhar 2006). An Iranian American PAC was organized in 2002, and the PAC contributed $19,000 to federal candidates in 2004.

◼ Organizational Models for Ethnic Groups

We identified several organizational models for ethnic groups. The first is the AIPAC model, where the organization strives to be the clearinghouse of information regarding foreign policy for the homeland of the ethnicity. The AIPAC model consists of developing separate funding, research, and lobbying organizations; the funding arm raises significant financial resources, which are then used to fund the research institutions and professional in-house lobbyists. The organization employs a sophisticated grassroots operation, which includes state and local chapters. AIPAC also has an affiliated charitable organization, the American Israel Education Foundation, which funds educational programs. One area in which AIPAC does not participate is direct campaign contributions: AIPAC does not organize a PAC, although scholars assert that, nonetheless, the organization plays a significant role in funding congressional candidates. For example, Mearsheimer and Walt contend that "AIPAC makes sure that its friends get financial support so long as they do not stray from AIPAC's line," either through campaign contributions from AIPAC leaders or by screening and then connecting congressional candidates to major Jewish and pro-Israel donors and PACs (2007, 154).

There are a number of ethnic organizations that are organized in a similar fashion to the AIPAC model, the most notable example being the Cuban American National Foundation, which modeled itself expressly after AIPAC (Haney and Vanderbush 1999). Likewise, leaders of the Armenian Assembly of America and the American Hellenic Institute acknowledge their organizations are also patterned after AIPAC (Mufson 2000; Watanabe 1984). Other ethnic organizations, such as the Armenian National Committee of America, the American-Arab Anti-Discrimination Committee, and the Arab American Institute all appear to be structured like AIPAC. Additionally, many, but not all, of these groups are associated with a PAC, which, while technically separate from the ethnic group, is organized by the leaders or directors of the overall organization. Like AIPAC, many of these organizations are affiliated with a 501(c)(3) institute dedicated to educational, cultural, and other nonprofit endeavors. Contributions from individuals to 501(c)(3) institutes and organizations are often tax-deductible, which helps provide a monetary incentive for individuals to donate to the organization. Thus, these institutes can fund educational and informational projects that contribute to the overall goals of the organization, while also providing added tax advantages to the organization and its members.

A second pattern is for the group to function primarily as a PAC, collecting contributions from individuals that are then distributed to candidates and officeholders. Some PACs simply distribute campaign contributions, while other PACs have direct contact with elected officials as well. The US India PAC (USINPAC), the Irish American Democrats, the National Action Committee PAC (NACPAC), the National Organization for Political Action (NORPAC), and the Washington PAC all follow this pattern. The most sophisticated of these PACs look a great deal like traditional ethnic membership organizations, albeit with higher dues: their websites include policy information, rhetoric and talking points, and links to like-minded organizations. For example, the websites for NORPAC, the Washington PAC, and NACPAC provide issue positions and value-based arguments for US support of Israel, and the organizations encourage mobilization. In doing so, these PACs use purposive appeals to encourage individuals to contribute to the PAC and help fund the stated mission of the organization. The PACs also often use social rewards, hosting fundraisers and receptions where PAC members and donors can meet candidates and celebrities. Ethnic PACs not only make contributions to candidates, but some also host fundraisers for candidates, and guests to the fundraisers make their contributions directly to the candidates and not the PAC itself. It is not uncommon for such fundraisers to raise six figures: an amount significantly higher than the contribution a single PAC can make to a candidate in an election cycle.

Some PACs also encourage members to contact policymakers directly to reiterate the goals of the organization. For example, while NORPAC underscores the ability of the organization to link with lawmakers, it also encourages its members to provide "personal support" to members of Congress, such as educating members on positions or "providing the emotional assurance that a public position taken is appreciated within our community" (NORPAC 2007). In addition to trying to pull Indian Americans into the political process through its website, USINPAC tries to cast a wider net by distributing its literature through other, mostly nonpolitical, Indian American groups to their members. Other ethnic PAC websites do not necessarily include a "Get Involved" link on the site or a mechanism that encourages visitors to write their representatives or allows visitors to send e-mail to their members of Congress. Instead, these ethnic PACs focus on the electoral connection and the need to elect members of Congress who share the views of the PAC. NACPAC's website states that donations to the organization will be used to elect and "build relationships with pro-Israel Congressmen," as well as target "unfriendly incumbents for defeat" (NACPAC 2007). These PACs also emphasize their efforts to personally connect with members of Congress. For example, the Washington PAC, which was founded in 1981 by Morris Amitay,[15] states that its "Capitol Hill location enables it to meet with Representatives and Senators on an almost daily basis" (Washington PAC 2007).

Most of the organizations that follow the PAC mobilization model are pro-Israel, and many of these PACs gave hundreds of thousands of dollars to federal candidates between 1997 and 2004. For example, over the 1998–2004 election cycles, NACPAC contributed $607,000 to federal candidates, NORPAC gave over $617,000, and the Washington PAC distributed almost $700,000. However, in some cases federal candidates declined to accept those contributions: for example, candidates returned to NORPAC over $40,000 in contributions. While NACPAC boasts that it is the "nation's largest pro-Israel political action committee," another pro-Israel PAC contributed much more from 1997 to 2004: the National PAC (NATPAC) distributed almost $1.1 million in contributions during that time period. However, NATPAC and a few other large pro-Israel PACs like the Desert Caucus do not maintain websites that help pull citizens into the political process.

A third organizational prototype is the not-for-profit 501(c)(3) advocacy model. Such organizations choose to remain nonprofit for tax reasons, and their 501(c)(3) status allows individual contributions to the group to be tax-deductible in many cases. The TransAfrica Forum, Japanese American Citizen League, NCSJ, and the United Jewish Communities are examples of not-for-profit ethnic organizations that seek to influence foreign or intermestic policies. These organizations focus a great deal on monitoring, collecting and distributing information, and education, all of which are designed to help promote the missions of the organizations. Although such organizations are prohibited from spending funds on lobbying, many do participate in advocacy work. Many see the distinction between "lobbying" and "advocacy" as trivial at best, and Chapter 3 will discuss lobbying by nonprofit organizations further. However, 501(c)(3) organizations can attempt to persuade policymakers directly as long as they are not spending funds directly on lobbying, and nonprofits can engage in grassroots lobbying.

Ethnic nonprofit organizations do both. For example, NCSJ is part of a network of Jewish organizations and acts as the "central coordinating agency . . . for policy and activities on behalf of the estimated 1.5 million Jews in the former Soviet Union" (NCSJ 2007). NCSJ monitors emigration, tracks anti-Semitism, distributes information and analysis, hosts conferences, and provides support to Jewish communities within the former Soviet empire. Likewise, TransAfrica states that it "serves as a major research, educational, and organizing institution for the African-American community offering constructive analyses of issues concerning U.S. policy as it affects Africa and the Diaspora in the Caribbean and Latin America. . . . [W]e sponsor seminars, conferences, community awareness projects and training programs. These activities allow us to play a significant role in presenting to the general public alternative perspectives on the economic, political, and moral ramifications of U.S. foreign policy" (TransAfrica Forum 2007). By providing information to policymakers, these nonprofit organizations hope to influence both the agenda-setting and the policymaking stages. In addition, many advocacy groups build grassroots networks to help lobby policymakers indirectly.

A final model is an entrepreneurial model, where the organization is run by an individual or two, and these few people wear all of the hats, including fundraising, public relations, advocacy, and contacting members of Congress and their offices. Many of these organizations are run by the same individual(s) who founded the group, and some of these founders stated they established the organization because of the absence of ethnic entities that focused on foreign policy. Despite their relatively small size, such organizations can have an influence. For example, the Polish American Congress, described in 1998 as one of Washington's most effective ethnic lobbies, is "literally a mom-and-pop shop," operated by Casimir and Myra Lenard for over thirty years (Longworth 1998). The Irish National Caucus was founded by Father Sean McManus after he found that no Irish American organizations were present in Washington in the mid-1970s, and the organization played a significant role in shepherding the MacBride Principles into law over a period of more than a decade. Yet, the organization is small and centered on Father McManus, and he often answers calls placed to the organization's main phone number. Other examples of the entrepreneurial model include the American Kurdish Information Network and the Albanian American Civic League.

▦ Conclusion

The universe of ethnic American organizations is as diverse as the nation itself, and ethnic American groups vary greatly in terms of their size and resources, how they are organized, and the issues on which they focus. While most ethnic American groups focus on cultural or domestic issues, a subset consisting of several dozen lobbies are active in foreign policy and intermestic policy realms. The array of ethnic lobbies focused on foreign policy has changed over time, as new ethnic communities have immigrated to the United States and other more established ethnic communities have begun to become involved in foreign policy making. Other ethnic communities no longer are especially active in foreign policy making, in part because they have assimilated to the point that foreign policy is no longer salient to most members. Other factors have also contributed to the changing nature of the ethnic lobby universe, as external events like the end of the Cold War have reduced the saliency of foreign policy for some ethnic communities.

The next chapter analyzes the strategies and tactics that ethnic groups and organizations use to influence the policymaking process, including direct lobbying, grassroots lobbying, campaign contributions, and coalition building. The chapter will also examine in depth the scope and nature of political action committee expenditures by ethnic organizations.

▦ Notes

1. The Comprehensive Anti-Apartheid Act of 1986 set in motion the executive order by President Ronald Reagan (Weisman 2005).

2. Other *non*-ethnic-based organizations do exist for the purpose of influencing public policy toward Africa.

3. As will be explained more fully in the next chapter, 501(c)(3) organizations are tax-exempt charities and cannot use monies for lobbying activities. However, these organizations can (and do) attempt to sway the policymaking process through advocacy. In contrast, 501(c)(4) organizations are also nonprofits, but donations to these organizations are not tax-deductible. Because of this, these organizations are permitted to expend monies to lobby for legislation as long as shareholders do not benefit from the legislation.

4. We asked several of these policymakers why we found no organized Somali or Ethiopian lobbying effort, and one policymaker responded that these cultures are clan based, with a strong entrepreneurial spirit. Because of this, it is harder for Somalis and Ethiopians to create organizations across clans. A second policymaker agreed with this assessment.

5. In addition to USINPAC, Walt (2005) states that the Indian American Forum for Political Education (IAFPE) and the Indian American Center for Political Awareness (IACPA) are political lobbying organizations.

6. Still, according to Dudden and policymakers interviewed for this study, a more critical factor for HR 759 was the bipartisan support by Henry Hyde (R-IL) and Lane Evans (D-IL).

7. The formation of the Committee of One Million "remains cloaked in governmental secrecy," as one of the founding members may have worked for the Central Intelligence Agency (Bachrack 1976).

8. In his analysis, DeConde discusses the "powerful 'British and Scotch-Irish' group and its supporters" as having a significant influence on US policy toward Northern Ireland (1992, 176). Because of DeConde's analysis, we included the Anglo American lobby in the policymaker survey, despite the fact that we found no evidence of an organized Anglo lobby.

9. The MacBride Principles "set out equal opportunity and nondiscrimination guidelines for companies and projects in Northern Ireland receiving money from the" International Fund for Ireland (Carroll 1998, 10). The INC's focus on bipartisanship likely helped the organization's efforts to enact the MacBride Principles. According to Father Sean McManus, Democratic congressional leaders blocked efforts to pass the legislation. When Republicans took control of the House in 1995, Representative Benjamin Gilman (R-NY) became chair of the House Committee on International Relations, and Gilman shepherded the principles into law.

10. Remittances from ethnic communities in the United States to former or ancestral homelands are not limited to Latin American and Caribbean nations; remittances are important sources of economic development funds for Eastern European and Asian countries as well (Shain 1999).

11. There is no agreement regarding whether it is best to use the term "Jewish American lobby" or "Israeli American lobby." On the one hand, some observers assert that the proper term is "Israeli American lobby," since it includes all Americans who lobby or advocate on behalf of strong US-Israeli positions, including many Jewish Americans, but also non-Jews. For example, Mearsheimer and Walt argue that the "core of the (Israel) Lobby is comprised of American Jews who make a significant effort in their daily lives to bend U.S. foreign policy so that it advances Israel's interests . . . (but) also includes prominent Christian evangelicals (and) neoconservative gentiles" (2006, 14–15). Likewise, while Bard states that AIPAC is part of the formal lobby that represents American Jews, the "more accurate label" is the Israeli lobby "because a large proportion of the lobby is made up of non-Jews" (1991, 6). On the other hand, some contend that the term "Jewish American lobby" better captures the ethnoracial dynamic of individuals and groups who are joined by a common Jewish ethnoracial heritage.

12. Mearsheimer and Walt agree that Jewish Americans did affect Truman's deliberations, but they assert Truman's "decision to back Israel's creation and to recognize the new state was influenced (though not determined) by intercessions from Jewish friends and advisers" (2007, 118; see also Weil 1974). Mearsheimer and Walt also contend that both presidents Truman and Eisenhower purposely did not embrace Israel too closely in order to preserve US relations with Arab states.

13. Although the Arab American Leadership Council Political Action Committee is listed on the AAI website as being affiliated with the organization, it is technically an independent PAC. This distinction is important because it allows the PAC to seek and collect contributions from individuals who are not members of the AAI.

14. Although a majority of Arab Americans are Christian, some Arab Americans are Muslim.

15. Amitay is the former executive director of AIPAC, and he is credited with transforming AIPAC into a lobbying powerhouse (Frankel 2006).

3

Lobbying Strategies

Ethnic interest groups confront the same obstacles that other organized interests face in terms of gaining influence: ethnic groups must gain access to the policymaking process in order to influence policymaking. Thus, a central problem that ethnic groups must tackle is: Why should members of Congress or other policymakers, often overwhelmed by requests for meetings, take the time to meet with your organization? Even if you are allowed to meet with a member of Congress, why should the representative act on your requests? Often, the answer to the first question lies in the degree to which an organization can provide something of value to the member of Congress, such as information or electoral support in terms of votes and/or campaign contributions. And the answer to the second question is that groups can use a host of strategies in an attempt to influence and persuade policymakers, including direct lobbying, grassroots lobbying, coalition building, and monitoring the policymaking process. It will become clear that the answers to both questions are often interrelated: campaign contributions can be valuable to members of Congress, and those contributions may provide valuable access to interest groups so that they can attempt to persuade the policymaker by providing key information or rhetoric. This chapter first examines the main strategies used by ethnic groups to gain access and influence the policymaking process. Then, the chapter examines the degree to which ethnic groups engage in the electoral process through the use of political action committees. Finally, the chapter analyzes the use of direct lobbying and grassroots lobbying by ethnic groups.

Ethnic Group Strategies

Perhaps the best-known persuasion tactic is *direct lobbying,* where interest group leaders or their agents (i.e., lobbyists) speak directly to decisionmakers in an attempt to influence public policy. Interest groups, corporations, unions, and organizations often establish an office in Washington, DC, to expedite lobbying at the federal level, allowing their leaders close proximity to Congress, the White House, and executive agencies. Some organizations will dedicate one or more employees to the role of government relations, and the employees will work to develop relationships with policymakers in the hopes of gaining access to and, ultimately, influence with these decisionmakers. However, organizations are not required to have a Washington office to engage in direct lobbying: some groups rely instead upon hired representatives who will champion the organizations' interests to policymakers. The three forms of surrogate representation are "(1) multiple-client 'boutique' lobbying firms; (2) major Washington law firms; and (3) megafirms that provide one-stop shopping for all public relations and government relations needs" (Shaiko 2005, 6). Even organizations that employ professional in-house government-relations experts may also hire surrogate representation for certain issue campaigns or for long-term help with promoting their agenda.

It is commonly believed that 501(c)(3) organizations, those nonprofit entities that most people conceptualize as the tax-deductible charities, cannot engage in direct lobbying. In fact, many 501(c)(3) organizations do frequent Capitol Hill and are clearly attempting to influence the policymaking process, which they can do legally as long as lobbying is not the principal purpose of the organization and the organization does not spend money in an attempt to influence legislation. From the perspective of the Internal Revenue Service (IRS), "where there is no expenditure by the organization for lobbying, there is no lobbying by the organization" (Smucker 1999, 51). Therefore, as long as volunteers are used (and are not reimbursed for their expenses), or the organization does not spend money directly in its attempt to persuade lawmakers, the organization is not technically engaged in lobbying. While many 501(c)(3) charities refuse to label their advocacy work on Capitol Hill as "lobbying," many researchers don't split hairs. For example, in his research on lobbying, Anthony Nownes found that many charities, such as the American Cancer Society and the Alzheimer's Association, "lobby extensively" (2006, 14), and Nownes and others see no reason to use the term "advocacy" to describe the efforts by charities to influence policymakers.

Lobbying is often tied unequivocally to electioneering (Shaiko 2005), where organizations, companies, and unions are involved in the electoral process not only in hopes of influencing the composition of government, but also with the expectation of establishing access to politicians once they are in office. Businesses and unions are prohibited from contributing directly to political campaigns, but they can form political action committees and 527 organizations, which are funded by their employees and members. Many leaders of these organizations form "unaffiliated" PACs that are not connected directly to the organization, but are run as parallel operations. By remaining unaffiliated from the group, these PACs are allowed to solicit contributions from individuals who are not members of the organization. The 501(c)(3) nonprofit groups cannot engage in partisan electioneering activity at all: "working for the election of a particular candidate . . . is strictly prohibited and is cause for the nonprofit to lose its tax-exempt status" (Smucker 1999, 66).[1] The 501(c)(3) organizations can produce reports of voting records, which rate officeholders on various issues important to the organization, but these voting record reports must be produced throughout the year and not simply close to the election.

While campaign contributions are important to members of Congress, interest groups may possess another commodity that is valuable to elected officials: information. Fundamentally, interest groups gain access by acquiring and transmitting valuable information that "legislators need to make good public policy and get reelected" (Wright 2003, 2). John Wright posits that interest groups acquire and disseminate information about the "status and prospect of bills under active consideration; [the] electoral implications of legislators' support for or opposition to those bills; [and] the likely economic, social, or environmental consequences of proposed policies" (88). For instance, ethnic groups may provide valuable information about the prospects of a bill's passage, and they can also provide information to policymakers about the unintended consequences of a bill or the unseen value of including a key provision in the legislation. Indeed, ethnic groups may play an important function in helping secure sponsors and cosponsors for a bill, and then working to ensure the bill is shepherded through the legislative process. For example, AIPAC is credited with playing a key role in securing cosponsors and guiding bills through the legislative process, and part of the influence of AIPAC is grounded in its ability to provide members of Congress and staffers with information.

> For overstretched members of Congress and their staffs, who don't have the time or resources to master every subject in their domain, AIPAC makes itself an essential tool. It briefs. It lobbies. It organizes frequent seminars on subjects such as terrorism, Islamic militarism and nuclear proliferation. It brings experts to the Hill from think tanks in Washington and Tel Aviv. It provides research papers and offers advice on drafting legislation on foreign affairs, including the annual foreign aid bill. (Frankel 2006, 25)

Further, ethnic groups can provide important persuasive arguments and rhetoric that can help lawmakers justify the bill's passage (see, also, Mearsheimer and Walt 2007). For example, in 2006, Indian American groups trumpeted the economic value of the US-India Civilian Nuclear Agreement, as well as India's record in terms of democracy and nuclear nonproliferation.

Finally, ethnic groups may also detail how salient a piece of legislation is to important constituents and, explicitly or implicitly, to the reelection prospects of members of Congress. For example, the Serbian Unity Congress has issued action alerts that encourage Serbian Americans to write their members of Congress, state to their representative that the Serbian American community opposes Kosovo independence, and remind members of Congress of the electoral size of the community (Serbian Unity Congress 2007). To give another example, some Armenian Americans criticized then-representative James Rogan (R-CA) for not doing more to secure the passage of a resolution condemning the Armenian genocide of 1915, and the Armenian National Committee of America endorsed Rogan's opponent and the eventual winner of the race, Democrat Adam Schiff (Schmitt 2000).

The 2000 contest between Rogan and Schiff highlights the complexity of determining the influence of ethnic groups, since it is difficult to ascertain exactly why Rogan lost and Schiff won. The Armenian Genocide Resolution was not the only issue looming over the race for the California 27th Congressional District: Rogan also played a key role in the controversial impeachment proceedings against President Bill Clinton, and the contest was in many respects a proxy fight between supporters and opponents of the impeachment (Wallsten 2000). The race was also viewed as a bellwether for determining which party would control the House of Representatives, and the contest became the most expensive House race in history. For these reasons, it is difficult to know if Rogan and Schiff courted Armenian Americans because the Armenian voting bloc was important in and of itself or because the race was unusually close, and it is difficult to determine if the Armenian vote cost Rogan the election. However, observers noted that both candidates acted as if the Armenian American vote was extremely important: Rogan and Schiff each courted Armenian Americans to the point that both candidates accused each other of pandering, and both had campaign workers on staff who spoke Armenian (Wallsten 2000). Others seemed to agree that the Armenian vote was important, as Rogan secured a promise from House Speaker Dennis Hastert to allow a floor vote on the Armenian Genocide Resolution (Schmitt 2000).[2] Journalists estimated that the number of Armenian American voters in the district ranged from 17,000 to over 20,000, approximately 7 to 9 percent of the almost 216,000 individuals who voted in the district's 2000 general election (Wallsten 2000; Schmitt 2000).

Having thousands of ethnic brethren in a congressional district is not only helpful for electoral purposes, it can be critical for an ethnic interest group to engage in *grassroots (or indirect) lobbying*. Grassroots lobbying occurs when groups mobilize "those who share their views to participate in some way so their own voices will be heard by policymakers" (Berry 1997, 116). Such a strategy acknowledges that a group's members may be the best promoters of the group's cause. Whether it is because elected officials desire to be reelected or because they believe they have a responsibility to listen to constituents, grassroots campaigns can have a powerful effect on policymakers. Because of technological advancements, grassroots lobbying is becoming easier and cheaper for groups to employ. Groups have long used phone banks, postcards, and newsletters to inform and mobilize members, but the advent of e-mail alerts provided groups with a tool to rally members very quickly.[3] Further, elected officials may come to see ethnic groups as single-issue voters, where issues salient to the ethnic group are more critical than partisanship in determining the voting decisions for members of the ethnic group. In this sense, ethnicity may be a wedge, allowing an enterprising politician to pry a group away from their "normal" voting patterns. To give a marginally hypothetical example, although Armenian Americans may tend to vote Republican, a Democratic candidate might be able to convince voters of Armenian descent that she will support Armenia better than the Republican incumbent. Doing so allows the Democratic candidate to gain valuable votes from the Republican incumbent.

Groups can also attempt to *influence public opinion,* either in terms of mass opinion or attentive publics (Berry 1997). Attentive publics are "groups in the population concerned about particular issues who follow their development in Washington" (Berry 1997, 116). Since the media play an important role in shaping public opinion, ethnic groups often target the media to achieve the broader goal of influencing the public. Scholars assert the media have three main effects on mass opinion (Erikson and Tedin 2005). First, the media acts as an agenda setter and can influence public discourse in its selection of issues that are reported. As media coverage of an issue increases, the public tends to view the issue as more significant. Second, the media can "prime" the public so that a particular issue becomes more important in evaluating the president or other political figures. That is, the media can affect which issues the public uses to judge major political leaders. Finally, how news stories are presented or "framed" can significantly influence how the public considers the issues. Framing involves "selecting and highlighting some facets of events or issues, and making connections among them so as to promote a particular interpretation, evaluation, and/or solution" (Entman 2004, 5). News frames can play an important role in shaping opinions about foreign policy and building consensus regarding foreign affairs, and the media, presidents, and other elites can at times offer competing (and diverging) news frames (Entman 2004).

So important is the role of the media in influencing to what the public is exposed and in affecting how the public views an issue that Tony Smith contends that "perhaps no alliance is more important [to a group] than that with the media" (2000, 120). Groups also fund and disseminate research that supports the group's positions, and this research can be used to influence the media, policymakers, and the general public. Finally, groups use demonstrations, histrionics, and rallies to garner media coverage and draw attention to the groups' positions. Media campaigns, research, and demonstrations all may indirectly influence policymakers by shifting the opinion of their constituents. Of course, policymakers also may be exposed to the advertisements, research, and media coverage of rallies, and such exposure may influence the opinion of policy-makers directly.

There are numerous examples of ethnic groups attempting to influence public opinion, often by framing issues or events as critical to the national interest. For example, Martin Weil states the success of the Polish American and Jewish American lobbies during the Cold War was due in part to their ability to successfully equate the ethnic group's foreign policy positions as being identical to the national interest (1974, 121). The Israel lobby is especially adept at framing support for Israel as being in the strategic interest of the United States and ensuring "that the mainstream media's coverage of Israel and the Middle East consistently favors Israel and does not call U.S. support into question in any way" (Mearsheimer and Walt 2007, 169). Other ethnic groups work to frame their ancestral homeland in a positive light and the enemies of their homeland in a negative manner. For example, in the early to mid-1990s, Armenian Americans were successful in framing Azerbaijan's efforts to reassert control over the Nagorno-Karabagh region as an act of aggression and perhaps an extension of the 1915 Armenian genocide (Ambrosio 2002a). Likewise, during the Balkan conflict of the early 1990s, Serbian American organizations attempted to frame Serbia as the victim of Croat aggression similar to the 1941–1945 "civil war in which the Croatian Fascists, collaborators of the Nazi regime . . . murdered between 600,000 and 1,200,000 Serbs" (Paul 2002, 106).

Of course, groups can employ a combination of strategies to influence policymaking. For example, while a group directly lobbies members of Congress and others, the group also mobilizes its members to contact their members of Congress and support the group's position. Scholars contend that factors exogenous to the group, such as the saliency of the issue and the stage of the policymaking process, affect interest group strategies (see Kollman 1998). In addition, the group's resources likely affect the strategies they can and do employ (Gerber 1999). For example, larger and diffuse groups have an important resource (members) needed to implement a grass-roots campaign, with members targeting members of Congress across the country. On the other hand, media campaigns are expensive endeavors, and groups that are financially rich have the resources needed to implement public relations campaigns.

Increasingly, organizations also form *coalitions* with other interest groups, policymakers, and other actors in order to develop initiatives, plan strategies, and enact policies (Schlozman and Tierney 1986). Kay Schlozman and John Tierney found that a large majority of organized interest groups consult congressional committee staff members, members of Congress, friends in other private organizations, and/or the personal staffers of members of Congress when planning political strategies on policy matters (1986, 275). Indeed, they found that "among the most important links in Washington interest politics are those that connect organized interests to one another," and entering into coalitions was the second most common technique used by groups (Schlozman and Tierney 1986, 278). Many groups enter coalitions because "they view them as the most effective way to shape policy outcomes" (Hula 1995, 241). Developing and participating within coalitions has the advantage of stretching organizational resources, as different coalition partners may provide the coalition with distinct resources. For example, one coalition partner may enjoy broad contacts with the media, while another partner may possess valuable contacts within the policymaking process. Another coalition member may maintain an extensive grassroots organization that can be mobilized. Indeed, coalition partners may have complementary grassroots organizations, allowing the coalition to target members of Congress and other policymakers using multiple constituencies. In addition to entering a coalition in order to influence a specific policy or issue, groups may also join coalitions in order to attain selective benefits, such as information, or as a symbolic gesture to their members or to the other groups in the coalition (Hula 1995).

Although coalitions can be formal associations, coalitions typically "maintain highly informal organizational arrangements under which participating organizations are simply expected to contribute time, professional help, clerical services, and the like, according to their resources and their stake in the matter at issue. This informality has the dual advantage of minimizing power struggles and jurisdictional disputes" (Schlozman and Tierney 1986, 48). Coalition members often have different roles and goals, with some groups acting as core members critical to forming the coalition, other organizations operating as specialists or "players" who join the alliance for tactical reasons, and other groups tagging along at the periphery (Hula 1995). Coalitions are often fluid, with groups joining because of a specific issue, and some groups leaving the alliance as the focus of the coalition shifts. Coalitions can also be ad hoc in nature, forming to champion a specific policy and then dissolving once the policy is decided. This does not preclude the coalition (or a similar coalition) from forming in the future; in fact, the alliance might form very quickly, since the organizations worked together on a previous issue, thereby overcoming the collective action problem.

Finally, groups work to *monitor* the policymaking process closely. In the words of Tony Smith, a "hallmark of a successful ethnic lobby is its ability to closely monitor, and if possible actually define, the policymaking process" (122). Although Smith was discussing ethnic groups, his words apply to *all* types of interest groups; successful groups spend a great deal of time and resources monitoring the policy process. A strong network of information providers must be developed, and contacts must be made in Congress, the White House, in agencies, and with the media, in order for a group to monitor the policymaking process well. Such monitoring may enable groups to kill an initiative or a change in the status quo long before policy-makers have an opportunity to deliberate on the proposal. Although having a member of the ethnic group serve in Congress can be helpful, nonbrethren can also serve the group well. Thus, while it can be useful for an ethnic group to have one of its own in Congress, it is not necessarily needed to monitor the policymaking process and promote the group's interests.[4] Congressional caucuses can help advocate the views and goals of ethnic interests as well. Regular meetings and contacts with agencies are important, and institutionalized organizations are more likely to earn this valuable access. "Money and votes cannot buy this kind of access, which is gained instead by patience, intelligence, determination, and the time to build up an infrastructure of influence—attributes that neither single individuals nor an ethnic community alone can provide but which are hallmarks of an institutionally effective lobby" (Smith 2000, 124). In other words, while modern technology can make a small, neophyte group look like an impressive organization, slick newsletters and PowerPoint presentations do not gain the access that AIPAC and other established groups have earned through years of work and developing connections to policymakers and other elites.

Monitoring also helps groups understand the needs of policymakers, especially in terms of information, votes, and campaign contributions. Wright (2003) argues that one of the reasons that lobbyists make the rounds on Capitol Hill is to identify what information is needed by members of Congress and congressional staffers. Congressional offices often seek out information from interest groups, thus making interest groups a sort of on-demand research bureau.[5] Indeed, some scholars now argue that policymakers can and do use ethnic interest groups to further their own policymaking goals. For example, Smith asserts that, at times, elected officials "rouse ethnic constituencies to pressure their representatives" to support and demand policies that are promoted by the elected officials (2000, 100). Likewise, Paul Watanabe argues that policymakers may "aggressively court ethnic groups and encourage their activism" (1984, 53). In a sense, successful groups are able to develop a symbiotic relationship with members of Congress and other policymakers, where interest groups are valued by policymakers and, thus, enjoy access to these policymakers (Haney and Vanderbush 1999).

Having a member of Congress as champion of the cause can be especially helpful. Although many ethnicities count on ethnic brethren to be a "horse" for the lobby, it is not necessary for the lobby and the member of Congress to share the same ethnicity. Senator Bob Dole (R-KS) championed Armenian issues because the doctor who nursed him back to health after World War II was Armenian (Greve 1995). Having a member of Congress act as an advocate for a lobby has many advantages, both inside and outside of Congress. Inside the institution, the horse may call on the group to testify at committee hearings, use committee procedures to influence the executive branch, propose legislation and offer amendments to other bills, or use procedural innovations to influence executive agencies (Tierney 1994). In addition, the horse may facilitate the group's efforts to lobby other members of Congress. Outside of Congress, a member of Congress may greatly aid the group's efforts in going public: a member of Congress can gain valuable face time to champion an issue, which better allows a lobby to influence public opinion (Tierney 1994). The relationship can be beneficial to the horse as well as the ethnic group: like other types of interest groups, ethnic groups will often work enthusiastically to help elect and reelect representatives who champion their issues. Ethnic groups can host fundraisers for the candidate, direct PAC contributions to the candidate, and encourage members of the organization to contribute directly to the candidate. Groups may also provide candidates with much-needed organizational and grassroots support that can be critical in close elections.

Examining the Role of Ethnic PACs in Elections and Lobbying

As noted earlier, electioneering, direct lobbying, and grassroots lobbying are often very much linked. For example, groups contribute money to campaigns, write and distribute "report cards" that rate candidates on issues dear to the group, make in-kind contributions to campaigns, and make independent expenditures for and against candidates. All of this is done to influence the policymaking process either by determining who will be elected into the policymaking process or by encouraging those elected to support or oppose the issue positions of those engaged in the electioneering.

Although campaigns have always involved money to some degree, congressional and presidential campaigns have become exceedingly expensive over the past several decades. The degree to which money dominates congressional and presidential campaigns has led many to conclude that groups and even individuals can "buy" candidates and officeholders (see Hall and Wayman 1990 for discussion). While he believes the concern over PACs is exaggerated, Wright does acknowledge that "PACs are probably the primary source of cynicism and distrust of politics in the United States today" (Wright 2003, 115). While ethnic groups are no strangers to the electoral arena, several high-profile races have fueled discussions that ethnic groups have increased their impact on the policymaking process. For example, the Israeli lobby has been credited with defeating congressional candidates viewed as being less than supportive of Israel and with providing critical campaign contributions to friends of Israel (Felton 1984a). In the mid-1980s, the National Association of Arab Americans began targeting members of Congress who the organization believed were hostile to Arab interests (Pressman 1985). Pakistani Americans and Indian Americans have waged a virtual ethnic war in congressional elections by backing opposite candidates in recent elections

(Morgan and Merida 1997; Curtiss 2000), and Eric Uslaner (2002) asserts that at least five ethnic groups (American Jews, Arab Americans, Latinos, Cuban Americans, and Armenian Americans) worked to affect congressional races or the presidential race in 2000. Ethnic clashes in campaigns are not limited to national races: a Pakistani American group gave Democratic Louisiana gubernatorial candidate Kathleen Blanco $50,000 at least in part because her Republican opponent, Bobby Jindal, is of Indian heritage (Moller 2003). In a conscious effort to flex the political muscles of the Indian American community, USINPAC contributed more than $200,000 in the 2004 and 2006 election cycles (McIntire 2006).

All of this has led some scholars to warn that ethnic groups and their PACs are exercising too much influence in the electoral arena. For example, Smith contends:

> The key characteristic of campaign financing regulations that offers these [ethnic] groups influence is that individuals from *outside* a congressional district may make contributions for races in which they are not themselves eligible to vote. With their contributions, small ethnic communities, some almost utterly lacking in voting strength, may nonetheless find politicians willing to represent their interests. (2000, 101, emphasis in original)

Surprisingly, aside from PACs representing Jewish or pro-Israel interests, virtually no research has examined the scope of ethnic PAC contributions. We know little about which ethnicities are the most active in the electoral realm, how much money they are contributing to candidates, and what trends have emerged. This section tries to answer these questions by examining the nature and scope of ethnic PAC activity from 1998 to 2006.

A political action committee is "a specialized form of organization that contributes money and other kinds of campaign support directly to federal candidates" (Herrnson 2005, 26). While many PACs are instituted by corporations, labor unions, and interest groups as an extension of the organization designed to influence elections, some PACs are self-created and independent. PACs can contribute up to $5,000 to individual congressional candidates for each phase of the election cycle, meaning most congressional candidates can receive a total of $10,000 from a single PAC: $5,000 for the primary, and $5,000 for the general election. If a candidate faces a further runoff election, then the PAC can contribute up to an additional $5,000. PACs can also contribute up to $5,000 to presidential candidates during the nomination phase, as well as $5,000 to presidential candidates who forgo federal funds for the general election.

Interest groups and their political action committees may use one of two main strategies when deciding how to distribute funds (Rozell and Wilcox 1999). One strategy is to focus on *access* to lawmakers, where the group makes campaign contributions in an effort to open a dialogue with office-holders who can influence legislation pertinent to the group's interests. Since overwhelming percentages of members of Congress are reelected, PACs that use an access or legislative strategy give the vast majority of their contributions to incumbents. PACs will often give money to both parties, in order to ensure that they can access key lawmakers on both sides of the aisle. In a sense, the access strategy is an extension of direct lobbying: the campaign contributions better enable the group to later lobby the member of Congress directly, and groups with the ability to raise more funds are likely to have more opportunities to gain access through the use of PACs. The financial prowess of the group can be influenced by the size of its membership rolls and the wealth of those members.

Alternatively, the second strategy is to support candidates who support the policy positions of the interest group, and oppose candidates who are hostile to the goals of the group, in hopes of affecting the composition of Congress. This *electoral* strategy places a premium on supporting candidates who will champion the issues and positions of the interest group. Implicitly, such a strategy acknowledges that members of Congress who have established positions are not likely to change those positions. Rather than attempt to persuade lawmakers who disagree with the group's positions, it is believed to be a more rational use of the group's resources to work toward replacing hostile lawmakers with more favorable individuals. This does not mean that PACs that use electoral strategies neglect to contribute to incumbents: PACs will provide supportive lawmakers with donations in order to help ensure that these members of Congress will be reelected. However, groups that utilize such an electoral strategy are more likely to give to challengers than groups that pursue a pure access strategy. Of course, a group can choose a mixed strategy: giving some funds to incumbents in order to increase the opportunity for access, as well as contributing some funds to individuals whose positions are especially congruent with those of the group. Indeed, Mark Rozell and Clyde Wilcox assert that "PACs making contributions to congressional candidates generally pursue a mixture of access and electoral strategies" (1999, 84–85).

In many respects, the contribution strategies of interest groups reflect their overall approach for influencing the policymaking process. For example, groups require access if they seek to lobby members of Congress directly, and one way they may try to gain access is by providing valuable factual information or persuasive rhetoric. Electoral contributions may assist a group in gaining access, thus improving their ability to influence the policymaking process with their information and persuasive arguments. At the same time, groups can attempt to influence the composition of Congress by recruiting candidates and providing (or withholding) valuable grassroots resources. Further, campaign contributions may lead to access if the electoral contributions provide a member of Congress a cue that an attentive group of constituents is active in the district.[6]

The question remains: Just how involved are ethnic groups in financing campaigns? In order to ascertain the degree to which ethnic groups participate in campaign financing, and the contribution strategies utilized by ethnic political action committees, the electronic archives of the Federal Election Commission were searched for ethnic-based PACs with some interest in foreign affairs or intermestic politics. While PAC contributions only represent one aspect of financing campaigns—the other major part being individual contributions—they provide a good starting point for examining the degree of participation of ethnic groups in elections.

The term *ethnic-based PACs* was operationalized as those PACs that focused on promoting, strengthening, or using ethnic identities to further the PACs' activities. Once such a PAC was identified, all monetary and in-kind contributions to federal candidates (i.e., candidates seeking a seat in the US House of Representatives, the US Senate, or the US presidency), independent expenditures for or against a federal candidate, and contributions to federal PACs were catalogued. Data were collected on the candidate's name, party affiliation, office being sought (including state and house district), incumbency status (coded as incumbent, challenger, or open seat), the contribution amount, and the date of the contribution. Following FEC coding, contributions made after the general election in even-numbered years were counted as contributions to the next election cycle.[7] For example, a contribution made to an incumbent on December 31, 2002, was coded as a contribution for the 2004 election cycle.

Both the FEC and the Center for Responsive Politics include data from the 1998, 2000, 2002, 2004, and 2006 election cycles, meaning that campaign contributions made after the 1996 congressional midterm election on November 5, 1996, should be included in the dataset. Not including Jewish PACs, the analysis identified a total of seventy PACs representing twenty-six ethnicities active in at least one of the five election cycles. In addition, we identified forty-three PACs associated with Jewish American or Israeli interests, the latter being identified through resources provided by the Center for Responsive Politics. Indeed, the Center for Responsive Politics has catalogued these groups as having industry-level status, which the center labels "Pro-Israel." No other ethnicity merits its own industry, and the Center for Responsive Politics classifies most of the other ethnic-based PACs as being interested in either "Foreign & Defense Policy" or "Human Rights."

A potential concern is that a PAC's name may not be transparent, and the PAC's name may not indicate that the organization is ethnic based. Such a worry is raised by Smith, who argues it is "often impossible" to analyze ethnic PAC contributions because at least some ethnic PACs wish to remain hidden (Smith 2000, 106). Likewise, the *Washington Report on Middle East Affairs* argues that many pro-Israel PACs operate with ambiguous names, such as SunPAC or National PAC (McMahon 2004). In order to help identify such stealth PACs, we asked ethnic leaders, congressional staffers, and members of Congress to identify ethnic PACs that our methodology may have missed. We found little evidence to suggest that non-Jewish ethnic groups are utilizing a stealth PAC strategy, and only two other ethnic PACs were identified: USINPAC, which the Center for Responsive Politics now calls US India PAC, and a Hispanic-based PAC called Committee for Hispanic Causes (CHC)–Building Our Leadership's Diversity. The Center for Responsive Politics has also launched an effort to identify and categorize stealth PACs, and there are currently very few PACs that are no longer matched with an industry or cause. In many respects, we are not surprised that the vast majority of ethnic PACs are transparent. While we acknowledge that some PACs may indeed wish to remain anonymous, we also assert that a PAC that is contributing to congressional campaigns as part of an access strategy will desire a certain amount of transparency. That is, the PAC will want a targeted member of Congress to know that the ethnic group or its interest group supported the congressperson, thereby increasing the likelihood that the member of Congress will grant access to the PAC in the future.

The Scope of Ethnic PAC Distributions

Before addressing the scope of ethnic contributions to candidates, it might be useful to examine how much money is needed by candidates to run a credible campaign. Recent research shows that the "typical House incumbent involved in a two-party contested race raised just under $1.4 million in cash and party coordinated expenditures in 2006," while candidates in open seat elections raised an average of nearly $1.6 million (Herrnson 2008, 167). But in competitive races, the average House incumbent collected more than $2 million in contributions in 2006, while the average Republican challenger raised $2 million and the typical Democratic challenger garnered $1.1 million.[8] On average, both Republican and Democratic candidates in competitive open House seat contests raised $2.2 million in 2006. The average candidate in a competitive Senate race collected over $11 million in 2006, while Senate candidates in uncompetitive races raised nearly $6 million. Altogether, House candidates raised over $871 million in 2006, while Senate candidates collected nearly $558 million.

With those figures in mind, the amount of financial and in-kind contributions flowing from ethnic PACs to federal candidates is surprisingly modest, especially the PACs that are not focused on supporting US-Israel relations. The non-Jewish PACs analyzed for this study contributed a total of $4,486,401 to federal candidates and their campaigns across the five election cycles, for an average of $890,000 in contributions per election cycle (see Table 3.1). The level of financial assistance provided by ethnic PACs to federal candidates varies remarkably, ranging from a few dozen dollars in several cases to over

Table 3.1 Federal Contributions by Largest Ethnic PACs, 1998–2006 (in dollars)

Name of PAC	Federal Expenditures	Contributions to Candidates	Returned Contributions	Net Candidate Contributions	Contributions to Other PACs	Independent Expenditures
US-Cuba Democracy PAC	846,764	760,624	0	760,624	74,500	11,640
Congressional Black Caucus PAC	532,000	497,000	10,000	487,000	15,000	30,000
Arab American Leadership Council PAC	490,563	494,063	6,500	487,563	3,000	0
Black America's PAC	393,111	378,111	5,000	373,111	15,000	5,000
CHC–Building Our Leadership's Diversity	341,000	318,000	6,500	311,500	29,500	0
US-India PAC (USINPAC)	294,599	244,999	2,500	242,499	52,100	0
Free Cuba PAC	291,218	269,718	2,500	267,218	24,000	0
Armenian American PAC (ARMENPAC)	263,869	300,369	47,000	253,369	10,500	0
Albanian American Public Affairs Committee	162,350	153,800	5,500	148,300	14,050	0
American Task Force for Lebanon Policy Council PAC	126,900	125,775	0	125,775	1,125	0
Hispanic Unity USA	121,000	127,500	6,500	121,000	5,000	0
Italian American Democratic Leadership Council	115,448	83,698	0	83,698	31,750	0
Irish American Democrats	106,942	88,350	0	88,350	4,250	14,342
Armenian National Committee PAC	66,350	66,350	0	66,350	0	0
Hispanic PAC USA Inc.	58,000	53,000	0	53,000	0	0
Iranian American PAC	51,500	41,500	0	41,500	10,000	0
Taiwanese American Action Council	50,950	50,950	0	50,950	0	0
Latino Alliance	38,244	26,535	0	26,535	5,052	6,657
Armenian Americans Legislative Issues Committee	32,355	7,000	0	7,000	5,000	20,355
Latino Citizens for Respect	32,122	1,500	0	1,500	0	30,622
Taiwanese American Victory Fund	23,900	24,400	500	23,900	0	0
Pakistani American Physicians PAC (PAK-PAC)	22,950	21,950	0	21,950	1,000	0
Asian American Action Fund	22,676	26,676	4,000	22,676	0	0
National Japanese American PAC	22,000	26,000	4,000	22,000	0	0

(continues)

Table 3.1 continued

Name of PAC	Federal Expenditures	Contributions to Candidates	Returned Contributions	Net Candidate Contributions	Contributions to Other PACs	Independent Expenditures
Hispanic Democratic Organization	21,500	21,500	0	21,500	0	0
National Association of Arab-Americans/NAAA-ADC PAC	31,120	28,120	0	28,120	3,000	0
Coalition for Asian Pacific Americans	21,299	20,680	1,381	19,299	1,000	1,000
Greek American PAC	20,666	19,200	0	19,200	1,000	466
Arab American PAC	20,571	18,153	0	18,153	1,670	748
Republican Italian American PAC	20,000	20,000	0	20,000	0	0
Japanese American Republicans	19,888	19,300	0	19,300	0	588
Indian American Republican PAC	18,750	15,750	0	15,750	3,000	0
Hellenic American Council Inc. PAC	12,796	12,796	0	12,796	0	0
Italian American Republican Coalition	10,500	11,500	1,000	10,500	0	0
United States–Cuba PAC	10,500	8,500	0	8,500	2,000	0
Armenian American Public Affairs Committee	10,151	10,151	0	10,151	0	0
Hellenic American PAC	10,100	10,000	0	10,000	100	0
Dynamis—A Hellenic Association Federal PAC	10,000	10,000	0	10,000	0	0
31 other PACs, with contributions of less than $10,000 each	76,036	72,883	9,300	63,583	9,760	2,693
Totals	4,820,688	4,486,401	112,181	4,374,220	322,357	124,111

Source: Federal Election Commission.
Note: Does not include Jewish or pro-Israel PACs.

$550,000 by the US-Cuba Democracy PAC in 2006. Only thirteen non-Jewish PACs spent more than $100,000 in total federal expenditures[9] over the five election cycles: the US-Cuba Democracy PAC, the Congressional Black Caucus PAC, the Arab American Leadership Council PAC, Black America's PAC, CHC–Building Our Leadership's Diversity, US-India PAC (USINPAC), the Free Cuba PAC, the Armenian American PAC, the Albanian American Public Affairs Committee PAC, the American Task Force for Lebanon Policy Council PAC, Hispanic Unity USA, the Italian American Democratic Leadership Council, and the Irish American Democrats. Of these PACs, all but the Italian American Democratic Leadership Council and the Irish American Democrats contributed more than $100,000 to individual candidates over the five election cycles. On average, non-Jewish PACs contributed $28,221 per PAC per election cycle to federal candidates. The median ethnic PAC contributed only $7,875 in an election cycle, a figure skewed by the relatively large number of ethnic PACs that make only a few donations to federal candidates in any given election cycle.

By comparison, the forty-three pro-Israel and Jewish PACs contributed a combined $13.4 million to federal candidates over the five election cycles, ranging from $1.9 million in combined contributions in 2000 to over $3.3 million in aggregated donations in 2004 (see Table 3.2). By all measures, pro-Israel and Jewish PACs dominate the ethnic PAC universe: the pro-Israel and Jewish PACs account for 75.4 percent of the ethnic PAC contributions to federal candidates and 74.0 percent of ethnic PAC federal expenditures from 1998 to 2006. On average, these pro-Israeli PACs contributed a little more than $72,979 per PAC per election cycle to federal candidates, and the median PAC contributed $52,015 to federal candidates in an election cycle.

Aside from the Jewish American community, the Cuban American lobby was the most active in terms of contributions to federal candidates, with Cuban American PACs contributing more than $1 million over the five election cycles (see Table 3.3). In addition to donations to federal candidates, the Cuban American PACs contributed over $100,000 to other federal PACs, usually leadership PACs created by prominent members of Congress. While the activities of the Free Cuba PAC, the political action committee for the Cuban American National Foundation, have declined over the past two election cycles, the US-Cuba Democracy PAC emerged in 2004 as a major ethnic organization. The US-Cuba Democracy PAC distributed over $750,000 in the 2004 and 2006 election cycles to federal candidates, by far the greatest amount of any ethnic PAC (including pro-Israel PACs) over a four-year period. The African American and Hispanic American lobbies were also very active, and PACs representing these ethnicities distributed $865,000 and $538,000, respectively, over the five election cycles to congressional candidates. While it is still dwarfed by the pro-Israel lobby, the combined contributions from the Arab American and Lebanese American

Table 3.2 Federal Contributions by Largest Jewish and Pro-Israel PACs, 1998–2006 (in dollars)

Name of PAC	Federal Expenditures	Contributions to Candidates	Returned Contributions	Net Candidate Contributions	Contributions to Other PACs	Independent Expenditures
National PAC	1,291,750	1,316,750	37,500	1,279,250	12,500	0
Washington PAC	936,650	939,650	5,000	934,650	2,000	0
National Action Committee (NACPAC)	866,000	858,500	4,000	854,500	11,500	0
Women's Alliance for Israel	849,250	857,250	8,500	848,750	500	0
NorPAC	827,698	850,070	58,286	791,784	35,914	0
Joint Action Committee for Political Affairs	827,069	786,860	9,291	777,569	49,500	0
Desert Caucus	825,000	818,500	18,500	800,000	25,000	0
Citizens Organized PAC	646,750	664,750	20,500	644,250	2,500	0
Friends of Israel PAC/Northern Californians for Good Government	569,000	571,500	2,500	569,000	0	0
MOPAC	508,250	504,000	4,250	499,750	8,500	0
Florida Congressional Committee	480,300	491,300	11,000	480,300	0	0
Americans for Good Government	473,300	492,300	21,500	470,800	2,500	0
Republican Jewish Coalition	455,900	435,900	2,000	433,900	22,000	0
Hudson Valley PAC	442,650	451,650	9,000	442,650	0	0
Americans United in Support of Democracy	360,700	364,700	6,500	358,200	2,500	0
Heartland PAC/Youngstown PAC	316,000	316,000	9,500	306,500	9,500	0
St. Louisians for Better Government	315,000	320,000	5,000	315,000	0	0
City PAC	304,000	306,000	2,000	304,000	0	0

(continues)

Table 3.2 continued

Name of PAC	Federal Expenditures	Contributions to Candidates	Returned Contributions	Net Candidate Contributions	Contributions to Other PACs	Independent Expenditures
Bi-County PAC	275,500	275,500	0	275,500	0	0
Mid Manhattan PAC (MIDPAC)	268,620	244,620	3,000	241,620	27,000	0
SunPAC	254,750	254,750	0	254,750	0	0
Maryland Association for Concerned Citizens	239,500	235,500	0	235,500	4,000	0
Louisiana for American Security	197,250	197,750	500	197,250	0	0
Women's Pro-Israel National PAC	189,450	192,450	3,000	189,450	0	0
Grand Canyon Caucus	153,500	157,500	4,000	153,500	0	0
To Protect Our Heritage PAC	149,366	155,630	7,250	148,380	0	986
Young Jewish Leadership PAC	103,561	77,300	0	77,300	1,250	25,011
Delaware Valley PAC	97,650	103,150	6,500	96,650	1,000	0
Northwest PAC	89,000	88,000	0	88,000	1,000	0
National Jewish Democratic Council PAC	78,233	74,562	500	74,062	675	3,496
Georgia Peach PAC	73,500	76,500	3,000	73,500	0	0
BAYPAC	72,025	68,750	0	68,750	2,650	625
California PAC	51,115	53,115	3,500	49,615	1,500	0
Greater Los Angeles PAC	29,250	23,650	0	23,650	5,600	0
PAC of Cherry Hill, NJ	27,500	27,500	0	27,500	0	0
8 other PACs, with contributions of less than $10,000 each	43,337	42,337	0	42,337	1,000	0
Totals	13,688,374	13,694,244	266,077	13,428,167	230,089	30,118

Source: Federal Election Commission.

Table 3.3 Federal Contributions by Ethnicity of PACs, 1998–2006 (in dollars)

Ethnicity	Election Cycles	Federal Expenditures	Net Candidate Contributions	Federal PAC Contributions	House Contributions	Senate Contributions	Democratic Percentage	Republican Percentage
African American	1998–2006	932,658.00	865,398.00	30,260.00	723,117.00	142,281.00	57	43
Albanian	1998–2006	162,350.00	148,300.00	14,050.00	128,000.00	17,200.00	27	63
Arab	1998–2006	542,254.00	533,836.00	7,670.00	463,341.00	70,277.00	72	27
Armenian	1998–2006	374,225.00	338,370.00	15,500.00	265,770.00	72,500.00	61	39
Asian	1998–2006	56,825.00	51,325.00	4,500.00	30,226.00	20,099.00	97	03
Bangladeshi	2006	1,000.00	1,000.00	0.00	1,000.00	0.00	100	00
Caribbean	2000–2002	4,650.00	4,650.00	0.00	3,000.00	1,650.00	78	22
Central and Eastern Europe	1998; 2004	1,250.00	1,250.00	0.00	1,250.00	0.00	20	80
Croat	1998	50.00	50.00	0.00	50.00	0.00	100	00
Cuban	1998–2006	1,151,482.00	1,038,342.00	101,500.00	728,924.00	297,918.00	43	56
Eritrean	2004	2,850.00	2,850.00	0.00	2,850.00	0.00	65	35
Hellenic (Greek)	1998–2002; 2006	53,562.00	51,996.00	1,100.00	34,296.00	17,700.00	56	44
Hispanic	1998–2006	614,766.00	537,935.00	39,552.00	455,035.00	82,900.00	95	05
Indian	1998; 2002–2006	325,295.00	266,195.00	59,100.00	211,945.00	54,250.00	46	54
Iranian	2004–2006	51,500.00	41,500.00	10,000.00	19,500.00	22,000.00	51	49
Irish	1998–2006	106,942.00	88,350.00	4,250.00	55,950.00	32,400.00	99	00
Italian	1998–2006	152,648.00	120,898.00	31,750.00	84,450.00	36,448.00	70	30
Japanese	1998–2006	41,888.00	41,300.00	0.00	26,800.00	9,500.00	41	59
Jewish	1998–2006	13,688,374.00	13,428,167.00	230,089.00	5,587,930.00	7,783,987.00	60	40
Korean	1998; 2004	7,000.00	7,000.00	0.00	4,000.00	1,000.00	80	20
Lebanese	1998–2006	127,500.00	126,375.00	1,125.00	97,950.00	28,425.00	48	52
Lithuanian	1998–2002	5,993.00	4,800.00	500.00	4,250.00	550.00	00	100
Pakistani	1998–2006	25,750.00	24,750.00	1,000.00	17,750.00	7,000.00	74	26
Polish	1998	500.00	0.00	500.00	0.00	0.00	n.a.	n.a.
Salvadoran	2000	400.00	400.00	0.00	400.00	0.00	100	00
Taiwanese	2002–2006	74,850.00	74,850.00	0.00	46,850.00	27,000.00	80	20
Vietnamese	2000	2,500.00	2,500.00	0.00	2,500.00	0.00	60	40
Totals		18,509,062.00	17,802,387.00	552,446.00	8,997,134.00	8,725,085.00	60	40

Source: Federal Election Commission.

Note: Democratic Percentage and Republican Percentage represent the percentage of contributions made to congressional candidates in each party; n.a. is not applicable.

PACs totaled $660,000 from 1998 to 2006. The Armenian American and Indian American lobbies each contributed over a quarter of a million dollars to congressional campaigns, with the Indian American lobby giving over $100,000 to federal candidates in 2004 and 2006. The Albanian American and Italian American lobbies were the only other ethnic lobbies to exceed $100,000 in federal campaign contributions over the course of this study.

Paul Herrnson's analysis of PAC contributions in the 2006 election cycle provides a useful benchmark for ethnic PAC activity. Herrnson calculates that PACs contributed approximately $348.5 million to congressional candidates in the 2006 campaign cycle. However, "a very small group of PACs is responsible for most PAC activity," with only 351 PACs accounting for $243 million in PAC contributions to congressional candidates (Herrnson 2008, 136). Each of these 351 PACs, which Herrnson calls the "all-stars" of the PAC universe, gave more than $250,000 to federal candidates in 2006. While encompassing only 7 percent of the PAC community, the all-stars account for a whopping 65 percent of the PAC contributions made in 2006. An additional 451 PACs gave between $100,001 and $250,000 to federal candidates in 2006, a group that Herrnson labels as "major players." These major players comprise 9 percent of registered PACs, and account for 19 percent of PAC contributions. Herrnson asserts that "the all-stars and major players are particularly influential because their wealth allows them to contribute to virtually every candidate whose election is important to them" (2008, 136). "Players" are PACs that contribute between $50,001 and $100,000 and thus "have the resources to give a significant contribution to many but not all of the candidates they wish to support," while the "junior varsity" PACs are "clearly constrained by their size" and only contribute between $5,001 and $50,000 to candidates in an election cycle (Herrnson 2008, 136–137). Herrnson labels the PACs that contribute $5,000 or less as the "little league," and these PACs play only a limited role in financing congressional elections.

Using Herrnson's benchmarks, only three ethnic PACs (the US-Cuba Democracy PAC, Women's Alliance for Israel, and the National Action Committee) gave more than $250,000 in 2006 to merit the "all-star" label. These three PACs gave 23.3 percent of all ethnic PAC contributions to federal candidates in 2006. An additional twelve PACs representing four ethnic groups gave between $101,000 and $250,000, accounting for 45.4 percent of ethnic PAC receipts in 2006. These include the Congressional Black Caucus PAC, the Hispanic-based CHC–Building Our Leadership's Diversity PAC, the US-India PAC, and nine pro-Israel PACs such as the Washington PAC, NorPAC, and the Friends of Israel PAC. Another twelve PACs (including the Arab American Leadership Council PAC, the Armenian American PAC, and ten pro-Israel PACs) gave between $50,001 and $100,000 in 2006, and these "players" accounted for 19.5 percent of ethnic PAC contributions. The twenty-seven "junior varsity" ethnic PACs were responsible for 11 percent of ethnic PAC contributions, while the twenty "little league" ethnic PACs accounted for just 1.1 percent of ethnic PAC receipts in 2006.

As they did in the aggregate analysis from 1998 to 2006, Jewish and pro-Israel PACs played the largest role by far in the ethnic PAC universe in 2006, with eleven of the fifteen ethnic PAC "all-stars" or "major players" being Jewish or pro-Israel. In all, Jewish and pro-Israel PACs contributed over \$3.1 million to federal candidates in 2006, or 68.2 percent of the \$4.6 million given by ethnic PACs in that election. However, it is worth noting that ethnic PACs make up a small segment of the PAC universe, a universe dominated by corporate, labor, and trade PACs. Again, PACs gave approximately \$348.5 million to federal candidates in 2006, meaning that Jewish and pro-Israel PACs were responsible for less than 1 percent of all PAC receipts in 2006, not an especially overwhelming percentage. Further, as will be shown later in the chapter, the top recipients of Jewish and pro-Israel PAC contributions do not always win their elections.

Who Gets the Money: Examining the Distribution of PAC Contributions

Which candidates are more likely to receive contributions from ethnic PACs? For example, are ethnic PACs more likely to contribute to incumbents or challengers, or to Democrats or Republicans? It is well documented that PACs tend to give to incumbents, and although substantial variance exists across individual ethnic PACs, as a whole ethnic PACs behave a great deal like PACs in general: they give far more to incumbents than to challengers or candidates seeking an open seat. Across the five election cycles included in the study, 77.5 percent of congressional contributions made by ethnic PACs were given to incumbents, with challengers receiving 9.5 percent of contributions, and the remaining 13.0 percent going to candidates seeking open seats (see Table 3.4). In House contests, ethnic PACs gave 76.3 percent of their contributions to incumbents, with challengers receiving 11.6 percent of contributions, and the remaining 12.1 percent going to candidates seeking open seats. For contests for Senate seats, ethnic PACs gave 78.7 percent of their contributions to incumbents, with challengers garnering only 7.3 percent of contributions, and candidates seeking open seats receiving the remaining 14.0 percent. Clearly, either to gain access or help keep friends in Congress, ethnic PACs favor incumbents over challengers. Of course, this may also reflect the decline of competitive congressional races, with only a few dozen competitive races in any given election cycle from 1998 to 2004, although there was an increase in the number of competitive races in 2006 (Herrnson 2008). Since pro-Israel PACs constitute such a large segment of the ethnic PAC universe, Table 3.4 provides the total net contributions by

Table 3.4 Distribution of Ethnic PAC Contributions to Members of Congress

US House of Representatives	Incumbents	Challengers	Open Seats
Non-Jewish PACs, 1998–2006	$2,273,639 (66.7%)	$602,288 (17.7%)	$533,277 (15.6%)
Pro-Israel PACs, 1998–2006	$4,587,391 (82.1%)	$440,886 (7.9%)	$559,653 (10.0%)
Non-Jewish PACs, 2006	$883,146 (76.4%)	$158,700 (13.7%)	$114,602 (9.9%)
Pro-Israel PACS, 2006	$1,259,222 (86.5%)	$100,498 (6.9%)	$96,582 (6.6%)
All nonconnected PACs, 2006	71%	16%	13%

US Senate	Incumbents	Challengers	Open Seats
Non-Jewish PACs, 1998–2006	$568,626 (60.4%)	$145,673 (15.5%)	$226,799 (24.1%)
Pro-Israel PACs, 1998–2006	$6,302,151 (80.1%)	$491,474 (6.3%)	$990,362 (12.7%)
Non-Jewish PACs, 2006	$203,700 (62.8%)	$66,275 (20.4%)	$54,225 (16.7%)
Pro-Israel PACS, 2006	$1,359,206 (79.3%)	$179,809 (10.5%)	$174,476 (10.2%)
All nonconnected PACs, 2006	71%	18%	10%

House and Senate Combined	Incumbents	Challengers	Open Seats
All ethnic PACs, 1998–2006	77.5%	9.5%	13.0%
Non-Jewish PACs, 1998–2006	65.3%	17.2%	17.5%
Pro-Israel PACs, 1998–2006	81.4%	7.0%	11.6%

Sources: Federal Election Commission and Herrnson (2008).

both pro-Israel PACs and non-Jewish PACs for both House and Senate contests. Despite the media reports and other discussions that Jewish organizations punish members of Congress who are hostile to Israel, pro-Israel PACs were *less* likely to contribute to challengers, and were more likely to contribute to incumbents, than the non-Jewish PACs. For example, across the five election cycles examined, only 7.9 percent of House contributions and 6.3 percent of Senate contributions from pro-Israel PACs went to challengers, while incumbents in the House and Senate received 82.1 percent and 80.1 percent of pro-Israel PAC contributions, respectively. Such a contribution strategy suggests that pro-Israel PACs are defending the status quo through an access strategy. In contrast, non-Jewish PACs gave 17.7 percent of their House contributions to challengers, and 15.5 percent of their Senate receipts to challengers. Only 66.7 percent of contributions by non-Jewish

PACs to House candidates were distributed to incumbents, and only 60.4 percent of Senate contributions by non-Jewish PACs were made to incumbents.

Herrnson's examination of the 2006 PAC contributions also adds perspective to the above analysis. Most ethnic PACs are "nonconnected," meaning they are not sponsored by an organization, corporation, or union. In his analysis of nonconnected PACs, Herrnson determined that approximately 71 percent of contributions to House candidates went to incumbents, while challengers received 16 percent of PAC contributions, and candidates for open seats garnered 13 percent (2006).[10] For the Senate, incumbents received 71 percent of the 2006 PAC contributions, while 18 percent of contributions were given to challengers, and open seat candidates received 10 percent. If only the contributions by ethnic PACs to House candidates in the 2006 cycle are examined, incumbents received 82.0 percent, while challengers received 9.9 percent and open seat candidates received 8.1 percent. For Senate candidates, ethnic PACs gave 76.7 percent of their contributions to incumbents in 2002, while challengers received 12.1 percent, and 11.2 percent went to candidates seeking open seats. Thus, when examining the aggregate data or just considering the data from 2006, ethnic PACs appear to favor incumbents more than other nonconnected PACs, indicating that ethnic PACs, as a whole, exercise a strategy of access.

Of course, individual ethnic PACs implement different strategies. At times, evidence of an access strategy for particular groups is readily apparent. For example, the Armenian American PAC (ARMENPAC) made contributions almost exclusively to incumbents, even incumbents who were months away from retirement. Less than 2 percent of ARMENPAC contributions were made to challengers, and the PAC even gave contributions to two opposing candidates (an incumbent and the challenger) vying for the same seat in 2004. In several states, such as California, New Jersey, and New York, ARMENPAC contributed to a high percentage of the state's delegation, and did so across party lines. For example, ARMENPAC contributed to ten of the thirteen members of the New Jersey house delegation in 2004. Further, ARMENPAC made contributions in September 2004 to three member of Congress (James C. Greenwood, R-PA; Gerald D. Kleczka, D-WI; and Karen McCarthy, R-MO) who had announced their retirements earlier in 2004.

There is also evidence that some PACs use a mixed strategy. For example, the American Task Force for Lebanon Policy Council gave the lion's share of its contributions to incumbents (76.7 percent) but also clearly tried to help its friends, even if they were challenging incumbents. In 2002, the PAC gave $8,000 to Representative John Sununu (R-NH) in his bid to unseat Senator Robert Smith (a fellow Republican). The PAC gave Sununu $7,000 before the September 10, 2002, primary election, a move that would have surely cost the group access to Smith had Sununu lost his bid to unseat the incumbent.[11]

Several of the ethnic PACs, such as the Albanian American Public Affairs Committee and Dynamis, appear to be utilizing an electoral strategy. The Albanian American Public Affairs Committee, which was founded by former congressman Joseph DioGuardi (R-NY), gave almost a quarter of its contributions (23.3 percent) to challengers, and 8.8 percent of its contributions went to third-party candidates.[12] The US-Cuba Democracy PAC has funded candidates who challenged incumbents the PAC believed were hostile to the organization's interests. For example, the US-Cuba Democracy PAC contributed the maximum $5,000 to Republican Stan Barnes in his effort to unseat fellow Arizona Republican Jeff Flake, and then spent an additional $11,600 in independent expenditures against Flake. Also, the partisan PACs, such as the Irish American Democrats, Congressional Black Caucus PAC, and Black America's PAC, were much more likely than the nonpartisan organizations to support challengers.

In terms of the partisan composition of contributions to House and Senate candidates, ethnic PACs gave 60 percent of their contributions to Democrats, while Republicans garnered 39.8 percent of the ethnic contributions across the five election cycles (see Table 3.3). Democratic candidates for the House of Representatives received 61.2 percent of ethnic PAC contributions, while Republican candidates for the lower house received 38.5 percent of PAC monies. For the Senate, Republicans did only slightly better: Democrats received 58.8 percent, while Republicans received 41.1 percent of contributions.

Again, Herrnson's work provides valuable data from which to compare the ethnic PAC figures. After the 1994 midterm elections, in which Republicans took control of both the House and the Senate, contributions to Democrats from corporate PACs, trade association PACs, and nonconnected PACs declined as those PACs shifted money to Republicans. For example, while House Democratic candidates received almost 60 percent of corporate PAC contributions in 1994, House Republican contenders received over 60 percent of corporate PAC contributions in the elections following the shift in party control. Likewise, Republican House contenders received approximately 60 percent of contributions made by trade association PACs. Although we did not collect data from election cycles prior to the Republican takeover of Congress, ethnic PACs have chosen not to shun the Democratic Party. If the ethnic PACs that gave more than 95 percent of their contributions to a single party are removed from the analysis, then Democrats received 56.9 percent of ethnic PAC contribution over the five election cycles, while Republicans received 42.9 percent of ethnic monies. In other words, Democrats were still favored by ethnic groups, despite their loss of control of the congressional agenda until 2006. With Democrats capturing both chambers of Congress in 2006, the percentage of ethnic PAC contributions to the Democratic Party may increase in 2008.

▨   The Top Recipients of Ethnic PAC Contributions

An examination of which candidates and officeholders receive the most contributions by ethnic PACs reveals that congressional leaders, ethnic brethren, and key supporters received the lion's share of contributions made between 1998 and 2006 (see Table 3.5). Over that time period, four senators—Joe Lieberman (D-CT), Tom Daschle (D-SD), Barbara Boxer (D-CA), and Arlen Specter (R-PA)—and one representative—Shelley Berkley (D-NV)—each received more than $200,000 in contributions from ethnic PACs, and thirty-five members of Congress received at least $100,000 in contributions. Since pro-Israel PACs account for such a large share of the ethnic PAC universe, it is not surprising that the bulk of the contributions to these members of Congress came from these PACs. Table 3.6 details the top thirty Democratic and Republican recipients of contributions made by pro-Israel PACs, and these PACs contributed heavily to congressional leaders—like Senator Daschle, Senator Mitch McConnell (R-KY), and House Speaker Dennis Hastert (R-IL)—and Jewish members of Congress—like Representative Berkley, Senator Specter, Senator Boxer, and Representative Eric Cantor (R-VA). The pro-Israel PACs also gave sizeable contributions to incumbents who are strong supporters of Israel, but who are not themselves Jewish, such as Senator Sam Brownback (R-KS), Senator Patty Murray (D-WA), and Senator Tim Johnson (D-SD). Pro-Israel PACs gave $83,567 to Artur Davis (D-AL) and $61,500 to Denise Majette (D-GA), two challengers who in 2002 beat Democratic House incumbents who were viewed by some as being pro-Arab (Hawkings and Nutting 2003). However, the PACs did not always back winners, and some of the incumbents listed in Table 3.6 lost their high-profile races, including Senator Rick Santorum (R-PA) and Senator Conrad Burns (R-MT) in 2006, Senator Tom Daschle in 2004, Senator Jean Carnahan (D-MO) in 2002, Senator Charles Robb (D-VA) in 2000, and Senator Alfonse D'Amato (R-NY) in 1998.

Table 3.7 presents the top recipients of contributions made by all non-Jewish ethnic PACs. As was the case with the Jewish PACs, the top recipients tended to be ethnic brethren or champions of ethnic causes, but, surprisingly, fewer congressional leaders made the list. Since congressional leaders are critical to setting the policymaking agenda and play a significant role in terms of gatekeeping, such a finding suggests that non-Jewish groups are focused less on protecting the status quo than Jewish groups. Instead, the evidence suggests that these other ethnic groups use PAC contributions to help support members of Congress who serve to champion the issues and goals important to their group. Arab American and Lebanese American PACs helped propel several Arab American members of Congress to the top of the list, including Senator John Sununu (R-NH), Representative Nick Rahall (D-WV), former senator Spencer Abraham (R-MI),

Table 3.5 Top Recipients of Ethnic PAC Contributions by Party, 1998–2006 (in dollars)

Democratic Candidates	Total Contributions	Republican Candidates	Total Contributions
Sen. Joe Lieberman (CT)	$277,843	Sen. Arlen Specter (PA)	$216,500
Rep. Shelley Berkley (NV)	$254,543	Sen. Jon Kyl (AZ)	$151,925
Sen. Thomas A. Daschle (SD)	$223,080	Rep. Eric Cantor (VA)	$142,430
Sen. Barbara Boxer (CA)	$207,972	Sen. Rick Santorum (PA)	$139,700
Sen. Robert Menendez (NJ)	$174,693	Rep. Mark S. Kirk (IL)	$137,132
Sen. Harry Reid (NV)	$171,277	Sen. Sam D. Brownback (KS)	$132,100
Sen. Patty Murray (WA)	$164,043	Sen. Ileana Ros-Lehtinen (FL)	$126,000
Sen. Russ Feingold (WI)	$153,310	Sen. Conrad Burns (MT)	$115,960
Sen. Bill Nelson (FL)	$149,371	Sen. Mitch McConnell (KY)	$114,410
Sen. Tim Johnson (SD)	$143,587	Rep. Dennis J. Hastert (IL)	$109,300
Sen. Ron Wyden (OR)	$139,310	Sen. Mike DeWine (OH)	$106,500
Sen. Debbie Stabenow (MI)	$136,106	Sen. Jim Talent (MO)	$101,510
Sen. Kent Conrad (ND)	$123,850	Rep. Thomas D. DeLay (TX)	$98,700
Sen. Mary L. Landrieu (LA)	$120,300	Sen. Robert F. Bennett (UT)	$90,250
Rep. Eliot Engel (NY)	$120,018	Sen. Alfonse M. D'Amato (NY)	$87,050
Rep. Steny Hoyer (MD)	$111,075	Sen. Jim Bunning (KY)	$83,100
Sen. Charles S. Robb (VA)	$110,321	Sen. Charles E. Grassley (IA)	$81,800
Rep. Tom Lantos (CA)	$107,350	Sen. George Allen (VA)	$72,000
Sen. Richard J. Durbin (IL)	$103,600	Rep. Clay Shaw Jr. (FL)	$71,855
Sen. Ben Nelson (NE)	$102,760	Sen. Richard C. Shelby (AL)	$70,500
Sen. Carl Levin (MI)	$102,529	Sen. Christopher S. Bond (MO)	$70,100
Rep. Joseph Crowley (NY)	$100,157	Sen. Gordon H. Smith (OR)	$68,750
Sen. Christopher J. Dodd (CT)	$100,000	Sen. Slade Gorton (WA)	$66,750
Sen. Evan Bayh (IN)	$98,600	Sen. John S. McCain (AZ)	$65,600
Sen. Joseph M. Cleland (GA)	$98,150	Sen. Spencer Abraham (MI)	$62,027
Sen. Max Baucus (MT)	$97,550	Rep. Benjamin A. Gilman (NY)	$61,068
Sen. Byron Dorgan (ND)	$96,750	Sen. Mel Martinez (FL)	$59,250
Sen. Jean Carnahan (MO)	$95,822	Sen. John Ensign (NV)	$57,700
Rep. Martin Frost (TX)	$94,225	Sen. Lisa Murkowski (AK)	$57,600
Rep. Richard A. Gephardt (MO)	$88,015	Sen. Wayne Allard (CO)	$57,500

Source: Federal Election Commission.

and Representative Ray LaHood (R-IL). Arab American PACs also helped fund Representative Cynthia McKinney (D-GA) and Representative James Moran (D-VA), two members of Congress who have been seen as critical of Israel. Other candidates received contributions from a host of different ethnic groups. For example, former representative Ben Gilman (R-NY), who is tenth on the list, received $31,600 in contributions from a host of ethnic PACs from 1998 until his retirement in 2003, including the Albanian American Public Affairs Committee (totaling $22,500), the Free Cuba PAC ($6,500), American Task Force for Lebanon Policy Council PAC ($1,600), and ARMENPAC ($1,000). Over those three election cycles, Representative Gilman also received $29,468 from pro-Israel PACs. In many respects,

Table 3.6 Top Recipients of Jewish and Pro-Israel PAC Contributions by Party, 1998–2006 (in dollars)

Democratic Candidates	Total Contributions	Republican Candidates	Total Contributions
Sen. Joe Lieberman (CT)	$254,843	Sen. Arlen Specter (PA)	$210,000
Rep. Shelley Berkley (NV)	$247,543	Sen. Jon Kyl (AZ)	$140,425
Sen. Tom Daschle (SD)	$213,580	Rep. Eric Cantor (VA)	$135,930
Sen. Barbara Boxer (CA)	$182,373	Rep. Mark S. Kirk (IL)	$133,132
Sen. Patty Murray (WA)	$164,043	Sen. Sam D. Brownback (KS)	$124,350
Sen. Harry Reid (NV)	$154,777	Sen. Rick Santorum (PA)	$123,000
Sen. Russ Feingold (WI)	$153,310	Sen. Mitch McConnell (KY)	$107,660
Sen. Ronald L. Wyden (OR)	$139,310	Rep. Dennis J. Hastert (IL)	$107,200
Sen. Robert Menendez (NJ)	$132,193	Sen. Conrad Burns (MT)	$103,960
Sen. Debbie Stabenow (MI)	$130,606	Sen. Mike DeWine (OH)	$101,000
Sen. Tim Johnson (SD)	$130,587	Sen. Ileana Ros-Lehtinen (FL)	$99,750
Sen. Bill Nelson (FL)	$126,371	Sen. Jim Talent (MO)	$93,010
Sen. Kent Conrad (ND)	$123,850	Sen. Robert F. Bennett (UT)	$87,250
Sen. Mary L. Landrieu (LA)	$112,750	Rep. Thomas D. DeLay (TX)	$84,700
Rep. Eliot Engel (NY)	$106,018	Sen. Alfonse M. D'Amato (NY)	$80,050
Sen. Charles S. Robb (VA)	$103,821	Sen. Jim Bunning (KY)	$75,900
Rep. Steny Hoyer (MD)	$103,575	Sen. Christopher S. Bond (MO)	$70,100
Sen. Ben Nelson (NE)	$102,760	Sen. Gordon H. Smith (OR)	$67,750
Sen. Richard J. Durbin (IL)	$100,100	Sen. Richard C. Shelby (AL)	$67,500
Sen. Carl Levin (MI)	$99,029	Sen. Slade Gorton (WA)	$66,750
Sen. Joseph M. Cleland (GA)	$98,150	Sen. Charles E. Grassley (IA)	$62,800
Sen. Max Baucus (MT)	$97,400	Rep. Clay Shaw Jr. (FL)	$61,355
Sen. Byron Dorgan (ND)	$96,750	Sen. Lisa Murkowski (AK)	$57,600
Sen. Christopher J. Dodd (CT)	$94,000	Sen. John S. McCain (AZ)	$57,500
Sen. Jean Carnahan (MO)	$93,422	Sen. Susan M. Collins (ME)	$56,500
Sen. Evan Bayh (IN)	$90,500	Sen. Wayne Allard (CO)	$55,500
Rep. Martin Frost (TX)	$88,725	Sen. Olympia J. Snowe (ME)	$51,250
Rep. Artur Davis (AL)	$83,567	Sen. George Allen (VA)	$51,000
Rep. Joseph Crowley (NY)	$76,157	Sen. Ben Nighthorse Campbell (CO)	$49,250
Rep. Richard A. Gephardt (MO)	$75,915	Sen. Tim Hutchinson (AR)	$47,900

Source: Federal Election Commission.

the contributions to Gilman are hardly surprising, given that he was the chair of the House Committee on International Relations from 1995 until 2001. Likewise, from 1998 to 2006, Senator Barbara Boxer received contributions totaling $25,599 from the Coalition for Asian Pacific Americans ($9,599),[13] USINPAC ($6,500), Hispanic Unity USA ($5,000), Iranian American Political Action Committee ($2,500), and ARMENPAC ($2,000). By comparison, Senator Boxer received $182,373 from pro-Israel PACs over those five election cycles.

In order to examine which candidates were the top recipients of PAC contributions by non-Jewish PACs, Table 3.8 lists the top recipients for Cuban American, African American, Hispanic American, Arab American, Armenian

Table 3.7 Top Recipients of Non-Jewish PAC Contributions by Party, 1998–2006 (in dollars)

Democratic Candidates	Total Contributions	Republican Candidates	Total Contributions
Sen. Robert Menendez (NJ)	$42,500	Sen. John E. Sununu (NH)	$43,150
Rep. Nick J. Rahall II (WV)	$40,720	Rep. Benjamin A. Gilman (NY)	$31,600
Rep. Brad Sherman (CA)	$36,316	Sen. Spencer Abraham (MI)	$30,777
Rep. Tom Lantos (CA)	$35,000	Rep. Dana Rohrabacher (CA)	$29,250
Rep. Henry R. Cuellar (TX)	$34,000	Rep. Joseph K. Knollenberg (MI)	$28,286
Rep. Cynthia A. McKinney (GA)	$33,000	Rep. Ileana Ros-Lehtinen (FL)	$26,250
Rep. John T. Salazar (CO)	$32,500	Rep. Ray LaHood (IL)	$24,500
Richard M. Romero (NM)	$30,000	Rep. Darrell E. Issa (CA)	$23,750
Sen. Hillary R. Clinton (NY)	$28,500	Sen. George Allen (VA)	$21,000
Rep. David Wu (OR)	$28,100	Sen. Charles E. Grassley (IA)	$19,000
Rep. Adam Schiff (CA)	$27,300	Sen. Rick Santorum (PA)	$16,700
Rep. James P. Moran Jr. (VA)	$26,850	Sen. John E. Ensign (NV)	$16,500
Sen. Barbara Boxer (CA)	$25,599	Sen. Mel Martinez (FL)	$15,750
Rep. Patrick J. Kennedy (RI)	$25,500	Jennifer S. Carroll (FL)	$15,000
Dario Herrera (NV)	$25,000	Rep. Donald Manzullo (IL)	$15,000
Rep. Joseph Crowley (NY)	$24,000	Rep. Mike Pence (IN)	$14,500
Sen. Bill Nelson (FL)	$23,000	Rep. Thomas D. DeLay (TX)	$14,000
Rep. Gary L. Ackerman (NY)	$22,500	Rep. Christopher H. Smith (NJ)	$14,000
Rep. David E. Bonior (MI)	$22,218	Rep. John E. Sweeney (NY)	$14,000
Democratic Senatorial		Michael Steele (MD)	$13,725
Campaign Committee	$21,000	Ronnie B. Greer (WI)	$13,500
Rep. Chris John (LA)	$20,500	Pres. George W. Bush	$13,218
Rep. John D. Dingell (MI)	$20,200	Dylan C. Glenn (R-GA)	$12,500
Rep. Corrine Brown (FL)	$20,000	Rep. Thaddeus McCotter (MS)	$12,100
Rep. Julia Carson (IN)	$20,000	Michael J. Bouchard (MI)	$12,075
Rep. Frank Pallone (NJ)	$19,650	Sen. Conrad Burns (MT)	$12,000
Rep. John Conyers Jr. (MI)	$19,600	Sen. Lincoln D. Chafee (RI)	$12,000
Rep. Ciro D. Rodriguez (TX)	$18,500	Sen. Orrin Hatch (UT)	$12,000
Rep. Nick Lampson (TX)	$18,200	Clinton B. Lesueur (MS)	$12,000
Rep. Dennis Cardoza (CA)	$18,000	Rep. Tom Feeney (FL)	$11,500
Rep. Solomon Ortiz (TX)	$18,000		

Source: Federal Election Commission.

American, and Indian American PACs over the five election cycles examined. Contributions by African American PACs and Hispanic American PACs are dominated by partisan PACs, which contribute to either Democrats or Republicans, but not both parties. For example, the Congressional Black Caucus PAC contributed only to Democrats from 1998 to 2006, while Black America's PAC gave 99.5 percent of its contributions to Republicans. Because of their partisan nature, both of these PACs are more likely to contribute to challengers than the typical PAC. In a similar fashion, virtually all of the contributions made by the CHC–Building Our Leadership's Diversity PAC, Hispanic PAC USA, Hispanic Unity USA, and the Hispanic Democratic Organization PAC were given to Democrats, while the Latino Alliance

Table 3.8 Top Recipients of PAC Contributions for Selected Ethnicities, 1998–2006

Recipient from Cuban American PACs	Contributions	Ethnic Brethren	Recipient from African American PACs	Contributions	Ethnic Brethren	Recipient from Hispanic American PACs	Contributions	Ethnic Brethren
Rep. Patrick J. Kennedy (D-RI)	$21,500	No	Rep. Cynthia A. McKinney (D-GA)	$20,000	Yes	Richard M. Romero (D-NM)	$25,000	Yes
Sen. Bill Nelson (D-FL)	$21,000	No	Rep. Corrine Brown (D-FL)	$15,000	Yes	Rep. Henry R. Cuellar (D-TX)	$23,000	Yes
Sen. Joseph I. Lieberman (I-CT)	$20,000	Yes	Jennifer S. Carroll (Chal: R-FL)	$15,000	Yes	Rep. John T. Salazar (D-CO)	$17,500	Yes
Sen. Robert Menendez (D-NJ)	$16,000	Yes	Rep. Julia Carson (D-IN)	$15,000	Yes	Rep. Ciro D. Rodriguez (D-TX)	$16,500	Yes
Rep. J. Salazar (D-CO)	$15,000	No	Democratic Senatorial Campaign Committee	$15,000	n.a.	Rep. Dennis Cardoza (D-CA)	$15,000	Yes
Rep. Gary L. Ackerman (D-NY)	$14,000	No	Rep. Major Robert Owens (D-NY)	$15,000	Yes	Dario Herrera (D-NV)	$15,000	Yes
Sen. John Ensign (R-NV)	$13,000	No	Ronnie B. Greer (R-WI)	$13,500	Yes	Rep. Linda Sanchez (D-CA)	$14,500	Yes
Sen. Bob Graham (D-FL)	$13,000	No	Rep. David A. Scott (D-GA)	$12,500	Yes	Carlos J. Nolla (D-KS)	$14,000	Yes
Sen. Harry Reid (D-NV)	$13,000	No	Dylan C. Glenn (Chal: R-GA)	$12,000	Yes	Eddie Diaz (D-FL)	$13,000	Yes
Sen. Conrad Burns (R-MT)	$12,000	No	Clinton B. Lesueur (Chal: R-MS)	$12,000	Yes	Annie Betancourt (D-NM)	$11,000	Yes
Rep. Debbie Wasserman-Schultz (D-FL)	$12,000	No	Michael Steele (R-MD)	$10,125	Yes	Sen. Robert Menendez (D-NJ)	$10,500	Yes
Rep. Eliot Engel (D-NY)	$11,500	No	L. Louise Lucas (OS: D-VA)	$10,005	Yes	5 Candidates	$10,000	
Rep. David Wu (D-OR)	$10,500	No	8 Candidates	$10,000				
Sen. Lamar Alexander (R-TN)	$10,000	No						
Rep. Allen Boyd (D-FL)	$10,000	No						

(continues)

Table 3.8 continued

Recipient from Arab American PACs	Contributions	Ethnic Brethren	Recipient from Armenian American PACs	Contributions	Ethnic Brethren	Recipient from Indian American PACs	Contributions	Ethnic Brethren
Rep. Nick J. Rahall II (D-VA)	$31,720	Yes	Rep. Brad Sherman (D-CA)	$24,700	No	Rep. Ileana Ros-Lehtinen (D-FL)	$17,750	No
Sen. John E. Sununu (R-NH)	$26,000	Yes	Rep. Joseph K. Knollenberg (R-MI)	$16,418	No	Rep. Eni Faleomavaega (D-AS)	$15,000	No
Rep. James P. Moran Jr (D-VA)	$21,000	No	Rep. David E. Bonior (D-MI)	$8,500	No	Rep. Tom Lantos (D-CA)	$12,500	No
Rep. Ray LaHood (R-IL)	$17,000	Yes	Sen. Robert Menendez (D-NJ)	$8,500	No	Rep. Joseph Crowley (D-NY)	$12,000	No
Rep. John Conyers Jr. (D-MI)	$16,500	No	Howard Kaloogian (R-CA)	$8,252	Yes	Rep. Donald A. Manzullo (R-IL)	$12,000	No
Rep. Darrell E. Issa (R-CA)	$16,000	Yes	Rep. Adam Schiff (D-CA)	$8,150	No	Sen. Charles E. Grassley (R-IA)	$10,000	No
Sen. Spencer Abraham (R-MI)	$15,277	Yes	Rep. Thaddeus G. McCotter (R-MI)	$7,100	No	Jobs, Opportunities & Education PAC	$10,000	No
Rep. John D. Dingell (D-MI)	$15,000	No	Sen. Amy Klobuchar (D-MN)	$7,000	No	DCCC	$9,000	No
Rep. Dennis Kucinich (D-OH)	$14,500	No	Sen. Paul S. Sarbanes (D-MA)	$5,800	No	Sen. Evan Bayh (D-IN)	$7,600	No
Rep. David E. Bonior (D-MI)	$12,218	No	Sen. Mitch McConnell (R-KY)	$5,750	No	Rep. Michael R. Pence (R-IN)	$7,500	No
Rep. Chris John (D-LA)	$12,000	Yes	Rep. Frank Pallone Jr. (D-NJ)	$5,650	No	Sen. Richard G. Lugar (R-IN)	$7,000	No
Rep. Cynthia McKinney (D-GA)	$11,000	No	Democratic Senatorial Campaign Committee	$5,000	No	Superior California Federal Leadership Fund	$7,000	No
Sen. Lincoln D. Chafee (R-RI)	$10,000	No	National Republican Congressional Committee	$5,000	No	Sen. Barbara Boxer (D-CA)	$6,500	No
Rep. Jesse L. Jackson Jr (D-IL)	$10,000	No	Rep. E. Clay Shaw Jr. (R-FL)	$5,000	No	Rep. Frank Pallone Jr. (D-NJ)	$6,500	No
Rep. Barbara Lee (D-CA)	$9,500	No	Rep. Joseph Crowley (D-NY)	$4,500	No	2 Candidates	$6,000	No

Source: Federal Election Commission.
Note: Ethnic brethren are those who share the ethnic heritage of the PAC.

contributes exclusively to Republicans. Although the African American PACs do contribute to nonblack candidates, every candidate who received at least $9,000 in combined contributions from the African American PACs was black. Likewise, all but one of the sixteen candidates who received at least $10,000 from the Latino American PACs were Hispanic.

Arab American PACs are also supportive of ethnic brethren running for federal office, and six of the top recipients of contributions from these PACs were Arab Americans. However, because they have far fewer brethren seeking public office, the other ethnic groups that have active PACs give far more contributions to candidates who do not share their ethnic heritage. For example, only one of the top recipients from Armenian American PACs was of Armenian descent, and none of the top recipients of Indian American PACs was an Indian American. Instead, many of the top recipients from Armenian American PACs are incumbents who represent states with large numbers of ethnic brethren. Nine of the top recipients of Armenian American PAC contributions hailed from California, Michigan, New Jersey, or New York, all states with sizable Armenian communities. Arab American PACs were also more likely to give contributions to candidates who hail from states with larger populations of Arab Americans. For example, Arab Americans have contributed to a number of candidates from Michigan, including former senator Spencer Abraham (a Republican who is also of Lebanese descent), Representative John Dingell (D), Representative David Bonior (D), and Representative John Conyers (D).

▪ How Ethnic Contributions Compare to Others

How do contributions by ethnic PACs compare to the amount of campaign contributions made by other types of PACs? Some of the amounts discussed earlier in this chapter seem very large: thirty-five members of Congress received at least $100,000 over five election cycles from various ethnic groups. But, are the amounts of money being contributed by ethnic PACs excessive, especially when one considers all the campaign contributions a candidate receives in total? The answer in most cases is no. Take the top recipient of ethnic PAC contributions over the course of the study: Senator Joe Lieberman, who received $277,843 in ethnic PAC contributions. Lieberman collected 61 percent (nearly $170,000) of the ethnic PAC contributions in 2006, when he faced the fight of his political life. With voters unhappy with his support of the Iraq War, Senator Lieberman lost the Connecticut Democratic primary to challenger Ned Lamont. Lieberman then ran in the general election as an Independent, eventually winning the three-way race for the Senate seat. Lieberman, one of the strongest supporters of Israel on Capitol Hill, collected $171,843 from pro-Israel PACs from 2001 to 2006, approximately 7.1 percent of the $2.4 million he received from all PACs for his 2006 reelection bid (Center for Responsive Politics). In addition to collecting data on PAC activities, the Center for Responsive Politics codes large individual contributions with the industry associated with the individual contributor, and Lieberman received a total of $1.4 million in PAC and individual contributions from the pro-Israel lobby from 2001 to 2006. There is no question that $1.4 million is a great deal of money, and Joe Lieberman was the number one recipient of pro-Israel contributions in 2006. However, Lieberman raised more than $20 million for his campaign, and four other industries (lawyers and law firms, securities and investment, real estate, and retirees) gave more money to Lieberman than did the pro-Israel lobby. A total of twelve industries, ranging from alternative energy to pharmaceuticals, gave more money to Lieberman in 2006 than any other congressional candidate. According to the Center for Responsive Politics, the pro-Israel contributions accounted for just 6 percent of Lieberman's total fundraising.[14] Approximately 3 percent of Connecticut's population is Jewish, so the percentage of Lieberman's fundraising from pro-Israel sources exceeded the percentage of his Jewish constituents. However, candidates often turn to ethnic and religious networks to raise campaign contributions (Brown, Powell, and Wilcox 1995), so given Lieberman's religion and established positions on Israel, it is not surprising that he tapped Jewish networks to finance his reelection bid.

Prior to 2006, the member of Congress who received the greatest amount of ethnic PAC contributions was Senator Tom Daschle, who received over $223,000 in ethnic PAC contributions from 1998 to 2004. Daschle, who was the highest-ranking Democrat in the Senate in 2004, received $150,075 from ethnic PACs in the 2004 election cycle, including $5,000 from the Congressional Black Caucus PAC, $2,500 from the Iranian American PAC, and $1,000 each from ARMENPAC and the Taiwanese American Action Council PAC. But the vast majority of the ethnic PAC money received by Daschle, $140,575, came from pro-Israel PACs, and Daschle received a total of $262,775 in PAC and individual contributions from the pro-Israel lobby. However, Daschle received over $19 million in individual, PAC, and other contributions for his 2004 reelection campaign, and the pro-Israel lobby accounted for only 2 percent of Daschle's campaign war chest, not an especially significant percentage of his overall fundraising.[15] It is also worth noting that while Daschle was the number one recipient of pro-Israel campaign dollars, it is difficult to argue that Jewish patrons had an undue influence on the contest: Daschle lost the race by 3,500 votes to an opponent who collected just $750 from Jewish PACs.

Admittedly, the 2006 Lieberman and 2004 Daschle contests were unusual: they were closely watched Senate races, and control of the Senate was at stake (Koszczuk and Stern 2005). Because of this, both Lieberman and

Daschle attracted a great deal of campaign contributions from other sources, which may have reduced the overall impact of the pro-Israel contributions. What of other congressional recipients of ethnic dollars? To what extent do ethnic contributions dominate their fundraising? Nevada Democrat Shelley Berkley received the second highest amount of contributions from ethnic interest groups from 1998 to 2006, totaling over $254,000. First elected to the House in 1998 by a margin of 5,775 votes, Berkley was reelected by a more comfortable margin of 17,000 votes and 7 percentage points in 2000 against Jon Porter, a serious challenger who would be elected to the US House in 2002 in another district. After her reelection in 2000, Berkley earned a seat on the House Committee on International Relations in 2001. According to the Center for Responsive Politics, Berkley received $612,000 in campaign contributions from pro-Israel PACs and individual contributors from 1998 to 2006, or approximately 8.9 percent of her total fundraising across the five election cycles.[16] Does that represent a significant proportion of her fundraising? The answer likely depends on how one looks at the question and one's point of view. Approximately 4.4 percent of the Nevada 1st District was Jewish in 2000, meaning that Jewish contributions made a greater percentage of Berkley's fundraising than simply their proportion of the district's population. However, the growth of Las Vegas's Jewish population is one of the fastest in the nation, and a recent study estimated that 6 percent of the area's residents are Jewish (Friess 2004; Sheskin 2007a). Further, given Berkley's ethnic heritage and religion (she is Jewish), it is not surprising that she tapped Jewish networks to finance her congressional runs. Do Jewish PACs and donors have an undue influence on Berkley? That is doubtful: Berkley would likely support Israel regardless of the support of the pro-Israel lobby. Berkley's parents immigrated to the United States from Eastern Europe, and Berkley has discussed how the immigration experience of her family has shaped her life (Tetreault, 2003; Hawkings and Nutting 2003). Further, Berkley appears to be making defending the interests of the casino and gambling industry her first legislative priority (Hawkings and Nutting 2003), and the gaming industry is a larger source of her campaign contributions.

The best example of pro-Israel contributions accounting for a very high percentage of a candidate's overall fundraising is the 2002 primary contest between Representative Earl F. Hilliard and challenger Artur Davis. Davis received more than $200,000 in pro-Israel PAC and individual contributions, which accounted for 22 percent of Davis's fundraising in 2002. There are other candidates who receive strong support from pro-Israel contributors, but, unlike Davis, most of these candidates are Jewish. For years, Senator Carl Levin (D-MI) has received substantial support from pro-Israel contributors, usually totaling hundreds of thousands of dollars per election cycle (Babcock 1991). In his 2002 reelection bid, Levin received nearly $340,000 from pro-Israel supporters, accounting for approximately 12 percent of his fundraising. In response to a 1991 *Washington Post* report on pro-Israel campaign contributions, Levin's campaign manager Gordon Kerr indicated the numbers should not be surprising given that Levin is a "long-standing believer in the U.S.-Israel strategic relationship, and he's a Jewish senator, for gosh sakes" (Babcock 1991, A21). Likewise, Senator Ron Wyden (D-OR) received a total of $470,000 in pro-Israel campaign contributions in his 1998 and 2004 reelection bids, accounting for 6.6 percent of his fundraising. The same trend appears in some House races. For example, Representative Tom Lantos (D-CA) raised $270,000 from pro-Israel campaign sources from 1998 to 2006, which accounted for 9.2 percent of his fundraising. Representative Sander Levin (D-MI) received almost $218,000 in pro-Israel campaign contributions, accounting for 6.3 percent of his fundraising.

However, for many of the Senate's top recipients of pro-Israel contributions, the percentage of contributions from pro-Israel donors is less than 4 percent of their overall fundraising, in part because most of the major recipients of pro-Israel dollars are senators who raise millions of dollars over the course of their six-year term. For example, in the 2004 Senate election cycle, pro-Israel contributions accounted for just under 2 percent of Senator Patty Murray's reelection dollars and approximately 1.6 percent of Senator Barbara Boxer's campaign war chest. Overall, Murray and Boxer raised $8 million and $10.5 million in campaign contributions, respectively. The percentage of pro-Israel dollars can be higher in some House races, at times ranging from 3 to 7 percent of the funds raised by members of Congress. For example, the pro-Israel lobby accounted for 3.4 percent of the contributions raised from 2000 to 2006 by Eric Cantor, one of the few Jewish Republicans to serve in the House during this study. The pro-Israel lobby accounted for 6.8 percent of the contributions for Eliot Engel (D-NY) from 1998 to 2006. In his 2004 and 2006 reelection bids, Artur Davis received 3.3 percent of his campaign contributions from pro-Israel sources. Even in her 2002 effort to unseat Cynthia McKinney, only 4.8 percent of Denise Majette's fundraising came from pro-Israel contributors and PACs, not an especially high amount given the discussion by journalists and analysts that Jewish organizations had targeted McKinney. There is little doubt that the pro-Israel lobby is a formidable presence in campaign financing, accounting for nearly $38 million in contributions to federal candidates and political parties from 1998 to 2006. The Center for Responsive Politics ranks the pro-Israel lobby as the forty-first most active industry in federal elections from 1990 to 2006. However, with the exception of a few candidates and a few races, pro-Israel contributors, including both individual and PAC donors, do not account for a remarkably large percentage of the campaign contributions collected by members of Congress.

Because the Center for Responsive Politics does not code large individual contributions made by the ethnic groups that are not focused on Israel, we have to rely on ethnic PAC contributions to examine the other ethnic lobbies.

Based on these data, most of the other ethnic communities appear to be dwarfed in the arena of campaign finance by other sources of campaign contributions. Take the top recipient of Cuban American PAC contributions, Representative Patrick Kennedy (D-RI). Kennedy received a total of $21,500 from Cuban PACs, including $10,000 in 2002. However, Kennedy raised $640,000 in PAC contributions in 2002, meaning that Cuban PAC donations only accounted for 1.5 percent of the PAC money contributed to Kennedy. Kennedy raised a total of $2.2 million in individual and PAC contributions in 2002, and, when one compares the large donors to Cuban American PACs with the large individual donors of Kennedy's campaign, there is no evidence that Kennedy's coffers were filled with large individual contributions from Cuban Americans. To give another example, the top recipient of Armenian American PAC money was Representative Brad Sherman (D-CA), who received $24,700 from Armenian PACs from 1998 to 2006. Over those five election cycles, Sherman collected more than $2.2 million in PAC contributions alone, meaning that Armenian American PAC receipts accounted for 1.1 percent of Sherman's PAC contributions.[17] Sherman received $8,000 from the Armenian National Committee PAC in 2002, the fifteenth largest PAC contribution for that year. However, a host of other industries contributed far more to Sherman in 2002. For example, PACs associated with unions gave Sherman over $190,000, and real estate PACs gave him almost $70,000. Sherman's district has one of the largest Armenian populations in the nation, and the percentage of Armenian PAC contributions made to Sherman is lower than the percentage of Armenian Americans in his district.

Finally, the top recipient of Arab American PAC dollars was Representative Nick Rahall (D-WV), who received $39,720 from Arab and Lebanese American PACs over the five election cycles. Overall, ethnic PAC contributions account for 2.6 percent of the funds raised by Rahall from 1998 to 2006. A third of those contributions were made in 1998, and they accounted for approximately 10.5 percent of the $121,575 Rahall raised in that cycle. That is not an insignificant proportion of Rahall's fundraising in 1998, but the proportion was caused more by low overall fundraising by Rahall than by high contributions from ethnic PACs: Rahall did not need to raise a great deal of money in 1998 because Republicans did not field an opposition candidate in either 1996 or 1998. Further, it is unlikely that contributions from Arab and Lebanese American PACs had undue influence on Rahall, who is of Lebanese heritage. Rahall has served in Congress since 1977, and he is known as "a frequent critic of Israel and an advocate of closer ties to Arab states" (Duncan and Nutting 1999, 1480). There is no evidence that the ethnic PAC money helped buy Rahall's election or his vote.

Again, tracking ethnic-based campaign contributions is difficult at the level of the individual contributor, and some critics argue that these contributions to some members of Congress are quite significant. For example, in his 2001 analysis of the foreign aid appropriation process, Michael Dobbs asserts that Representative Frank Pallone (D-NJ) received more than $100,000 in Armenian American contributions in 1998, which would mean that between 20 and 25 percent of his contributions from individual donors came from Armenian Americans. Dobbs also contends that Armenian American contributors raised more than $200,000 for Senator Mitch McConnell (R-KY) and the Republican Party of Kentucky. Armenian American organizations have not necessarily been modest regarding Armenian participation in campaign financing: in 2005, the Armenian National Committee of America (ANCA) announced that Armenian Americans had contributed at least "$3.9 million in documented donations and an estimated $5 million in total campaign contributions" to federal campaigns during the 2004 election cycle (ANCA 2005). Assuming the ANCA data are correct, Armenian Americans gave nearly $1.3 million in large individual contributions to congressional candidates in 2004, and the report states that Representative Pallone, Representative Joe Knollenberg (R-MI), Senator McConnell, Representative Schiff, and Representative George Radanovich (R-CA) received the highest levels of campaign contributions.[18]

Critics have also cited the Cuban American community as using campaign contributions to influence foreign policy. The Center for Responsive Politics tracked large contributions from Cuban Americans from 1980 to 2000, finding that Cuban Americans gave nearly $643,000 in federal contributions in 1998 and nearly $1.2 million in federal contributions in 2000 (Center for Responsive Politics n.d.). Those figures include contributions to party committees, which account for 45 percent of all individual contributions by Cuban Americans over the span of the study. If contributions to parties and presidential candidates are removed from the equation, then Cuban Americans gave approximately $354,000 to congressional candidates in 1998, and approximately $495,000 to congressional candidates in 2000. In 2000, $210,000 in individual contributions from Cuban Americans went to just five congressional candidates: Florida Senate candidates Bill Nelson (D) and Bill McCollum (R), Senator Robert G. Torricelli (D-NJ), Representative Robert Menendez (D-NJ), and Representative Lincoln Diaz-Balart (R-FL). In 1998, Cuban Americans gave over $204,000 to just four candidates: Representative Lincoln Diaz-Balart, Senator Bob Graham (D-FL), Representative Menendez, and Representative Ileana Ros-Lehtinen (R-FL).

While the above figures are large, the amounts of individual contributions given to congressional candidates by Cuban Americans do not appear especially high, given the size of the Cuban American community nationwide, as well as the size of the communities in the districts of the candidates. For example, of the 1.2 million Cuban Americans living in the United States in 2000, over 830,000 resided in Florida and over 77,000 lived in New Jersey. Further, Diaz-Balart, Menendez, and Ros-Lehtinen are all Cuban Americans, and they likely tapped ethnic networks when engaging in fundraising.

The Center for Responsive Politics also notes that Cuban American contributions are actually declining somewhat, even as the cost of campaigns, and the amount of money being raised by congressional and presidential candidates, increase significantly.

While more research is clearly needed on tracing ethnic contributions at the individual donor level, the initial findings do not suggest that overall individual-level contributions by ethnic communities are especially significant, given the overall cost of campaigns. Instead, it appears from the individual contribution trends of the Cuban and Armenian lobbies that ethnic lobbies focus individual contributions on a few members of Congress and candidates who champion the interests of the lobby, thereby leveraging the resources of the group. A simple examination of PAC contributions does not reveal the true level of ethnic support for these members of Congress who support the ethnic communities the most. Additional research could focus on these and other ethnic groups that are already established in terms of PAC contributions, including the Greek, Lebanese, Irish, and Indian American lobbies, to determine if this pattern holds true for these lobbies. This preliminary research indicates that fundraisers and bundling, where individuals and groups collect contributions from individual donors and then deliver the checks to the candidate, could play a significant role in ethnic group politics.

The Scope of Ethnic Lobbying

Aside from campaign contributions, the second way in which interest group activities conjure mistrust among the public is through lobbying, and as "lobbying has grown in recent years, anxiety has mounted over the consequences of interest group politics" (Berry 1997, 1). In order to examine the degree to which ethnic organizations participate in direct lobbying, we examined lobbying disclosure reports filed from 1998 to 2006 with the secretary of the Senate. While many business and trade organizations may see electioneering as directly connected to lobbying, ethnic organizations largely abstain from direct lobbying, at least lobbying activities that require direct expenditures that must be disclosed. We identified only three dozen ethnic-based organizations that reported direct lobbying expenditures (see Table 3.9), and several of those organizations reported spending less than $10,000 on each of their semiannual reports. Some of the organizations included in Table 3.9 concentrate entirely on foreign affairs, while others focus both on foreign affairs and domestic issues.

AIPAC leads all ethnic-based organizations in terms of lobbying expenditures, averaging almost $1.2 million in lobbying costs per year from 1998 to 2006. All told, Jewish-based organizations averaged slightly more than $2 million a year in lobbying expenditures. The second most active. ethnic

Table 3.9 Total Lobbying Expenditures by Ethnic-Based Groups, 1998–2006

Organization	Years Active	Total Expenditures (dollars)
American Israel Public Affairs Committee (AIPAC)	1998–2006	10,565,017
United Jewish Communities	1998–2006	2,188,083
Armenian Assembly of America	1998–2006	1,820,000
American Jewish Committee	1998–2006	1,442,540
Hebrew Immigrant Aid Society	1998–2006	1,296,616
Zionist Organization of America	1998–2006[a]	996,700
Republican Jewish Coalition	1998–2006	774,215
Mexican American Legal Defense and Education Fund	1998–2006[a]	724,108
National Council of Jewish Women	1998–2006	720,000
American-Arab Anti-Discrimination Committee (NAAA-ADC)	2002–2006	480,000
Washington Office on Africa	1998–2004[a]	450,000
American Coalition for Filipino Veterans, Inc.	1998–2006	412,000
American Jewish Congress	2004–2006	375,000
Cuban American Foundation	1998–2001	349,409
Formosan Association for Public Relations	2000–2001; 2003	320,000
Friends of Ukraine	2002–2003	320,000
Alliance for a New Kosovo	2005–2006	270,000
Africa-America Institute	2001–2004	240,000
Albanian American Civic League	1998–2006[b]	200,000
United Hellenic American Congress	1998–2006[a]	130,000
American Friends of the Czech Republic	1998 2001	110,000
Assyrian American League	2002–2003	100,000
Hellenic-American Heritage Council	2001–2006[a]	100,000
African Hebrew Israelites of Jerusalem	2004	80,000
Save Darfur Coalition	2006	80,000
Polish American Congress	1998	70,000
World Jewish Congress (American Section)	2005–2006[a]	40,000
Cuba Democracy Public Advocacy Corp.	2005–2006[a]	23,088
Indian American National Foundation	2001–2002[a]	20,000
American Hellenic Institute Public Affairs Committee	1998–2006[c]	Minimal Activity
Asian-American Resource Center	2005–2006[c]	Minimal Activity
Croatian American National Advisory Council	2001–2003[c]	Minimal Activity
Hmong International Human Rights Watch	2002–2004[c]	Minimal Activity
Iranian Trade Association	1998–2001[c]	Minimal Activity
Joint Baltic American National Committee	1998–2006[c]	Minimal Activity
Korean Institute for Human Rights (Utah Chapter)	2001[c]	Minimal Activity
National Federation of Croatian Americans	2001–2006[c]	Minimal Activity

Notes: a. Includes at least one year in which reported semiannual lobbying expenditures were less than $10,000.

b. Organization did not report activity in 2001 and 2003.

c. Organization reported less than $10,000 in lobbying expenditures in every semiannual report.

group is the Armenian Americans, and the Armenian Assembly of America spent a little over $200,000 per year on lobbying. The American-Arab Anti-Discrimination Committee (ADC) began reporting lobbying expenditures midway through the study, and the lobby has averaged $96,000 annually in lobbying expenditures since 2002. The Cuban American Foundation, the lobbying arm for the Cuban American National Foundation, was active for the first four years of the study, averaging over $87,000 in lobbying expenditures per year from 1998 to 2001. However, the Cuban American Foundation has not reported any lobbying expenditures since 2002. All told, ethnic organizations simply do not rely on hired lobbyists and direct lobbying to the same degree as other sectors or industries. For example, the total amount spent by AIPAC on lobbying expenditures from 1998 to 2006 was $10.5 million. Dozens of nonethnic organizations spent more than $11 million in 2006 alone. Most of those organizations are businesses, but even some grassroots organizations, like AARP, greatly exceed the lobbying expenditures of AIPAC: in 2006, AARP spent $23.1 million on lobbying, while AIPAC spent a little more than $1 million.[19]

It is important to keep in mind that the type of lobbying tracked by the lobbying disclosure reports is just one aspect of direct lobbying. As explained earlier, organizations, even 501(c)(3) organizations, can engage in lobbying and advocacy activities that do not require direct expenditures, such as simply meeting with members of Congress and their staffers. Such efforts to influence the policymaking process do not require disclosure under current regulations and are very difficult to track. Thus, organizations such as the Irish National Caucus, the Armenian National Committee of America, and USINPAC can and do engage in direct lobbying, even though these organizations are not dedicating funds that can be tracked through disclosure reports.

In contrast to most of the organizations that dominate in terms of direct lobbying expenditures, most ethnic organizations are mass-based organizations, and the primary resource of mass-based organizations is not money, but people. Because of this, most of the ethnic groups identified for this study focus a great deal on grassroots mobilization, where the organization encourages members of the group, the ethnicity, or the broader public to contact members of Congress and other policymakers about an issue or position. At the most basic level, ethnic organizations provide action alerts, which present facts and rhetoric about an issue and call upon members and visitors to contact their representatives. Some ethnic groups use Capwiz or another "astroturf" Web program, which allows individuals to easily e-mail their elected representatives about an issue, giving the illusion of a grassroots campaign. Some organizations go much further, showing members and others who visit the website how to become more engaged in policymaking and how to more effectively influence their representatives. For example, the ADC has a "Get Active!" section on its website, which describes in detail how individuals can become more effective citizen lobbyists. Policymakers interviewed for this project identified a number of ethnic groups as having excellent grassroots networks, including the Jewish, Cuban, Armenian, and Greek lobbies. Policymakers also noted that AIPAC has the most sophisticated grassroots network of any ethnic-based organization.

Finally, many ethnic organizations leverage their grassroots and other resources by working with other ethnic organizations (often associated with other ethnicities), human rights groups, and other nongovernmental organizations on issues not related directly to their own ethnicity. ANCA works with non-Armenian groups to recognize and stop human rights abuses and genocide, such as working with the National Association for the Advancement of Colored People (NAACP) and other groups to bring attention to the crisis in Darfur. Working on Darfur and other issues like it may increase the ability for the ANCA to position itself as a credible expert on genocide and human rights; by broadening the scope of their focus, they may better address issues that are more central to the Armenian community, like the 1915 Armenian genocide. Armenian groups are by no means alone in terms of using coalitions. For example, Arab American groups worked with free speech organizations, like the ACLU, and libertarian groups to oppose the Patriot Act and racial profiling.

In interviews with ethnic group leaders, a number of individuals (who do not represent Jewish organizations) noted that Jewish groups are often very important coalition partners in terms of promoting human rights and foreign aid. For instance, Jewish organizations are working with African American and other groups to bring attention to the humanitarian crisis in Darfur and to provide assistance to refugees, and Jewish organizations play a prominent role in the Save Darfur Coalition. At times, Jewish organizations use ethnicity and historical trauma to mobilize Jews for causes that do not directly affect their ethnic brethren. For example, in its appeal for financial contributions to assist Sudanese refugees, the Hebrew Immigrant Aid Society issued an emergency appeal stating that "as Jews, it is our historical and moral imperative to help victims of this genocide" (Hebrew Immigrant Aid Society n.d.). Jewish organizations also work with other Jewish entities to champion issues important to the American Jewish community. For example, NCSJ works with a number of other Jewish organizations, and it provides some links on its Web page to its member agencies, other Jewish organizations, think tanks, and other organizations. NCSJ also provides links to Jewish-based initiatives and campaigns. For example, after the 2006 Israel-Lebanon conflict, NCSJ provided a Web link to the United Jewish Communities' Israel Emergency Campaign.

Conclusion

We found little evidence that ethnic organizations have undue influence in terms of campaign finance or direct lobbying. Across the five election cycles, the non-Jewish PACs analyzed for this study spent a *total* $4.8 million in net federal campaign activities. To put these figures in perspective, according to the Center for Responsive Politics, in the 2006 election cycle alone, *each* of the twenty largest PACs contributed at least $1.8 million to federal candidates, with the National Association of Realtors contributing almost $3.7 million to federal candidates. Pro-Israel PACs contributed a total of $3.0 million to federal candidates in 2006, $3.1 million in 2004, $2.7 million in 2002, $1.9 million in 2000, and $2.1 million in 1998. Yet, combined contributions of all pro-Israeli PACs are less than the amount of money distributed by some single corporate and union PACs. Again, contributions by pro-Israel PACs constitute less than 1 percent of the PAC universe. In terms of direct lobbying, ethnic organizations, both Jewish and non-Jewish, account for an even smaller percentage of the direct lobbying universe than they do of the campaign finance realm.

Rather than money, the strength of ethnic groups and organizations is their membership, and ethnic groups focus their energies and strategies on using their membership rolls to influence public policy. The next chapter will examine the importance of the size of an ethnic group's population, as well as other factors, in helping to explain ethnic group influence.

Notes

1. Indeed, the IRS investigated the National Association for the Advancement of Colored People (NAACP) because of its criticism of President George W. Bush in 2004, which some Republican members of Congress complained amounted to electioneering (Fears 2006). The IRS eventually declared that the remarks did not violate the organization's tax-exempt status.

2. Under pressure from the executive branch, Hastert would later rescind the promise in October of 2000. ·

3. While electronic communication may be a valuable tool for groups to mobilize their members, e-mail and fax communications are not as valuable for influencing policymakers. Traditional letters and telegrams, which require more effort, have a greater impact on elected officials. E-mail and fax campaigns often appear to be "manufactured," and while e-mails and faxes are not ignored by members of Congress, "they are easier to discount" (Berry 1997, 137).

4. Of course, simply having ethnic brethren in Congress does not necessarily mean the ethnic community will successfully influence the policymaking process. Serbian American leaders believed initially that Ohio senator George Voinovich would champion the perspectives of the organized Serbian American community. That has not necessarily been the case.

5. Wright's argument differs from the traditional service bureau model of interest group behavior offered by Bauer, Pool, and Dexter (1963). Wright contends that interest groups have an opportunity and, at times, an incentive to deceive policymakers by withholding key information or by presenting misinformation.

6. A member of Congress may also meet with constituents not out of a fear of electoral retribution, but out of a genuine interest in providing good representation.

7. In the few cases where candidates faced a runoff election following the general election, the date of the runoff election was used to distinguish the election cycle for which the contribution was made.

8. In uncompetitive races, the typical incumbent raised just over $1 million, while the average challenger raised approximately $100,000 in 2006.

9. Total federal expenditures for a PAC include contributions to congressional and presidential candidates, independent expenditures for or against a federal candidate, and contributions to other federal PACs.

10. Herrnson's analysis examines major party-contested races. However, his analysis does provide a useful benchmark with which to compare ethnic group contribution.

11. The PAC contributed $5,000 on February 26, 2002, to Sununu for his primary race, plus made a $1,000 contribution on the same date for his general election campaign, as well as an additional $1,000 contribution on April 15, 2002, for Sununu's general election campaign.

12. However, some of those contributions were made to DioGuardi's own campaigns to return to Congress.

13. The Coalition for Asian Pacific Americans also spent $1,000 in the form of independent expenditures in support of Senator Boxer in 2004.

14. The Center for Responsive Politics has coded $24,128,416 of the $31,712,957 in contributions that Lieberman received from 2001 to 2006. The $1,435,940 in pro-Israel contributions is 5.95 percent of $24.1 million that the center has coded.

15. The Center for Responsive Politics has coded $13,246,819 of the $15,528,784 in contributions that Daschle received from 1999 to 2004. The $262,775 in pro-Israel contributions is 1.98 percent of $13.2 million that the center has coded.

16. Across all PAC and individual contributions, Berkley raised $7.7 million according to the Center for Responsive Politics, and the center has coded $6.9 million of those contributions.

17. Overall, Sherman collected more than $5.7 million in individual and PAC contributions from 1998 to 2006.

18. The report does not spell out contribution amounts to members of Congress, but that information can be extrapolated by subtracting contributions to presidential candidates (a little more than $800,000) and contributions to the national party and congressional committees (roughly $817,000).

19. Since 1999, AARP has spent at least $4 million annually on lobbying, and it spent $36.3 million in 2005.

4

Accounting for Varying
Levels of Clout

Despite the interest generated in ethnic groups and foreign policy over the past thirty years, little research has been conducted to determine which ethnic groups enjoy the most influence in foreign policy. Aside from the Jewish American lobby, which is routinely appraised as being the most influential ethnoracial lobby in the United States, most of the analyses on ethnic groups list a number of ethnic communities as having significant influence, without discussing the degree to which some of those lobbies are more influential than others. For example, R. C. Longworth (1998) contends that the Cuban, Greek, Armenian, Polish, and Baltic lobbies are among the most effective ethnic American lobbies. Likewise, Frank Greve (1995), quoting then-representative Lee Hamilton (D-IN), indicates the Taiwanese, Cuban, Armenian, and East European lobbies are emulating the successes of the Jewish American lobby to influence foreign policy. What is missing from these discussions is a better sense of which ethnic groups are more successful than others, and the degree to which ethnic lobbies can influence the policymaking process compared to other types of lobbies. This chapter examines the first question of which ethnic groups are perceived as being the most influential. However, before turning to the analysis of which ethnic groups have the most influence in the foreign policy–making process, we will examine the major factors that may help explain which ethnic groups should be the most influential.

■ Explaining Ethnic Group Influence

Over the past decade, several scholars have addressed the phenomenon of ethnic mobilization, positing a host of factors that may determine the political success of ethnoracial groups and movements.[1] For example, Milton Esman hypothesized that seven factors determine the success and sustainability of ethnic political mobilization: the political opportunity structure, leadership, ideology, organization, resources, goals, and strategies/tactics. Speaking more broadly, Mohammed Ahrari (1987) asserts that three characteristics predict the power or influence of ethnic groups in the United States: the degree of congruence between the interests promoted by an ethnic group and the strategic interest of the mother country to the United States, the degree of assimilation of the ethnic group, and the homogeneity of the ethnic group. The analysis presented in this chapter focuses on several broad factors that may help explain the influence of ethnic groups: the size and dispersion of their population, their resources, the saliency of foreign policy issues to the ethnic groups, their assimilation into American society, and the degree to which their goals are an attempt to alter the status quo. The factors to be analyzed expand the aspects of influence offered by Ahrari by including resources available to an ethnic group that may then be used for mobilization or advocacy purposes. This analysis differs from Esman by focusing less on the factors that are elite driven and, thus, can change quickly as some individuals leave leadership roles and others arrive. It is clear that leadership, ideology, and strategies matter a great deal to mobilization, and the following qualitative analysis will address these important pieces of ethnic group influence. However, these factors are difficult to study systematically across thirty-eight ethnic groups and their representative organizations. By focusing on population, issue saliency, resources, assimilation, and goals of the ethnic groups included in the project, we can assess more methodically why some ethnic groups emerge as more influential than others.

Population

A key component to the success of interest groups and social movements is mobilization, and ethnic groups with larger populations may have a greater influence on policymaking than smaller ethnic communities because the main political power of grassroots organizations is linked directly to their main resource: people, or more specifically, people who vote (Gerber 1999). Although any given ethnic lobby makes up a small percentage of the population, voting is "an important way in which ethnic communities make their voices heard in Washington" (Smith 2000, 95). Like other grassroots groups, it is likely that successful ethnic groups are better able to mobilize members of the ethnic community to communicate with their elected representatives, meet with members of Congress and staffers, and work to persuade their representatives to champion or at least support the issues that are important to the ethnic group. Access is the first step toward influence (Wright 2003), and the degree of geographic concentration of an ethnic group may influence the group's ability to gain access to members of Congress. For example, a member of Congress might be more likely to schedule a meeting with an Armenian American organization if the district includes a sizeable population of Armenian Americans. This would mean that size of the interest group *within an individual congressional district* is an important predictor of the group's ability to gain access to (and ultimately influence) an individual member of Congress. Thus, while we might expect a group with a million members nationwide to have greater access to Congress than a group with 10,000 members, the smaller group might have greater access if its 10,000 members are concentrated in one congressional district, and the members of the larger group are scattered across all 435 congressional districts. In such a scenario, the smaller group is very likely to be large enough to demand the attention of the member of Congress who represents its district, where the larger group might not have such a critical mass in any one district to demand the attention of a member of Congress.

In addition, a geographically concentrated population is also likely to help the ethnic community maintain its ethnic identity. Tony Smith argues that immigration patterns in the early twentieth century facilitated ethnic group influence in foreign affairs. Most of the immigrant groups were geographically concentrated, thus "increasing the likelihood of a strong ethnic identification and giving them more electoral clout" (Smith 2000, 51). Indeed, Smith states that this concentration of Irish and German Americans helped stall US involvement in World War I, and then retarded US involvement after the war. In a related manner, according to Carole Uhlaner et al., low levels of political participation among Asian Americans may be linked in large part to their geographical dispersion, which creates an insufficient incentive for ethnic and political leaders to mobilize political activity among Asian Americans. They argue that "the lack of geographic concentration makes ethnic politics more expensive and less valuable for Asian Americans" (Uhlaner, Cain, and Kiewiet 1989, 218).

The second manner in which the population of an ethnic community can expand its influence is when the group's population is diffused across many congressional districts. A dispersed population allows an ethnic community to target many members of Congress through a grassroots campaign since, first and foremost, members of Congress desire to be reelected (Mayhew 1974), and few members of Congress will refuse to listen to constituents (or have their staff members at least meet with constituents). Having constituents across the country increases the opportunity for a group's message to have an effect, since it increases the number of members of Congress who can be targeted through a grassroots campaign. If the group faces no significant other grassroots or constituent opposition, and if members of Congress are not opposed to the group's position a priori, then the group may be able to persuade individual members of Congress to support the group's position across a number of districts.

From this discussion, there are two testable hypotheses to examine the ways in which the population of an ethnic community can be an asset to its political efforts: first, ethnic communities that have large populations in concentrated areas can help elect representatives to Congress who can champion the issues of relevance to the ethnic community; and second, ethnic communities that are dissipated across a large number of congressional districts can work to influence a large number of members of Congress to support (or oppose) measures that are important to the ethnic group. The research hypotheses are:

H1: Ethnic communities that have large populations have greater influence in the foreign policy–making process.

H2: Ethnic communities that are dissipated across a large number of congressional districts have greater influence in the foreign policy–making process.

While the final section of this chapter will formally test these hypotheses, it is clear that ethnic organizations believe that size matters: some ethnic group leaders interviewed for this project complained that US Census figures underestimate the number of Americans who share their ancestry, and, at times, ethnic organizations assert that the actual number is much higher. For example, one Italian American organization states there are "more than 26 million Americans of Italian descent" (Order Sons of Italy in America 2007), almost 9 million greater than the 2005 census estimate. Likewise, an Albanian group states there are 400,000 Albanian Americans (Albanian American Civic League 2007), a figure almost triple the estimate made by the US Census. The American Jewish Committee commissioned a 2006 study which concluded that an earlier survey conducted by the United Jewish Communities underestimated the number of Jews in America by 1.2 million. Some groups go to great lengths to explain why they believe their ethnicity is undercounted by the US Census. For example, while the US Census gauges the size of the Arab community in the United States as 1.4 million in 2005, the Arab American Institute asserts the figure is at least 3.5 million, and the organization's website includes a methodological justification based on survey data for the higher estimate. It would appear that, at least in the minds of the leaders of these ethnic organizations, a larger ethnic population translates into the potential for increased influence.

Table 4.1 shows the overall population of ethnic American groups included in the study, as well as the populations for selected ethnic groups that are not active in foreign policy. Except for Jewish Americans and Kurdish Americans, the data are based on US Census figures. Data for Jewish Americans are based on the Glenmary Research Center's study of religious congregations and membership (Jones et al. 2002), and data for Kurdish Americans are based on journalistic accounts (Chandrasekaran 2007).[2] Because the

Table 4.1 Population of Ethnicities in 2005

Ethnicity	Population	Percentage of US Population
US population	288,378,137	
African American	36,844,565	12.78
Albanian	151,411	0.05
Arab	1,400,345	0.49
Armenian	421,291	0.15
Asian	13,879,891	4.81
Baltic	825,840	0.29
Caribbean (West Indian)	2,233,125	0.77
Central and Eastern European	15,514,450	5.38
Colombian	730,510	0.25
Croat	401,208	0.14
Cuban	1,461,574	0.51
Czech	1,555,767	0.54
Danish	1,434,060	0.50
Dutch	5,079,268	1.76
English	27,761,546	9.63
Eritrean[a]	17,787	0.01
Estonian[a]	25,034	0.01
Ethiopian	128,408	0.04
Filipino	2,807,731	0.97
German	49,178,839	17.05
Greek	1,291,381	0.45
Guatemalan	758,898	0.26
Hispanic	41,870,703	14.52
Hmong	188,900	0.07
Honduran	459,653	0.16
Indian	2,479,424	0.86
Iranian	377,618	0.13
Irish	34,668,723	12.02
Italian	17,235,187	5.98
Japanese	1,204,205	0.42
Jewish[b]	6,114,808	2.12
Korean	1,406,687	0.49
Kurdish[c]	40,000	0.01
Laotian	209,627	0.07
Latvian	88,474	0.03
Lebanese	464,119	0.16
Lithuanian	712,332	0.25
Mexican	26,781,547	9.29
Nicaraguan	281,167	0.10
Norwegian	4,601,154	1.60
Pakistani	210,410	0.07
Polish	9,770,544	3.39
Salvadoran	1,239,640	0.43
Serbian	169,479	0.06
Somali[a]	36,223	0.01
Spanish[a]	2,024,004	0.72
Swedish	4,259,792	1.48
Taiwanese[a]	293,568	0.10
Turkish	164,945	0.06
Ukrainian	963,263	0.33
Vietnamese	1,521,353	0.53

Source: 2005 US Census American Community Survey.
Notes: a. Figures are based on 2000 Census data. b. Figures are based on Jones et al. (2002). c. Figures are based on Chandrasekaran (2007).

census relies on individuals to self-report ancestry, the figures presented in Table 4.1 almost certainly underestimate the number of Americans who share an ancestry with an ethnic group. However, just because an individual is of an ethnic ancestry does not mean the individual considers himself or herself to be a member of that ethnic community: for example, an American of Irish descent may not have any connections to the Irish American community and may not consider herself to be Irish. Because individuals must self-identify with a particular ancestry, the census data do help gauge the relative size of different ethnic American groups.

On the surface, there does not appear to be any significant pattern in terms of the size of the ethnic group and its ability to influence foreign policy. For example, there is little evidence that two of the largest ethnic groups in America, German Americans and Anglo Americans, have any organized presence in the foreign policy–making process.[3] Over 49 million Americans consider themselves to be of German ancestry, followed by Irish Americans (34.7 million) and English Americans (27.8 million). Other sizeable ancestries include Mexican (26.8 million), Italian (17.2 million), and Polish (9.8 million), while 20.5 million simply regard their ancestry to be "American." Combining the populations of the ancestries associated with the Captive Nations helps gauge the size of the Central and Eastern European lobby, an important ethnic lobby during and immediately after the Cold War, and 15.5 million Americans belong to one of the ancestries associated with the Captive Nations. There are approximately 6.1 million Jewish Americans, a figure comparable to Dutch Americans (5.1 million), Norwegian Americans (4.6 million), and Swedish Americans (4.3 million). Some ethnicities often associated with a significant presence in foreign policy had populations between 1 and 2 million, including Czech (1.5 million), Greek (1.3 million), and Cuban (1.4 million). Yet there are other ethnic groups of similar size that have virtually no activity in foreign policy, such as the Danish (1.4 million) and Spanish (2.2 million). The census also estimated that 1.4 million Americans are of Arab descent. Still other ethnicities often discussed as being players in the foreign policy–making process have small populations: there are only 420,000 Armenian Americans, fewer than 825,000 Baltic Americans, and fewer than 300,000 Taiwanese Americans.

In terms of race, there are now 5 million more Hispanic Americans (41.9 million in 2005) than African Americans (36.8 million) in the United States. Although a great deal of discussion has centered on the growth of the Hispanic vote and the potential increased influence of the Hispanic lobby (Navarro 2004), African Americans still constitute a much larger voting bloc than Hispanic Americans. Because 40.7 percent of Hispanics in the United States are not citizens, almost twice as many blacks (14 million) voted than Latinos (7.5 million) in November 2004 (Holder 2006). Likewise, 32.5 percent of Asians in the United States are not citizens, and only 2.8 million Asians voted in 2004.

Is a critical mass needed for an ethnic community to achieve influence in the policymaking process? Tony Smith hypothesizes that, coupled with a million-dollar budget for campaign contributions and the absence of a countervailing enemy group, the threshold for entry into the policymaking process is 250,000 voters across a small number of districts. Because some members of ethnic communities are not citizens and others are not registered to vote, voting turnout rates vary substantially across races. Further, one must account for the size of the adult population of the ethnic group, since only those citizens 18 or older may vote. According to the census, 28 percent of adult Hispanics voted in 2004, compared to 29.8 percent of adult Asians, 56.3 percent of African Americans, and 65.8 percent of whites who are not Hispanic (Holder 2006). Those turnout rates mean that many ethnic groups would need 900,000 adult members to achieve the 250,000 voter threshold. Based on this reasoning, a number of Asian American ethnicities may be poised to emerge as capable of influencing foreign policy, including Vietnamese (over 1 million adults in 2005), Koreans (1 million adults in 2005), and Indians (1.8 million adults in 2005). Even when accounting for lower voter turnout rates among Asians in the United States, Vietnamese Americans and Korean Americans each likely constituted a voting bloc of at least 250,000 in 2005, while Indian Americans likely constituted a voting bloc of at least 500,000. In contrast, although their growth rates are substantial, some of the Hispanic ethnic groups that may be interested in influencing foreign policy did not approach the 900,000 adult population threshold in 2005. For example, there were 326,000 adult Hondurans, 212,000 adult Nicaraguans, 546,000 adult Colombians, and 881,000 adult Salvadorans in the United States in 2005, according to the census. Because of low turnout rates among Hispanics in the United States, only Salvadoran Americans come close to constituting a voting bloc of a quarter of a million.

That is not to say that smaller ethnic groups cannot have influence; again, if the ethnic group has a concentrated population, then it may have the opportunity to persuade its congressional representatives to champion issues the ethnic group finds important. In order to examine the degree to which an ethnic group's population is concentrated or dispersed, a Gini Index for each ethnic group was computed using ethnic population data for all 435 congressional districts.[4] A Gini Index of 0 indicates that the ethnic group is evenly distributed across congressional districts, while an index of 100 implies that the entire ethnic group lives in one congressional district. Table 4.2 presents the Gini Index for the ethnic groups included in the study, as well as selected other groups. Not surprisingly, Irish Americans and Anglo Americans have the most evenly distributed populations in the United States, and European ethnic groups tend to be more evenly distributed than other ethnic groups. In contrast, Hmong Americans, with a Gini Index of 91.85, are very concentrated into a few congressional districts. The Gini Index scores confirm that other ethnic groups commonly associated with living in enclaves do in fact

Table 4.2 Dispersion and Concentration of Ethnic Groups

Ethnicity	Gini Index
Irish	25.34
Anglo	27.61
German	35.65
Dutch	37.56
Greek	44.51
Arab	44.67
Lebanese	45.65
Central & Eastern European	46.54
Latvian	47.94
Italian	48.15
Estonian	49.01
Baltic	50.23
Polish	50.30
Swedish	50.86
Lithuanian	52.36
Ukrainian	53.01
Czech	54.39
Turkish	54.40
Indian	54.67
African American	56.43
Asian	57.07
Danish	57.73
Croat	57.96
Korean	59.07
Hispanic	60.63
Serbian	61.27
Vietnamese	64.87
Pakistani	65.06
Norwegian	65.86
Guatemalan	68.83
Iranian	69.22
Filipino	69.26
Japanese	69.56
Honduran	69.88
Mexican	70.38
Laotian	70.64
Jewish	70.84
Albanian	72.51
Taiwanese	72.61
Caribbean (West Indian)	73.80
Armenian	73.96
Ethiopian	74.64
Colombian	75.08
Salvadoran	78.74
Somali	80.45
Nicaraguan	81.83
Cuban	82.06
Hmong	91.85

Note: A Gini Index of 0 indicates that the population of the group is distributed evenly across all 435 congressional districts, and a Gini Index of 100 indicates that the entire population of the ethnic group lives in one congressional district.

have concentrated populations, including Cuban Americans, Somali Americans, Armenian Americans, and Jewish Americans.

Previous research on ethnic group influence in foreign affairs has often centered on Jewish Americans, Cuban Americans, and Armenian Americans, and some have argued these groups enjoy greater influence because of their concentrated populations. Indeed, if Smith's logic is correct, then having an ethnic population concentrated in a few districts may be more important than having a larger population distributed across the nation. Little research has been conducted that helps explain how large an ethnic group (or any group of people who find a particular policy realm to be personally important) must be in order for the group to gain significant influence. It is highly probable that a group that comprises 10 percent of the district will be able to gain the attention of the member of Congress, especially if there is little opposition to the group within the district. Since congressional districts averaged approximately 650,000 in 2000, the 10 percent threshold is approximately 65,000. The same may very well be the case at the 5 percent or even 2.5 percent threshold. Even at 2.5 percent, the ethnic group would number approximately 16,250 residents, a figure large enough to potentially earn the attention of the member of Congress, especially if the group is highly organized and does not have opposition within the district.

In order to examine the degree to which ethnic groups are concentrated into specific congressional districts, we examined census data estimating the population of each ethnic group in every congressional district.[5] For each district, the estimate for each ethnic group was divided by the district's overall population. Table 4.3 shows the degree to which ethnic groups included in the study are concentrated and dispersed across congressional districts. Rows show the number of congressional districts in which the ethnic group composes at least 1 percent, 2.5 percent, 5 percent, 10 percent, 25 percent, or 50 percent of the district's population. For example, in 2000, African Americans and Hispanic Americans accounted for over half the population in twenty-five and twenty-four congressional districts, respectively, and Mexican Americans accounted for half of the population in ten districts, while Asian Americans made up half the population in one district. A number of other ethnic groups compose at least 25 percent (approximately 162,500) of the population of congressional districts, including Irish, Italian, Cuban, and Caribbean Americans. Fourteen ethnic groups, including Polish and Armenian Americans, make up at least 10 percent of the population in at least one congressional district, and twenty-one ethnic groups account for at least 5 percent of at least one congressional district's population.

Armenian Americans may be the best example of the influence that can be achieved by a small ethnic group, and one of the reasons cited for the success of the Armenian lobby is its concentration in a few congressional districts (Doherty 1996b; Wallsten 2000; Walt 2005). According to 2000 census data, almost one-third (123,000) of Armenian Americans lived in just

Table 4.3 Number of Congressional Districts with Significant Ethnic Populations, 107th Congress

Ethnicity	Number of Congressional Districts with Threshold Percentage					
	1 percent	2.5 percent	5 percent	10 percent	25 percent	50 percent
African American	406	348	253	154	65	25
Hispanic	415	308	235	155	62	24
Mexican	295	191	133	87	35	10
Asian	324	167	85	38	7	1
Irish	432	421	383	252	4	0
Italian	418	281	163	71	4	0
Jewish	194	110	55	21	4	0
Anglo	427	408	363	181	3	0
Cuban	17	7	7	2	2	0
Caribbean (West Indian)	53	20	10	6	1	0
Central and Eastern European	395	266	164	58	0	0
Polish	325	181	93	21	0	0
Filipino	77	21	11	3	0	0
Japanese	21	3	2	2	0	0
Armenian	6	3	1	1	0	0
Czech	44	9	3	0	0	0
Korean	39	9	3	0	0	0
Indian	73	18	2	0	0	0
Salvadoran	29	9	1	0	0	0
Arab	39	3	1	0	0	0
Colombian	10	2	1	0	0	0
Laotian/Hmong	11	3	0	0	0	0
Greek	33	2	0	0	0	0
Iranian	7	2	0	0	0	0
Ukrainian	30	1	0	0	0	0
Hmong	7	1	0	0	0	0
Lebanese	1	1	0	0	0	0
Baltic	15	0	0	0	0	0
Lithuanian	11	0	0	0	0	0
Croat	8	0	0	0	0	0
Taiwanese	2	0	0	0	0	0
Ethiopian	1	0	0	0	0	0
Laotian	1	0	0	0	0	0
Serbian	1	0	0	0	0	0
Somali	1	0	0	0	0	0

Source: 2000 US Census.

five districts of the 106th Congress (the California 27th, 26th, 29th, 24th, and 19th). Half of all Armenian Americans lived in just twenty congressional districts, and the number of Armenians in those twenty districts ranged from 2,500 to 74,000. A similar pattern emerges with Cuban Americans: 57 percent of Cubans lived in five districts (the Florida 21st, 18th, 20th, and 17th, and the New Jersey 13th), and 71 percent resided in just twenty districts. The number of Cuban Americans in those twenty districts ranged from 4,200 to 330,000. For both Armenian and Cuban Americans, their concentrated populations in a few states also translates into representation in the US Senate: California and New Jersey senators have championed the views of Armenians, and Florida and New Jersey senators have advocated the issue positions of Cuban Americans.

In contrast, the populations of other ethnic groups often associated with foreign policy influence are distributed across more districts. For example, the number of Greek Americans (1.3 million) is comparable to the number of Cuban Americans (1.46 million), but the Gini Index for Greeks is 44.51, while the Gini Index for Cuban Americans is 82.06. Only 6.8 percent of Greek Americans lived in the five congressional districts with the largest Greek populations (the New York 14th and 5th, the Massachusetts 6th, the Florida 9th, and the Illinois 13th), and only 19.3 percent of Greek Americans lived in the twenty largest congressional districts. In 2000, there were at least 2,000 Greeks in 206 congressional districts, and at least 1,000 Greek Americans in 317 congressional districts. Indian Americans, who numbered 1.67 million in 2000 and have a Gini Index of 54.67, follow a similar pattern: just 10 percent lived in the five congressional districts with the largest population of their brethren (the New York 6th, the California 13th and 14th, and the New Jersey 6th and 7th), and 27.3 percent of Indian Americans lived in the twenty largest congressional districts. In 2000, there were at least 2,000 Indian Americans in 224 congressional districts, and at least 1,000 Indian Americans in 332 districts.

Jewish Americans are unique in several regards. In 2000, there were a number of congressional districts with substantial Jewish populations, yet Jewish Americans also had substantial numbers across a large number of districts. For example, Jewish Americans composed 25 percent or more of four congressional districts in 2000, 14.4 percent of Jewish Americans lived in five congressional districts (the Florida 19th, the New York 8th, 9th, and 14th, and the California 29th), and 35.9 percent lived in the twenty congressional districts with the largest number of Jews. At the same time, there were at least 2,000 Jewish Americans in 280 congressional districts, and at least 1,000 Jews in 335 districts. In terms of raw numbers, the population dispersion of Jews mirrors that of Greek and Indian groups, yet Jews also have concentrated population centers similar to those of Irish and Italian Americans, two groups with substantially larger populations. Almost unquestionably, Jewish Americans who are interested in maintaining strong US ties to Israel benefit from the fact that evangelical Christians, another segment of the overall Israeli lobby (Mearsheimer and Walt 2006), have a population pattern that complements Jews extremely well: evangelical Christians are concentrated in many areas of the United States where Jews tend to be absent.

From a policymaking perspective, ethnic groups such as Jewish, Irish, and Italian Americans should enjoy distinct advantages for having both concentrated populaces and dispersed brethren. These ethnicities benefit from having members of Congress who, because they represent large ethnic populations, serve as leaders on the issues important to the community. At the same time, ethnic organizations tap into wide grassroots networks to lobby members of Congress across the country to support the positions of the ethnic community. There are also significant numbers of members of these ethnic groups serving in Congress and throughout the policymaking process. Smaller ethnic groups, such as Asian Americans or Polish Americans, also have both concentrated communities and dispersed brethren. The population patterns of African Americans, Hispanic Americans, and Mexican Americans show how these ethnic groups should be capable of influencing the foreign policy process if they are mobilized to do so. All have significant concentrated communities—communities so large that the groups are a majority of the population in a number of congressional districts. In addition, the groups make up a significant percentage of the population in other districts throughout the country.

Issue Salience

Having a population of several million members is of little consequence to an ethnic lobby if the members of the community are not motivated to participate politically by ethnic concerns. For example, while there are over 49 million Americans of German ancestry, German Americans have virtually no organized presence in the foreign policy–making process, and there is little evidence that German Americans find US-German relations to be a salient issue. Several scholars hypothesize that issue salience plays an important role in affecting foreign policy outcomes. For example, Rogers (1993) asserts that apartheid was highly salient to black Americans, thus mobilizing them to participate in the foreign policy process. At the same time, sanctions were not especially salient to business interests, thus limiting the degree to which business groups were mobilized to oppose sanctions. A highly salient issue may also help unify an ethnic community, and such unity can play a major role in determining the group's success (Smith 2000). Smith cites the unity among Jewish Americans in support of Israel as a sovereign state as a key reason for its successes, and unity over the support of Israel may have even created a single-issue constituency among Jewish Americans.

There are a number of sources of issue salience for ethnic Americans. First, many ethnic Americans feel a connection to or an affinity toward their ancestral homeland. The 2002 film *My Big Fat Greek Wedding* parodied the affection that many Greek Americans have toward Greece, but critics of ethnic-based involvement in foreign policy express concern that such affections can diverge from, or run counter to, the national interests of the United States. While the fear of conflicted loyalties is a matter of contention among scholars, there is little debate that ethnic organizations often work to maintain, reinforce, or strengthen the connections ethnic Americans have with their ancestral homelands. For example, according to a report issued by the United Jewish Communities:

> Since its founding in 1948 and particularly since the Six Day War in 1967, Israel has attracted the attention of American Jewry in a variety of ways. . . . the organized Jewish community sees Israel as a critical component of American Jewish identity, and it has invested considerable resources to reinforce the connection of American Jews with Israel. (Ament 2005, 3)

It would appear that the efforts of Jewish American organizations have paid off: according to the report, 69 percent of American Jews feel very or somewhat attached to Israel, and 84 percent strongly or somewhat agree that Israel is the spiritual center of the Jewish people (Ament 2005).

Because of attachments like these, many ethnic communities want to strengthen ties or maintain strong ties between their ancestral homelands and the United States. Perhaps this is most true with American Jews and the broader Israeli lobby, who contend that a strong Israel is in the national interest of the United States. However, there is no shortage of examples, and both established ethnic groups, such as Greek and Italian Americans, and recent immigrant groups, like Indian and Pakistani Americans, seek to strengthen or maintain strong ties between the United States and their former homelands. Still, the issue of relations between the United States and the ancestral homeland may not be imperative enough to rally many members of an ethnic group, who may be more concerned with domestic issues that impact their day-to-day lives, such as employment or health care. However, the existence or emergence of a crisis may be an important mobilizing factor for ethnic groups, and an ethnic organization is more willing to use its scarce resources when it perceives a crisis to be greatest (Goldberg 1990).[6] In addition, a perceived threat can be an important motivator for individuals to join ethnic organizations and become more engaged in the policy process (Watanabe 1984). Research has shown that individuals are more motivated by losses than by gains, a proposition that may have profound consequences on ethnic group politics (see Kahneman and Tversky 1979; Ainsworth 2002). For example, Jewish Americans might be more motivated to join AIPAC by the news that Iran's missile technology threatens Israel than by news of a major breakthrough in negotiations between Israelis and Palestinians. Or, to use another example, Pakistani Americans might be more motivated by the opportunity to defeat an Indian American running for elected office than by the chance to elect a member of their own ethnic community.[7]

There is ample evidence that the presence of an enemy of the ancestral homeland can be a motivating factor for ethnic communities, helping to make both ethnicity and foreign policy salient to individuals. Again, this is a major motivating factor for Jews and other supporters of Israel, many of

whom believe that Israel's survival is in part dependent upon military assistance from the United States to help keep Israel's enemies at bay. A major
focus of AIPAC at present is the containment of Iran and elimination of its
nuclear program. For Cuban Americans, the enemy of their homeland is the
leader of that country, Fidel Castro, and many Cuban Americans believe US
foreign policy should focus on ending Castro's reign. Smith calls Turkey a
"powerful foreign enemy that stirs deep emotional fears" among Greek
Americans (2000, 115), and many Armenian Americans also consider Turkey
to be the enemy of their homeland. The same may be true with Indian Americans in terms of US relations with Pakistan and vice versa.[8]

The pan-ethnic lobbies do not have the same phenomenon of an enemy
of the homeland spurring political participation among brethren in the United
States: since the pan-ethnic communities are comprised by individuals who
share a common continental-based geographical connection instead of a
state-based connection, there is not necessarily one foreign state or one dic-
tator to provide a stimulus for ethnic-based participation. With the exception
of apartheid, which clearly mobilized many African Americans who did not
trace their ancestry to South Africa, there is little evidence that the enemy of
a homeland can spur political participation among a race. For African Americans, there are other enemies of Africa, such as poverty, AIDS, and other
humanitarian crises, that do provide a stimulus for political participation on
the part of African Americans and African American elites. However, it is difficult at the present to identify an enemy of South and Central America that
can motivate the Hispanic American community to become more involved in
foreign policy making, and this may retard the ability of Hispanic elites to
mobilize Latino Americans.[9] The same is likely true for Asian Americans.
Even Arab Americans, many of whom may oppose Israel's policies toward
the Palestinians and Lebanon, do not appear to be mobilized in the same
capacity as country-specific ethnicities.

Finally, collective memories are an important component of identity,
since "ethnicity cannot be politicized unless an underlying core of memories,
experience, or meaning moves people to collective action" (Esman 1994, 14).
Indeed, research suggests that existence of a common historical trauma contributes to the success of the mobilization of organized ethnic interest groups
(Paul 1999). Further, the existence of a common historical trauma may provide unity to an otherwise diverse ethnic community, and unity may play a
major role in determining the group's success (Ahrari 1987; Smith 2000).
There is evidence that a number of ethnic groups included in this study are
motivated by historical traumas or use collective memories to motivate ethnic brethren. Of course, the Holocaust motivates many Jewish Americans to
support the state of Israel, and Armenian Americans are motivated by the
1915 genocide of Armenians during the waning days of the Ottoman Empire.
Some Korean and Chinese Americans mobilize because Japan refuses to

acknowledge the use of "comfort women" during World War II. Like an enemy of the homeland, such historical traumas may be a key to rally ethnic brethren to become active in the policymaking process.

From this discussion, three hypotheses about the influence of saliency on ethnic group influence can be tested.

H3: Ethnic groups that find foreign policy issues to be very salient have greater influence in the foreign policy process.

H4: The existence of an "enemy" of the ancestral homeland increases the influence of an ethnic group.

H5: The existence of a historical trauma increases the influence of an ethnic group.

In order to determine what issues are most salient to ethnic groups examined in the study, we analyzed the websites of ethnic organizations in 2004, 2005, and 2007 and journalistic accounts of the activities of ethnic groups. Table 4.4 presents the most salient issue or issues for each of the ethnic groups during the study. Foreign policy is an important concern to many of the groups included in the study, yet there is a great deal of variance regarding the issues that are most salient to the ethnic groups. Some ethnic groups, such as Czech Americans, are mainly interested in strengthening or maintaining bilateral relations between the United States and their ancestral homeland. Other ethnic groups, such as Armenian Americans, Greek Americans, and Taiwanese Americans, are interested in bilateral relations, but these ethnic lobbies also advocate for weaker relations between the United States and the enemies of their ancestral homelands. The Pakistani and Indian lobbies are similar in this regard, although these lobbies spend less energy and resources in an attempt to weaken US relations with the enemy of their ancestral homeland. While probably not rising to the level of an enemy, the Baltic lobby is clearly concerned over Russia's returning influence, and it has used Russia's efforts to increase its influence in the region to mobilize Baltic brethren. The Baltic lobby is unusual as an ethnic lobby, since it calls attention to foreign policy issues across Central and Eastern Europe and not just issues that affect the three Baltic nations. This is especially true concerning democratization and Russia's resurgent nationalism. For example, the Joint Baltic American National Committee (JBANC) pressured the Bush administration to denounce the 2004 Ukrainian election results as fraudulent, and JBANC sought to bring attention to allegations of voter intimidation and fraud in the 2006 national elections in Belarus. A few ethnic lobbies believe the United States should pressure the leaders and governments of their ancestral homelands. Cuban Americans are the best example of this, but Ethiopian Americans and Hmong Americans would like to see the United States use more hard-line tactics against the Ethiopian and Laotian governments, respectively.

Table 4.4 Most Salient Issues for Ethnic Groups Included in Study, 2004–2007

Ethnicity	Most Salient Foreign Policy or Issue
African	Global AIDS/HIV prevention and treatment
	Stronger actions by United States to stop genocide in Darfur
Albanian	Support of Kosovo independence
Anglo	No organization or issues identified
Arab	Greater support for Palestinians in Arab-Israeli conflict
Armenian	Recognition of the Armenian genocide
	Section 907 of the Freedom Support Act
	Foreign aid to Armenia
Asian	Immigration: Family preference categories
Baltic	US relations with the Baltic states
	Concern over Russia's influence in region
Caribbean	Economic development of the Caribbean
Central and	
Eastern European	Visa Waiver Program
Colombian	Socioeconomic development in Colombia
Croat	Economic and democratic support for Croatia
Cuban	Isolating Cuba and the Castro regime
Czech	Visa Waiver Program
Eritrean	Hard line against Ethiopia regarding border dispute
Ethiopian	Human rights and democracy in Ethiopia
	Opposition to the current regime
Filipino	Full benefits for Filipino veterans of World War II
	Immigration: Path to citizenship
Greek	Withdrawal of Turkish forces from Cyprus
	US-Greek relations
	Aegean Sea boundary dispute with Turkey
Hispanic	Immigration: Family preference categories
	Immigration: Path to citizenship
	Opposition to enacting CAFTA and expanding NAFTA
Hmong	Greater promotion of human rights for Hmong in Laos
Indian	US-India relations
	H-1B visas
Iranian	US-Iranian relations
Irish	Reunification of Ireland
	Civil rights in Northern Ireland
	Immigration and visas
Italian	US-Italian relations
Japanese	US-Japanese relations
Jewish	US-Israeli relations
	Iranian nuclear program
Korean	Reunification of Korea
	Comfort Women Resolution
Kurdish	Greater protections for Kurds in Turkey
Lebanese	US-Lebanese relations
	Restrain Israel response to Hezbollah[a]
	Ban of sale of cluster bombs to Israel[a]
Lithuanian	US-Lithuanian relations
	Growing Russian influence in region
Mexican	Immigration: Family preference categories
	Immigration: Path to citizenship

(continues)

Table 4.4 continued

Ethnicity	Most Salient Foreign Policy or Issue
Pakistani	US-Pakistani relations
Polish	Visa Waiver Program
Salvadoran	Immigration: Path to citizenship
	Opposition to enacting CAFTA and expanding NAFTA
Serbian	Opposing UNMIK and preventing an independent Kosovo
Somali	Ending Somali political unrest
Taiwanese	Independent Taiwan
	Easing travel restrictions for Taiwanese officials
Turkish	US-Turkey relations
	Opposition to US recognition of Armenian genocide
Ukrainian	Foreign aid for Ukraine
	Support for democracy in Ukraine

Note: a. Arose as a salient issue during the study.

Immigration is a salient issue for a number of groups, perhaps signaling that strong relations already exist between the United States and their ancestral homelands. Visa waivers emerged as an important issue during the study, as Central and Eastern European groups chafed at the fact that citizens of many European countries can visit the United States without visas, while citizens from Poland, Hungary, the Czech Republic, and the Baltic states (all members of NATO) cannot. Irish and Indian organizations champion immigration issues, and some Hispanic and Asian groups support retaining family preference categories, so that family members who live abroad can immigrate to the United States. Immigration is of much more concern than foreign policy itself for some ethnic groups. For example, Filipino and Mexican American organizations focus much more on immigration than on US relations with the Philippines and Mexico, respectively.

Foreign policy no longer commands the attention of some of the groups included in the study. For example, the Japanese American Citizens League (JACL), perhaps the most important Japanese American organization, now focuses exclusively on domestic issues such as civil rights. Indeed, the JACL has expanded the scope of its work to champion the civil rights of all Asian Pacific Americans.[10] We found no evidence that the JACL or other Japanese organizations lobby US policymakers about US-Japan relations, and policymakers interviewed for this project stated that Japanese Americans did not mobilize in opposition to the Comfort Women Resolution. In fact, Representative Mike Honda (D-CA), a Japanese American who spent part of World War II in a Colorado internment camp, introduced the resolution in the 110th Congress. Other emerging ethnic groups have failed to become institutionalized lobbies. For example, at the beginning of this study,

Colombian Americans appeared to be emerging as an organized force in foreign policy. However, some of the nascent Colombian American organizations are now inactive, and the remaining groups do not appear to be pursuing foreign policy per se. For example, the Colombian American Service Association coordinates humanitarian and economic development projects in Colombia, but the organization does not appear to be involved in the foreign policy–making process.

We examined websites of ethnic organizations from 2004 to 2007 to find evidence that groups use an enemy of the ancestral homeland or a historical trauma for mobilization purposes, and this information is presented in Table 4.5. There is also variance of the additional mobilizing factors, and some groups use the historical traumas and common enemies to mobilize brethren, while others do not. In some cases, ethnic groups, such as Hispanic Americans, Iranian Americans, Japanese Americans, and Mexican Americans, cite traumatic historical memories that occurred in the United States, such as bigotry, segregation, and discrimination against the ethnic group. While these memories may spur participation regarding civil rights, we found no evidence that these groups use the existence of an enemy or historical memories to mobilize brethren about foreign policy issues. In contrast, groups whose ancestral homelands are locked in conflict or disputes often use historical memories and rhetoric to mobilize brethren to become active in the foreign policymaking process. For example, Greek, Armenian, and Kurdish groups use stirring rhetoric about Turkey in an attempt to mobilize their members, and Turkish organizations return the favor. Albanian and Serb groups use inflammatory rhetoric to engage members regarding Kosovo independence. Although not central to their mobilization efforts, both Pakistani and Indian organizations have used harsh rhetoric in their literature as well. At first glance, Arab American organizations do not appear to use as much rhetoric against Israel as one might expect, but anger toward Israel is at times very evident. In a commentary posted in the Arab American Institute's press room, the author likened the 2006 Israel attack on Lebanon to events two decades ago: "In June 1982 in a genocidal mood, Ariel Sharon's Israel Defense Forces (IDF) invaded Lebanon to eliminate the PLO. According to western analysts nearly 18,000 Muslims were killed, about a million rendered homeless, another half-a-million awaiting death in Israeli seized territories of southern Lebanon" (Siddiqui 2006).

Resources

It should be of little surprise that ethnic communities with greater resources have a greater likelihood of influencing the political system, and there are a

Table 4.5 Mobilization Tools Used by Ethnic Organizations

Ethnicity	Enemy or Antagonist	Historical Trauma
African	Global apartheid	Colonial rule
Albanian	Serbia	Balkan conflict
Arab	Israel	Israeli settlements in Palestine; civil rights violations
Armenian	Turkey	Armenian genocide
Asian	None used	Discrimination
Baltic	Russia	Communism and Soviet occupation
Croat	Serbia	Balkan wars
Cuban	Fidel Castro	1959 Cuban Revolution
Czech	None used	Communism and Soviet occupation
Eritrean	Ethiopia	Eritrean-Ethiopian border dispute
Ethiopian	Mengistu regime	Mengistu dictatorship and civil war
Greek	Turkey	Turkey's invasion of Cyprus; 1922 massacre of Smyrna (now Izmir)
Hispanic	Discrimination	Discrimination and segregation
Hmong	Laos government	Secret War of Laos
Indian	Pakistan	None used
Iranian	Discrimination	Discrimination and bigotry
Irish	British government	Creation of Northern Ireland in 1920
Japanese	None used	Civil rights violations
Jewish	Iran; regional threats	1967 Six Day War; Holocaust
Korean	None used	World War II and Korean War; 1992 Los Angeles riots
Kurd	Turkey	Iraqi chemical attacks
Lebanese	Israel	2006 Israeli-Hezbollah War
Lithuanian	Russia	Communism and Soviet occupation
Mexican	Discrimination	Civil rights violations
Pakistani	India	Kashmir conflict
Polish	None	Communism and Soviet occupation
Salvadoran	None	Salvadoran Civil War
Serbian	Albania	Balkan wars; Kosovo independence movement
Somali	None used	Somali Civil War
Taiwanese	Communist China	Chinese Communist Revolution
Turkish	Kurdish separatists	PKK separatist conflict
Ukrainian	None used	Communism and Soviet occupation; Holodomor famine

Note: No evidence was found of use of enemy or historical trauma by Caribbean, Central and Eastern European, Colombian, Filipino, or Italian American organizations.

number of resources that can help an ethnic lobby achieve its goals. Most obviously, financial resources help ethnic lobbies contribute to political campaigns and engage in electioneering. Tony Smith contends that campaign contributions are a very important element in helping ethnic groups achieve influence. Since individuals outside a district can donate money, "small ethnic communities, some almost utterly lacking in voting strength, may nonetheless find politicians willing to represent their interests" (Smith 2000, 101). Smith argues that while businesses dominate campaign contributions, "contributions based on ethnic lobbying are also a critical part of the process" (2000, 101). Clearly, greater levels of income allow individuals to make more campaign contributions, and research demonstrates that the wealthy dominate this type of political activity (Verba, Schlozman, and Brady 1995), so it is likely ethnic groups with higher levels of household income will have greater opportunity to make financial contributions to candidates.

H6: Ethnic groups with greater financial resources have more influence in the foreign policymaking process.

Table 4.6 shows the median household and per capita incomes of the ethnic groups included in the study. Over two-thirds of the ethnic groups identified as being active in the foreign policy–making process are wealthier than the national average, at least in terms of median household income. In 2000, Indian Americans emerged as the wealthiest ethnic group, and by 2005 Indian Americans enjoyed a median household income of nearly $72,000. Many of the ethnic groups identified by scholars as being the most influential, including Taiwanese, Jewish, and Greek Americans, have median household incomes significantly higher than the national average. Most of the ethnicities with below average household incomes are Hispanic groups, and African Americans had the lowest incomes of any ethnic group included in the project. Of course, Hispanic Americans and African Americans are two of the largest ethnoracial groups in America, meaning that even with below average household incomes, the collective resources of these groups are greater than those of many smaller yet wealthier ethnic groups. Still, the lower levels of financial resources may impede participation on the part of some Hispanic and African ethnicities, such as Salvadoran Americans and Ethiopian Americans.

While campaign contributions may be important, financial resources are also necessary to establish and fund permanent organizations, which are then used to develop grassroots campaigns and monitor the policymaking process. Perhaps the most important tool for influencing public policy that can be obtained through financial resources is a permanent organization. Esman argues that formal organizations are "the indispensable weapon for political struggle" because they "aggregate material and human resources, prepare for the purposeful deployment, provide for the division of labor, maintain infrastructure for communication, and facilitate the socialization of individuals into the movement" (1994, 36). Permanent organizations, especially those located in Washington, DC, are critical because they institutionalize the ability of an ethnic community to be engaged in the political process. In the words of Smith:

Table 4.6 Median Household Income by Ethnicity in 2005

Ethnicity	Household Income (dollars)
Indian	71,932
Filipino	67,309
Lebanese	61,832
Iranian	61,365
Asian	59,925
Taiwanese	59,154
Lithuanian	59,056
Greek	59,016
Baltic	58,968
Croat	57,950
Italian	57,312
Polish	56,310
Central and Eastern European	55,973
Japanese	55,924
Serbian	55,676
Czech	55,018
Ukrainian	54,905
Jewish	54,000
Armenian	52,661
Anglo	52,442
Pakistani	52,395
Irish	51,937
Arab	50,538
Laotian	50,482
Korean	48,035
Albanian	47,445
Turkish	47,229
US population	46,242
Colombian	43,600
Caribbean (West Indian)	42,230
Hmong	39,225
Salvadoran	39,114
Cuban	38,395
Ethiopian	36,990
Hispanic	36,278
Mexican	35,464
African American	31,025

Source: 2005 US Census American Community Survey National Jewish Population Survey 2000–2001.

Like any interest group, an ethnic community becomes a seriously viable political force only when it has an organization whose chief purpose is to influence decisionmakers to adopt policies favorable to the group's interests. . . . Successful ethnic communities need specialized institutions whose major tasks can be broken into three broad categories: (1) ensuring organizational unity of the ethnic community itself; . . . (2) forming or supervising alliances with other social forces to call in unison for government actions; and (3) advocating policy positions and monitoring the behavior of government officials responsible for formulating and implementing policy. (2000, 109)

While entrepreneurs are often instrumental in forming movements, it is of critical importance for movements to become institutionalized to carry on if the entrepreneur leaves, retires, or dies. Permanent organizations are vital for advocacy and lobbying, since so much of both involves developing relationships with policymakers on Capitol Hill and elsewhere in the government. While individuals form those relationships, the organization also builds relationships with important policymakers. In addition, permanent organizations provide the infrastructure to develop and maintain institutes that produce another critical resource for ethnic lobbies: information. Fundamentally, having an organizational presence in Washington is critical for monitoring the political process and the government (Smith 2000). A strong organizational presence may be a reflection that foreign policy is important to an ethnic community, but strong organizations also maintain and increase the saliency of foreign policy to an ethnic community. Organizations help monitor the policymaking process and alert the ethnic community about potential changes to the status quo. They also develop persuasive arguments that help mobilize ethnic brethren and then provide information, rhetoric, and tools to help facilitate effective grassroots mobilization.

Strong organizations also beget greater resources by helping ethnic communities tap into governmental largesse. For example, the Cuban American National Foundation played a significant role in establishing funding for, and subsequent management of, Radio and TV Martí (Haney and Vanderbush 1999, 341), as well as processing Cuban immigrants from third countries (Newhouse 1992, 76–77). CANF is not the only ethnic organization to benefit from government contracts: the Armenian Assembly of America has received millions of dollars in grants from the US Agency for International Development (USAID). In 1998, the organization received approximately one-third of its income from US government grants (Dobbs 2001).

In addition, organizations can aid in building, maintaining, and mobilizing grassroots networks. Organizations can be instrumental in teaching an ethnic community how to become politically active and in providing opportunities for brethren to become engaged in the policy process.[11] A number of ethnic group leaders, including Armenian, Greek, Indian, and Jewish leaders interviewed for this project, stated that one of their main goals is outreach to the broader ethnic community to encourage political engagement (one leader summed up the message to ethnic brethren as: "Get involved, damn it."). Several organizations offer business and social networking for members, in part to help pull individuals into the organization and, eventually, the political process. Some organizations offer internships, which serve the dual purpose of engaging young people in the policy process and increasing the saliency of ethnic politics, but also identifying and training potential future leaders of the organization.

Many of the ethnic communities included in this study have ethnic-based organizations that focus primarily on foreign policy, while other ethnic organizations may focus only partially on foreign policy. Ethnic communities that are represented by an organization that focuses primarily on foreign policy may have greater influence in the foreign policy process. Table 4.7 lists the leading ethnic-based organizations identified as having some interest in foreign policy, as well as the primary focus of each organization. The ethnic organizations examined tended to focus on one or two of the following areas: influencing US foreign policy, protecting civil liberties and civil rights of ethnic brethren in the United States, promoting human rights outside the United States, influencing US immigration policies, supporting and promoting ethnic brethren, and encouraging political participation among ethnic brethren (see Appendix C for coding information).

The Armenian, Cuban, Greek, and Jewish communities all have sophisticated, well-funded, multifaceted organizations with decades of experience dedicated to foreign policy concerns, and all four of these ethnicities have organizations based on the AIPAC model. While these organizations may also engage in other activities, they are very much centered on influencing foreign policy. For example, while the Armenian Assembly of America states early in its mission statement that it seeks to represent "Armenian-American interests to the U.S. public and the policymaking community" and "to provide ever expanding opportunities for active participation of all Armenian-Americans in the American democratic process," the rest of the mission and vision statements are focused almost entirely on Armenia, Nagorno-Karabakh, and the Armenian genocide (Armenia Assembly of America 2007). Arab Americans also have two organizations that appear to be based on the AIPAC model, although these organizations also engage in domestic issues (such as civil rights and racial profiling) as well as focus on foreign policy. Both Arab organizations also promote the accomplishments of Arab Americans and encourage political participation among Arab Americans. As a result, it is difficult to argue that foreign policy is the central focus of the two Arab American groups; instead, foreign policy is but one of many concerns for these organizations. Baltic and Lebanese Americans have permanent organizations dedicated to foreign policy, and USINPAC was founded by Indian Americans in 2001 to increase the presence of Indian Americans in the foreign policy–making process. Some ethnicities included in this study do not have formal organizations aside from a PAC that operated at some point from 1998 to 2004. Because they lack formal organizations dedicated to foreign policy, it is likely that these ethnicities will not be ranked as being as influential as other ethnic groups that do have institutions dedicated to lobbying or advocacy work.

Table 4.7 Ethnic Organizations with Foreign Policy Interest

Ethnicity	Representative Organizations	Primary Focus
African	TransAfrica Forum	Foreign policy; human rights
Albanian	National Albanian American Council	Foreign policy
	Albanian American Civic League	Foreign policy
Anglo	None identified	
Arab	Arab American Institute	Mix, which includes foreign policy
	American-Arab Anti-Discrimination Committee	Mix, which includes foreign policy
Armenian	Armenian Assembly of America	Foreign policy
	Armenian National Committee of America	Foreign policy
Asian	National Council of Asian Pacific Americans	Brethren promotion; political participation
Baltic	Joint Baltic American National Committee	Foreign policy
Caribbean	Institute of Caribbean Studies	Brethren promotion
Central and Eastern Europe	American Central European PAC	Unknown
Colombian	Colombian American Service Association	Brethren promotion
Croat	Croatian American Association	Foreign policy
Cuban	Cuban American National Foundation	Foreign policy
Czech	American Friends of the Czech Republic	Foreign policy
Eritrean	Eritrean American Political Action Committee	Political participation; foreign policy
Ethiopian	Ethiopian American Civic Advocacy	Foreign policy; political participation
Filipino	National Federation of Filipino American Associations	Brethren promotion; political participation
Greek	American Hellenic Institute	Foreign policy
Hispanic	League of United Latin American Citizens	Brethren promotion; political participation
Hmong	Hmong International Human Rights Watch	Foreign policy; human rights
Indian	US-India PAC (USINPAC)	Foreign policy; civil rights
Iranian	National Iranian American Council	Brethren promotion; political participation
Irish	Irish National Caucus	Human rights; foreign policy
	Irish American Unity Conference	Human rights; foreign policy
Italian	National Italian American Foundation	Brethren promotion
Japanese	Japanese American Citizens League	Civil liberties; brethren promotion
Jewish	American Israel Public Affairs Committee	Foreign policy
	NCSJ	Foreign policy
	NORPAC	Foreign policy
Korean	National Association of Korean Americans	Brethren promotion; foreign policy
	Korean American Coalition	Brethren promotion
Kurd	American Kurdish Information Network	Human rights; foreign policy
Lebanese	American Task Force for Lebanon	Foreign policy
Lithuanian	Lithuanian American Community	Brethren promotion
Mexican	Mexican American Legal Defense and Educational Fund	Civil liberties; political participation
Pakistani	Pakistani American Congress[a]	Brethren promotion; political participation

(continues)

Table 4.7 continued

Ethnicity	Representative Organizations	Primary Focus
Polish	Polish American Congress	Brethren promotion; foreign policy
Salvadoran	Salvadoran American National Association	Brethren promotion; political participation
Serbian	Serbian Unity Congress	Brethren promotion; foreign policy
Somali	Somali American Community Association	Brethren promotion; foreign policy
Taiwanese	Formosan Association for Public Affairs	Foreign policy
Turkish	Assembly of Turkish American Associations	Brethren promotion; foreign policy
Ukrainian	Ukrainian Congress Committee of America	Brethren promotion; foreign policy

Note: a. Organization appears inactive since 2005.

H7: Ethnic groups that are represented by permanent organizations dedicated to foreign policy issues have greater influence in the foreign policymaking process.

We analyzed websites for evidence that ethnic organizations are engaged in the policymaking process through lobbying, advocacy, or otherwise meeting with elected representatives and government officials. We looked for evidence of a government affairs coordinator or team, articles or accounts of group officials meeting with policymakers, or evidence that the organization had testified in committee hearings. We also examined ethnic groups for evidence of grassroots mobilization, and there is wide variation across ethnic organizations in terms of their efforts to influence policymakers directly or indirectly through grassroots mobilization.

A final resource that may be overlooked is the degree to which an ethnic group possesses civic skills and emigrated from a country that promoted a civic and participatory culture. Civic skills are "communications and organizational capacities that are so essential to political activity. . . . Citizens who can speak or write well or who are comfortable organizing and taking part in meetings are likely to be more effective when they get involved in politics" (Brady, Verba, and Schlozman 1995, 273). Ethnic organizations and churches can help increase civic skills, but immigrant groups that already possess more civic skills are likely to have a greater influence than ethnic groups that must learn such skills. In addition, ethnic groups that hail from countries that exhibit a stronger civic culture, one that encourages voting and political participation, may find it easier to integrate into the American political process. Of course, civic skills and civic culture can be transferred to a group once in the United States, as the group becomes assimilated into the American social and political fabric. Assimilation is the final factor analyzed in this study.

■ Assimilation

Ahrari posits that assimilation is the second most important determinant of an ethnic group's power because the degree of assimilation experienced by members of the ethnic group affects the "capacity of group members to promote their foreign policy objectives in the United States" (1987, 156). Tony Smith (2000) and Eric Uslaner (2002) concur, contending that assimilation affects the unity of an ethnic community and, as an extension, its ability to mobilize politically. Assimilation into the American political community is essential for ethnic groups and individuals to first gain access to and then influence in the policymaking process.[12] Although individuals who are not citizens can influence the political process by meeting with policymakers, attempting to influence public opinion, and offering their time and energy to political causes and campaigns, noncitizens can neither vote nor make monetary contributions to campaigns. As a result, citizenship is an important step toward assimilation. In addition, some ethnic groups, especially those that emigrated from despotic states, may need to learn how to participate in democratic institutions and processes: they may need to be taught how to register to vote, that they can meet with public and elected officials, or that they may volunteer on a political campaign. Learning English may be an important assimilation milestone as well, since many elected officials and fellow citizens are not bilingual. In time, members of new ethnic communities may be encouraged to become involved in civic endeavors or to run for public office. Eventually, an ethnic community may become so assimilated that large numbers of its members become policymakers, either assuming elected positions or becoming part of the foreign policy–making process. Ethnic organizations are often critical for assisting in all of these assimilation stages.

And yet assimilation is a double-edged sword: if the ethnic group is too assimilated, then individuals will not be connected enough to the ethnic community as a whole, making it difficult to mobilize them ethnically or politically (Smith 2000; Uslaner 2002). Further integration into the American community may also lead later generations of an ethnic community to no longer consider themselves to be members of that particular ethnic community, but to have an ethnic heritage or to simply be "American." For example, a fifth-generation American of German descent may only identify with his German heritage when attending an Oktoberfest event. Thus, ethnic communities that desire to retain the political influence of their ethnicity must assimilate into the political system but also guard their ethnicity from complete absorption into the American culture lest their ethnicity become relegated to once-a-year cultural events. Assimilation is not simply a pedantic concern: some ethnic communities worry about interethnic marriage rates, since marriage to an individual outside the ethnic community may mean an erosion of the connection with the ethnic community and that the couple's children are not raised as part of the ethnic community. For example, research by Jewish American organizations shows:

> In-married Jews maintain more Jewish connections and greater engagement with Jewish life than intermarried Jews. The most significant differences between in-married and intermarried Jews are associated with synagogue membership and attendance in JCCs [Jewish Community Centers] and other Jewish organizations, . . . and keeping kosher. Less dramatic but still substantial differences between in-married and intermarried are associated with having close friends who are Jewish. . . . holding or attending a Passover seder, lighting Chanukah candles, fasting on Yom Kippur, and connections to Israel. . . . In-married and intermarried Jews differ dramatically in the extent to which they raise their children as Jews. Nearly all children (96%) in households with two Jewish spouses are being raised Jewish, compared to a third (33%) of the children in households with one non-Jewish spouse. (United Jewish Communities 2003, 18)

Jewish Americans are not alone in being concerned that assimilation may reduce, diminish, or even erase ethnic and cultural ties. For example, "from New York to Los Angeles, Japanese-Americans, the most integrated of Asian-American groups, are at a turning point in their century-long history in the United States. Many fear that their culture is dying and that there will never be enough new immigration from Japan to reinvigorate it" (Onishi 1995, A1).

Assimilation can also reduce the likelihood that ethnicity can be used to mobilize individuals to influence the foreign policy process. Nathan Glazer and Daniel Moynihan argued that the importance of ethnicity to prompt individuals to focus on the ancestral homeland "rarely survives the third generation in any significant terms" (1963, 313).[13] Smith contends Irish Americans have become so assimilated that, if Northern Ireland ceases to be a flashpoint, "Irish American activism with respect to foreign policy will become a subject for the history books, to join the stories of Italian American and German American ethnic activism" (2000, 117). Likewise, Robert Thompson and Joseph Rudolph assert the conflict in Northern Ireland "is not as pressing an issue for contemporary Irish-Americans as was Irish home rule in the nineteenth century" because of the thoroughness of Irish American "assimilation into the mainstream of American society" (1987, 150). In contrast, Ahrari argues that Jewish Americans "appear to have retained their paradoxical ability to assimilate enough yet still retain ample ethnic identification to pursue foreign policy goals affecting Israel" (1987, 156; see, also, Smith 2000). Glazer and Moynihan (1963) hypothesize that the fairly recent founding of Israel helps explain why Jewish Americans are so motivated by their ethnicity, despite many living in the United States for generations.

The argument that an ethnic group can become so assimilated that it loses its ability to affect foreign policy would seem to counter Alexander DeConde's assertion that Anglo Americans have more influence than is widely believed (see Chapter 2). After all, no ethnic group is more embedded in US society than Anglo Americans. However, DeConde's proposition focuses much more on the role that Anglo American elites play in formulating foreign policy than on mobilization by the Anglo American community. As such, DeConde may add an interesting twist to the assimilation argument: at some point a tipping point may be reached in the assimilation of an ethnicity, whereby the community influences policy more because it is *part* of the policymaking process, as opposed to using interest groups and movements to affect policymaking.

> H8: Ethnic groups that have assimilated into American society, but which still maintain ethnic connections, have more influence in the foreign policy–making process.

From a methodological standpoint, assimilation is a difficult concept to operationalize: How best does one capture the degree to which an ethnic group has integrated into American society? Likewise, what is the best method to measure the degree to which an ethnic group maintains its distinct cultural heritage? Although imperfect, two data sources provided by the US Census may help evaluate these two dynamics. First, length of time an ethnic community has lived in the United States may help gauge its assimilation. Newer immigrant groups are likely to be less assimilated than historic immigrant populations. The census collects data on the number of individuals who were born outside the United States for nearly all of the ethnic communities included in this study. Second, ethnic communities that continue to speak their traditional language are likely to maintain greater ethnic distinctiveness than ethnic groups that forgo maintaining their inherited language and only speak English. The census collects data measuring the number of individuals who speak a language other than English at home for most of the ethnic groups studied here.[14] Both of these sets of data are presented in Table 4.8.

The measures of assimilation reflect immigration patterns: European ethnicities, most of which began immigrating to the United States a century or more ago, have far lower percentages of brethren who were born outside the United States or who speak a language other than English at home than do non-European ethnicities. Still, some members of these European ethnicities retain their ancestral language: in many cases, a higher percentage of the European ethnicities speak a non-English language at home compared to the percentage of the ethnicity that was born outside the United States. For example, while only 2.7 percent of Czech Americans were born outside the United States, twice as many (5.4 percent) speak a language other than English at home. The same pattern holds for Italian, Polish, and Lithuanian Americans. Greek Americans exhibit the same pattern, although the percentage of foreign-born Greeks is higher (13.8 percent) than the other European ethnicities that were not under Soviet control. Notably, almost 28 percent of

Table 4.8 Indicators of Assimilation

Ethnicity	Percentage Foreign-Born	Percentage Who Speak a Language Other Than English at Home
African American	7.61	7.50
Albanian	57.09	69.10
Anglo	1.81	2.20
Arab	40.77	54.40
Armenian	42.72	56.20
Asian	61.45	71.10
Baltic	10.74	12.98
Caribbean (West Indian)	59.28	31.00
Central and Eastern European	7.06	10.23
Colombian	70.11	88.80
Croat	11.34	16.60
Cuban	60.62	84.60
Czech	2.74	5.40
Ethiopian	71.66	81.10
Filipino	55.30	58.20
Greek	13.77	27.80
Hispanic	40.05	78.20
Hmong	48.71	95.30
Indian	72.26	77.20
Iranian	65.62	75.60
Irish	0.75	2.50
Italian	3.28	7.60
Japanese	28.73	36.40
Jewish	11.90	11.50
Korean	69.23	73.50
Latvian	27.79	25.30
Lebanese	20.84	30.00
Lithuanian	6.92	9.50
Mexican	40.43	78.80
Pakistani	69.10	85.70
Polish	5.31	8.70
Salvadoran	68.35	94.50
Serbian	25.11	36.60
Taiwanese	78.30	89.10
Turkish	52.40	57.20
Ukrainian	29.30	32.10
Vietnamese	66.80	85.80

Sources: 2005 US Census American Community Survey; 2000 US Census.

Greek Americans speak Greek at home, again the highest percentage of any ethnicity whose homeland was not under Soviet control during the Cold War. Several of the ethnicities from Central and Eastern Europe have higher percentages of foreign-born than the rest of Europe, including Albanian, Estonian, Latvian, and Serbian Americans.

Most Asian American ethnicities have a high percentage of brethren who are foreign-born: in most cases, two-thirds or more of the ethnic group were born outside the United States. Of the Asian ethnicities, Japanese Americans appear to be the most assimilated, with only 27.8 percent of the ethnicity being born overseas, and only 36.4 percent speaking a language other than English at home. Among the remaining Asian ethnicities, Filipino and Indian Americans are more likely to speak English at home, followed by Korean Americans. However, while 77.2 percent of Asian Indians speak a language other than English at home, this figure may veil the ability of Indian Americans to easily integrate into the policymaking process because many immigrants from India also speak English (Vitello 2007). Hispanic ethnicities tend to follow a pattern similar to the Asian ethnicities: except for Mexican Americans, of whom 40.4 percent were born outside the United States, over two-thirds of other Hispanics were foreign-born. The Hispanic ethnicities included in the study all have very high percentages of speaking a language aside from English at home, ranging from 78.8 percent for Mexican Americans to 94.5 percent for Salvadoran Americans.

Approximately 12 percent of Jewish Americans were born outside the United States, while 21 percent of Lebanese Americans, 41 percent of Arab Americans, and 43 percent of Armenian Americans were born overseas. Generally speaking, the language percentages mirror the foreign-born percentages, although almost 10 percent more Arab and Armenian Americans speak another language at home.

Another way of conceptualizing assimilation is to examine the degree to which ethnic groups are integrated into the political process. For example, what are voter turnout levels for the ethnic group, how often do members of the ethnic community contact their members of Congress and other elected representatives, and to what degree are members of the ethnic community running for public office? Further increasing the political prowess of Jewish Americans is the fact that they participate at higher levels than most other ethnic communities. For example, voter turnout rates among Jews in presidential elections is higher than virtually all other demographic groups (Uhlaner 1989), and Jews vote at such high rates that they account for a higher percentage of the electorate than they do of the overall population: one scholar estimates that Jews may account for as much as 4 percent of the electorate (Sheskin 2007b). While data are not available for most of the other ethnoracial groups included in the study, some races do appear to participate at lower rates than others. Of course, some residents of the United States are not citizens, and they cannot vote, meaning that voter turnout rates among ethnic groups with large foreign-born populations will be lower than other groups. But even when accounting for citizenship, Uhlaner and her colleagues concluded that "Latinos and Asian-Americans register and vote at lower rates than whites and blacks" (1989, 217). Others agree that "a substantial difference" exists between the participation rates of Latino citizens and the rates of Anglos and African Americans, although they also conclude that substantial variation exists among Latino Americans (Verba, Schlozman, and Brady 1995, 231–232). For example, Americans of Cuban origin "engage in about as many political acts as the national average—indeed, somewhat more," while Americans from "Mexico, Puerto Rico, and other parts of Latin America are well below the national average; they average about half the number of political acts of Anglo-Whites" (Verba, Schlozman, and Brady 1995, 232).

Issue Goals in Relation to the Status Quo

Finally, the degree to which an ethnic lobby is defending the status quo may have a profound effect on the lobby's influence. Because the US policymaking process is decentralized, interest groups can gain access to the political system with "surprisingly little political capital" (Smith 2000, 93). Once involved in the policymaking process, organized interests that are defending established policies enjoy a strategic advantage compared to those interests that hope to change the status quo, since the decentralized policymaking process provides several opportunities to halt proposed changes. For example, legislation must pass both the House and the Senate, and then be signed by the president. If an interest group can convince either the House or the Senate not to ratify the bill, then the legislation dies. Often, bills die in congressional committees, as a committee may decline to forward the bill to the floor, or a committee chairperson may simply refuse to schedule a vote on the bill. For these reasons, many policies that enjoy wide support among the public, from health care reform to banning flag burning, are not enacted into law. From this discussion, the final research hypothesis is as follows:

> H9: Ethnic groups that are protecting established policies will have more influence in the foreign policy–making process.

In order to assess the degree to which ethnic groups were championing established policies or seeking to change the status quo, we coded the issue positions of ethnic lobbies presented in Table 4.4 in relation to existing US policies (see Appendix D for coding details, including established US policy at the time of the study). There is significant variance in the degree to which ethnic lobbies are protecting or challenging the status quo. In some cases, ethnic lobbies are challenging the status quo in terms of one policy, while working to protect another existing policy. For example, Armenian Americans are attempting to change the status quo in terms of the Armenian genocide, while the Armenian lobby is working to protect foreign aid flowing to Armenia. For some issues, there are elements of the status quo that the ethnic group supports, while there are other facets of existing policy that the group opposes.

For example, the American Hellenic Institute (2007) calls on the United States to "develop a 'special relationship' with Greece" and "expand and deepen its relationship with Greece through a coordinated program in the political, military, commercial and cultural fields." While the United States enjoys good relations with Greece, it also closed three of its four main Greek bases and stopped providing foreign assistance to Greece in the 1990s.

Examining the policy positions of ethnic lobbies in relation to existing US policies also helps illustrate how often ethnic lobbies are attempting to shift US policy, and it helps illustrate the obstacles these lobbies face. For example, the Baltic, Czech, and Polish American lobbies all seek to expand the Visa Waiver Program to include their ancestral homelands. In the wake of September 11, such an expansion appears to be unlikely, as subsequent legislation has increased the requirements for countries to participate in the program. On the other hand, some lobbies enjoy the strategic advantage of protecting the status quo. For example, US policies toward Israel and Cuba are very similar to what leading Jewish and Cuban American organizations desire.

▪ Summary of Factors Affecting Ethnic Group Influence

Scholars have posited that a number of factors, including population, assimilation, resources, and issue salience, help explain why some ethnic groups are more influential than others. These factors are likely to be interrelated in their effect on ethnic group influence. For example, while a concentrated ethnic population may be very helpful for maintaining ethnic solidarity and achieving influence in at least some congressional districts, a dispersed population is likely to be helpful in achieving broad support among members of Congress. However, maintaining ethnic ties across a dispersed population and then mobilizing that population are more difficult and take organizational and financial resources that some groups may lack. To use another example, issue salience likely plays a major role in affecting which groups are the most influential: a highly salient issue (or collection of issues) will motivate members of an ethnic group to take action, and this may very well help counteract the forces of assimilation, which tend to erode the importance of the ancestral homeland for later generations of the ethnic group. However, an ethnic group also needs resources and members in order to achieve influence. So, which factors matter the most? What is missing is a measure of ethnic group influence, a dependent variable, which can be used in an analysis to determine which factors are the most critical. The next chapter details how such a variable was created, and it discusses which ethnic groups are seen by policymakers as having the most influence.

Notes

1. In many respects, the dimensions used to analyze ethnoracial interest group formation and behavior are comparable to those employed by other social scientists to study nonethnic interest group and social movement formation as well (Truman 1951; Chong 1991; Woliver 1993; Tarrow 1994).

2. See Appendix B for details of data collection and analysis.

3. We did identify one German American organization, which states one of its objectives is to "foster friendship between the United States and Germany," but we found no evidence that the organization has attempted to influence the national government regarding any foreign or domestic policies (German American National Congress n.d.).

4. Because the annual American Community Survey only includes district-level data for larger ethnic groups, data from the 2000 US Census were used for the district-level analysis and to create the Gini Index.

5. See Appendix B for information on estimating the number of Jewish Americans in each congressional district.

6. Of course, policymakers and the ethnic brethren may not share the group's alarm. Ironically, if the US government also believes the issue is of dire consequence, the group's ability to influence policymakers may be retarded: "the more the government perceives a situation as threatening to its basic values and concerns, the less likely the nongovernmental group is to have direct and immediate access to or influence over decision makers" (Goldberg 1990, 11; see also Milbrath 1967 and Trice 1976). However, Trice asserts that there are circumstances when a group may be able to use widespread public interest to its advantage. For example, if the group may use public interest to "neutralize and isolate competing groups" while enlisting other actors and broadening its base of public support, the group "may be able to . . . gain indirect access to policy-makers" (1976, 22).

7. As noted in Chapter 3, the Pakistani-American Business Association of Louisiana held a $50,000 fundraiser for Louisiana gubernatorial candidate Kathleen Blanco in 2003 because her opponent, Bobby Jindal, was Indian American. One attendee, who was also the president of the Pakistani American Congress, stated, "I think it's a kind of unforeseen fear that if Bobby Jindal gets elected he might push things that are against the Pakistani interest" (as quoted in Moller 2003). He did not specify how the governor of Louisiana could influence Indo-Pakistani relations. Perhaps ironically, Jindal was defeated, but soon was elected to the US House of Representatives, where the opportunity to influence US relations with India and Pakistan is much greater than from the Louisiana governor's mansion.

8. However, some Indian American elites interviewed for this study were more focused on US-India relations, and they did not express concern that increased ties between the United States and Pakistan would retard the emerging US-Indo alliance. Others interviewed for this project disagreed with this assertion.

9. With the issue of immigration, it is possible that Hispanics could perceive nativist white Americans as racist, thereby creating an enemy that mobilizes the Hispanic American community. However, this is not the same as an enemy that threatens the homeland, thereby mobilizing Hispanic Americans to become more involved in foreign policy.

10. Other civil rights organizations have made similar moves. For example, the Mexican American Legal Defense and Educational Fund has expanded its scope to protect the civil and immigration rights of all Latinos.

11. For some ethnic communities, this is especially critical, since the communities emigrated from states that ban political participation.

12. The assimilation process may not be a positive experience for immigrant communities, and it may have a negative effect on future political participation. In examining why political participation rates among Asian Americans are low, even when controlling for citizenship and demographic factors, one study suggests that "Asian-American attitudes about the value of involvement in government may well reflect their history of discrimination and exclusion from government" (Uhlaner, Cain, and Kiewiet 1989, 218).

13. However, Glazer and Moynihan do acknowledge that race can extend beyond the third generation in terms of its ability to mobilize.

14. See Appendix B for information on assimilation estimates for Jewish Americans.

5

The Most Influential
Ethnic Lobbies

To better ascertain which lobbies are the most influential, fifty-four Washington insiders were interviewed, and each was asked to rate the influence of thirty-eight ethnic lobbies active in foreign policy making. For each lobby, respondents were asked to rate the lobby's influence in the foreign policy–making process on a scale of 0 to 100, with 0 meaning the lobby has no influence, and 100 meaning the lobby has a great deal of influence. Respondents were allowed to answer "don't know" if they had no opinion or knowledge of the lobby in question. In addition, many respondents offered qualitative information about their responses. We recognize that this survey does not measure actual influence. Instead, it gauges the *perceived* power of lobbies. Nonetheless, perceived power is important. A lobby that is perceived as powerful may find it easier to persuade policymakers, and such groups may prevent other groups from opposing them or cause other groups to mimic their strategies and tactics. We also acknowledge that individuals who were surveyed may not work with all groups, limiting their ability to speak to the influence of all of the lobbies. However, collectively these members of Congress, congressional staffers, committee staffers, and career professionals represent a very good sample of policymakers involved in foreign and intermestic policies: on average, the respondents had 12.9 years of experience with their current employers and possessed 14.2 years of foreign policy experience. In addition, it is important to note that the survey yields a snapshot of the role of ethnic lobbies in the foreign policy process during the study period of late 2005 to early 2007. Later studies may not yield the same results, as activities of different ethnic lobbies may increase or decrease their influence, and ethnic lobbies as a whole may lose or gain power.

The survey of policymakers and ethnic group leaders yielded both expected and surprising findings. Clearly, many policymakers dismissed the idea that the United States is experiencing a dramatic increase in the influence of ethnic lobbies: many respondents stated that the United States has a long history of ethnic groups attempting to influence the foreign and domestic policy–making processes, as well as politicians making direct appeals to ethnic groups for support. In addition, ethnic organizations have a long history of working with other organizations, such as human rights, religious, business, and labor groups, to achieve their objectives. What has changed, according to these respondents, is the actors: some ethnicities are becoming less influential, while other ethnic communities are discovering their voice. Several respondents noted that assimilation can mean that new generations of an ethnic community are less likely to find foreign policy issues related to their ancestral homeland to be salient. One bureaucrat stated: "The influence of individual ethnic groups changes because the ethnic communities dilute the longer they are here." As an example, the respondent then discussed how the Desis (young Indian Americans) are not as interested in US-India relations as the Antes (older Indian Americans who immigrated from India). Yet, as an immigrant group does assimilate, they are better able to influence the policymaking process as more members of the ethnic group become integrated into the political process.

Many policymakers noted the pluralistic nature of the US system, and that ethnic lobbies are just one type of actor that attempts to influence policymaking. One congressional committee staffer stated that "ethnic groups certainly have influence here in Congress. But except for a few Members (of Congress), ethnic groups have no more influence than other groups." The staffer went on to say that with all interest groups, "even with trusted groups, we take new information [they provide] with a grain of salt." Respondents also noted that ethnic communities do not speak with a monolithic voice: there are divisions of opinion even within the most influential communities. However, some ethnic communities are more divided than others, and ethnicities that are splintered are less effective in part because the different factions can work against each other. The Iranian American community was cited by several respondents as an example of this. Finally, a committee staffer noted that many ethnic (and nonethnic) groups simply are not especially skilled at advocacy work: "It is surprising that not many people know how to lobby Congress. The ones who do are the ones who have the influence you are looking for." So, which ethnic groups do know how to lobby Congress and influence the foreign policy–making process more broadly? This survey of policymakers helps shed some light on that question.

■ Survey Results: The Most Influential Ethnic Lobbies

As expected, the Israeli American lobby was ranked by far as the ethnic lobby that enjoys the most influence. It was ranked as the most powerful by 89.8

89.8 percent of respondents, and its mean influence rating was 81.7 (Table 5.1). The mean rating of the Israeli American lobby was a full 16 points higher than the next most influential lobby, the Cuban American lobby, which received a mean rating of 65.6. A cluster of seven ethnic lobbies was rated as the next most influential, ranging from 50 to 56. In many respects,

Table 5.1 Most Influential Ethnic Lobbies in Foreign Policy Making

Ethnic Lobby	Mean Influence	Standard Deviation	*N*
Israeli	81.7	15.9	49
Cuban	65.8	19.8	45
Irish	55.2	22.7	42
Armenian	53.6	19.5	44
Hispanic	52.5	22.0	41
Taiwanese	51.0	23.8	41
African	50.8	22.8	46
Greek	50.7	22.1	42
Indian	50.4	23.2	42
Italian	45.7	25.3	39
Mexican	44.8	21.4	42
Asian	43.3	22.0	40
Polish	39.1	22.6	39
Turkish	36.9	23.1	43
Anglo	36.7	29.2	34
Arab	35.7	16.1	43
Korean	35.7	18.3	42
Ukrainian	35.3	23.2	35
Pakistani	34.5	19.2	39
Lebanese	34.1	20.9	37
Kurd	32.4	17.7	37
Filipino	30.8	20.9	37
Iranian	30.1	20.4	37
Japanese	30.0	21.0	40
Central and Eastern European	29.0	21.3	34
Albanian	27.3	20.1	33
Ethiopian	26.7	21.8	25
Lithuanian	25.0	21.7	32
Caribbean	24.7	15.3	33
Laotian/Hmong	23.9	18.0	37
Serbian	23.2	18.2	37
Baltic	23.2	20.0	31
Colombian	22.5	17.8	31
Croat	22.4	17.8	33
Salvadoran	20.8	14.3	32
Eritrea	19.4	20.2	34
Somali	19.0	19.8	24
Czech	17.9	13.4	29

Source: Author survey, 2005–2007.
Note: Ratings are based on a scale of 0 to 100, with 0 meaning no influence and 100 meaning a great deal of influence.

the ranking of these seven lobbies is of little surprise: the Irish American, Armenian American, and Greek American lobbies all are cited as examples of influential ethnic lobbies, and all have been the subject of extensive case study analysis (Thompson and Rudolph 1987; Paul 2000; Hackett 1981; Hicks and Couloumbis 1981; Watanabe 1984). To a lesser extent, the same is true for the Taiwanese American and African American lobbies (Challenor 1981; Walters 1987; Scott and Osman 2002), and the Hispanic American and Indian American communities are often cited as ethnicities that are becoming increasingly influential (Pomper and Chatterjee 2000; Axtman 2003; Fitzgerald 2003; Navarro 2004; Forsythe and Trehan 2006; Curry 2006; McIntire 2006). The next sections discuss in depth the nine ethnic lobbies rated as the most influential.

The Israeli Lobby

Almost universally, those interviewed for this project believe the Israeli American lobby is the most influential ethnic-based lobby. Not only was the Israeli lobby given the highest score in the influence survey, but either the Israeli or Jewish lobby was cited the most often by respondents as an example of a lobby that can influence the policymaking process. One policymaker stated: "Every single policy toward Israel is affected by AIPAC and the Jewish lobby." Meanwhile, another stated that "the Jewish American lobby is always able to drive the agenda. If they have legislative priorities, those legislative priorities tend to translate into direct legislative action. [The lobby influences policies like] Iran, the Palestinian Authority, assistance to Israel." And another declared that the "Israeli lobby . . . dominates the agenda" of US-Israeli policy. Several respondents believe that the Israeli lobby is so powerful that it stifles open and honest debate in the United States about Middle East policies.

A number of policymakers (17.1 percent) cited the size of US foreign aid to Israel as evidence that the Israeli American lobby is influential. For example, one policymaker stated: "Every year, Israel is our number 1 aid recipient. Does Israel need more aid than Sudan, than the Congo?" Several policymakers noted that Jewish and pro-Israeli groups lobby to increase the overall foreign aid budget. According to one senior policymaker:

> We've made the decision to give foreign aid to Israel. It's a national policy, and Jewish Americans are helpful in terms of mobilizing support. They understand in broad terms that aid to Israel won't be there if foreign aid is not there. As a policy, they support foreign aid. Other groups say they want a bigger slice of the foreign aid pie. Jewish Americans say we want a bigger pie. Jewish Americans help with aid to Egypt because they consider that it's important that aid is spread out, so that Israel doesn't stand out. They also support aid to Africa.

Another policymaker made a similar contention, stating, "the annual foreign aid budget . . . is a big, big issue with pro-Israeli groups. . . . Israel [is] practically guaranteed foreign assistance every year. Everything else is open for debate." Other policymakers noted the degree and swiftness with which the United States supports Israel when Israeli-Arab conflicts emerge, and others argued that the Israeli lobby has a significant effect on US military policy toward both Israel and the Middle East more broadly.

Policymakers cited a host of factors as contributing to the influence of the Israeli lobby. For example, some policymakers noted that Jewish Americans and supporters of the Israeli lobby are an important source of campaign contributions for congressional candidates, while other policymakers discussed the saliency of Israel to Jewish Americans and other Americans who are supportive of Israel. For example, one senior policymaker noted that "a lot of (Americans) who are interested in Israel actually go back to Israel to visit. They send their kids to live on a kibbutz." However, the major theme to emerge from the interviews was that the Jewish American community is the best organized ethnic community. One committee staffer contended that if one wants to see which ethnic groups have influence, then one should ask:

> Who has people in Washington doing this full time? There are dozens of Jewish-American groups who have people in Washington getting their message out to policymakers, not just in the legislative and executive branches, but also with opinion leaders. Jewish Americans also have the Conference of Presidents of Major American Jewish Organizations, an umbrella organization which helps to unify their message. No other ethnic group has such an organization.

Policymakers contend that the Jewish community and broader Israeli lobby are adept at building broad, bipartisan support. For example, when the International Court of Justice considered a case that challenged the legality of the Israeli security barrier constructed in the West Bank, two US members of Congress, Steve Chabot (R-OH) and Robert Wexler (D-FL), testified at The Hague in support of Israel (Agence France-Presse 2004). Another policymaker noted the resolution by the House of Representatives that expressed support for Israel during the 2006 Lebanon War, which passed 410–8, stating that "no other ethnic lobby could muster that sort of support, and so quickly." In a related fashion, several policymakers noted the strong grassroots organization of the Israeli lobby, a resource that is unmatched by potential countervailing lobbies. Some policymakers attributed US support for Israel not just to the Jewish or Israeli lobby, but to a "natural affinity" Americans have toward Israel and the Holy Land. Others noted the ability of the Israeli lobby to argue that strong relations with Israel are in the national interest of the United States. One policymaker noted: "Jewish Americans do work to argue that what's in the US interest is also in Israel's interest, and they are conscious to make that argument instead of what is in Israel's interest is also in the US interest."

Nonetheless, some policymakers did not believe that the Israeli lobby dominates Middle East or even Israeli policy. One committee staffer declared: "There is no instance of an ethnic group single handedly delivering a policy. It's the same with aid to Israel. We aid Israel because it is in America's interest to aid Israel. It's the only democracy in the region. . . . The (policymaking) process on the Hill is very complex." The staffer pointed out that ethnic groups are just one component of that process. Another policymaker agreed with that sentiment, stating: "Israel is the only democracy in the region. They are a long-standing ally. They may do stuff we disagree with, but after September 11, a lot of folks empathized with Israel."

Despite the fact that the survey did not mention AIPAC by name, the pro-Israel organization was discussed by 39 percent of policymakers and 36.5 percent of respondents. For many, if not most, individuals interviewed for this project, there was little doubt that AIPAC is very influential. For example, one bureaucrat stated: "Every single policy toward Israel is affected by AIPAC and the Jewish lobby." A committee staffer commented that "AIPAC is the prototypical example of an ethnic group."

Respondents offered a host of reasons why AIPAC is so effective. Several policymakers emphasized the ability of AIPAC to mobilize grassroots campaigns across all congressional districts. Other policymakers discussed the degree to which members of AIPAC find Israeli policies to be extremely salient. Some policymakers stated that AIPAC is extremely good at connecting with congressional offices and providing information to members of Congress and staffers. For example, one personal staffer noted that in 2005,

> AIPAC held a one day seminar for congressional staffers, specifically about the money in the foreign aid bill. It had both factual presentation (here is how much money is being proposed for Egypt) and persuasive arguments (it should be economic aid and not military). Their efforts worked: The bill was amended to affect Egypt's foreign aid, making it economic and not military. This happens a lot with appropriations bills.

Committee staffers also noted that they hear often from AIPAC, with one staffer stating, "I get something, an e-mail or fax or something from AIPAC almost every day." Other policymakers stated that financial contributions by members of AIPAC to members of Congress help increase the influence of the organization. For instance, one policymaker remarked that members of AIPAC "help raise a lot of money to help contribute to members of Congress. That's something members can't ignore or find it difficult to ignore." One congressional staffer argued that AIPAC is the type of interest group that can have a "chilling effect" on members of Congress, where "you don't necessarily become their friend, but you try to avoid being their enemy." When asked to elaborate, the staffer stated:

> AIPAC is really good at what they do. They're organized, mobilized, motivated. They don't make threats, but you prefer to be on their side. They do have an ability to motivate your opponent. They are the one ethnic lobby that has been imbued with the reputation of: you cross them and they will come after you. That reputation may not be fair, since AIPAC focuses more on policy and not on elections.

Another policymaker, when asked if the influence of ethnic groups was increasing in congressional elections, stated: "I'm sure it's increasing. Ten years ago, it was political suicide to go against AIPAC, and it still is political suicide."

Still, some respondents indicated that AIPAC's reputation of influence is overblown. One senior policymaker, who stated that AIPAC is very good at keeping congressional offices up-to-date, also argued that many members of Congress already have a position on Israel before AIPAC seeks them out.

The Cuban American Lobby

While the Cuban lobby was ranked by respondents as the second most influential lobby, and the lobby was often cited as the second most powerful ethnic lobby after the Israeli lobby, a few respondents did indicate the Cuban lobby's influence, while still formidable, is declining. For example, one policymaker stated: "the CANF is the big dog of Cuban politics. They are effective, but less somewhat since [CANF's founder Jorge] Mas' death."[1] Some spoke of a generational shift among Cuban Americans, where Cuban exiles desire to return to Cuba but those born in the United States have little desire to move to Cuba, a trend documented by journalists as well (Gonzalez and Goodnough 2006). Some respondents asserted that a rift of sorts exists within the Cuban American community, with older Cubans supporting efforts to isolate Castro by restricting cash remittances and travel to Cuba, while younger Cubans find such measures to be too extreme. Other respondents made similar observations, noting that the debate over Cuba is now more open, and the Cuban exiles no longer control the policy debate, at least the policy debate outside of Florida and New Jersey. One policymaker noted that, in contrast to other ethnic lobbies, Cuban Americans cannot lead congressional delegations on fact-finding trips to their ancestral homeland, a perk that helps win over both members of Congress and congressional staffers.

Still, respondents as a whole viewed the Cuban lobby as being highly organized, very active, with a formidable and powerful presence in Washington. Many respondents stated that the concentration of Cuban Americans in Florida helps to accentuate the influence of the lobby, both because their representatives in Congress are sensitive to a key constituent group and because Florida is a key state in presidential elections. As a result, presidential candidates attempt to woo the Cuban vote, and several respondents stated that the Elián González controversy in 2000 helped elect George W. Bush. One policymaker asserted that the Cuban lobby retains some of its influence because there is little reason for most members of Congress to oppose the lobby. "Only recently, from farm state guys, do they [Cuban Americans] get blow-back from members." For most members of Congress, their reasoning is that "as long as I don't hear from my constituents, I can go along with it." A number of respondents also noted the support the lobby enjoys from a number of key members of Congress, not only from Cuban American representatives like Ileana Ros-Lehtinen (R-FL), Lincoln Diaz-Balart (R-FL), and Mario Diaz-Balart (R-FL), but also from non-Cubans like Senator Joseph Lieberman (I-CT). Another respondent argued that the Cuban lobby also has friends in the executive branch, noting that the Bush administration has a particularly aggressive attitude toward Cuba. This respondent also contended that there are bureaucrats in the State Department and Treasury who support the embargo and are sympathetic to the Cuban lobby, and some of these careerists have risen through the ranks over the past six years. Policymakers also viewed programs like Radio Martí as evidence of the success of the Cuban lobby, and some viewed the lobby as active in human rights.

The Irish American Lobby

The Irish lobby was rated as the third most influential ethnic lobby, although the mean influence rating for the lobbies ranked as the third through ninth are similar, and in many cases there is no statistical difference in the mean ratings of these seven ethnicities. Many respondents acknowledged that the Irish lobby has a long history of influence, and several indicated that the Irish lobby is somewhat unusual since most ethnic communities with such a long history in the United States are no longer active in foreign affairs. As with the Cuban lobby, some policymakers indicated that the Irish lobby derives part of its influence from concentrated and politically active communities in New York, Chicago, Boston, and elsewhere. Unlike the Cuban community, the Irish community is very large and widely dispersed, and several policymakers asserted that part of the power of the Irish lobby stems from the number of Americans who consider themselves Irish or who are sympathetic toward the Irish.[2] At least one senior policymaker stated that the Irish lobby is fairly homogeneous and speaks with one voice, thereby amplifying its effect on foreign policy. Other policymakers noted that some Irish American members of Congress champion the interests of the lobby, while one policymaker stated that some Irish American members of Congress do not vote in lockstep with the wishes of the Irish lobby. A few policymakers indicated that the Irish lobby's influence is waning, and other ethnic lobbies for which foreign policy is very salient, such as the Armenian and Cuban lobbies, have greater sway in foreign affairs. Others stated that the Irish lobby is more active when violence erupts in Northern Ireland, and the lobby has been less visible in foreign affairs because of the relative calm in Belfast.

Nonetheless, the Irish lobby was routinely named in open-ended questions as one of the most influential ethnic lobbies, and policymakers cited the lobby's effect in foreign policy, foreign aid, human rights, and especially immigration. Although the Irish lobby was credited by policymakers as having an effect on US involvement in the peace talks in Northern Ireland, foreign aid to Ireland, and the passage of the MacBride Principles, respondents were most likely to note the Irish lobby is very active with immigration policy: 19.5 percent of policymakers credited the Irish lobby with having a substantial influence in immigration policy, the highest percentage of any ethnic lobby.[3] One policymaker argued that the impact of the lobby has declined in immigration policymaking in part because fewer Irish nationals desire to emigrate from Ireland. At least one policymaker cited the amount of US aid to Ireland as a sign that the lobby has too much influence, since the standard of living in Ireland is now quite high.

The Armenian American Lobby

It is clear from the policymaking interviews that the Armenian lobby has established itself as one of the most influential of the ethnic lobbies, and policymakers perceive the lobby as very organized and active in the foreign policy–making process. Unlike the Irish and Greek lobbies, which a few policymakers indicated may be slowly eroding in influence, no respondent suggested that the Armenian lobby might be fading. Indeed, the Armenian lobby was cited frequently in examples of ethnic politics, and many respondents indicated the lobby is one of the most successful in Washington. In the words of one staffer: "Jewish Americans and Armenian Americans are absolutely the best around. They're the best motivated, the best mobilized, the best messaged." Policymakers credited Armenian Americans with being very interested in foreign policy and their organizations as being very good at mobilizing Armenian Americans to contact their members of Congress and congressional staffers. Others noted that because Armenian Americans have relatively concentrated populations in several districts in California and New York, the members of Congress who represent these districts are closely identified with Armenian American causes. In addition, other members of Congress who do not have significant Armenian populations in their districts have become champions of Armenian issues, and a few members of Congress, such as Representative Anna Eshoo (D-CA) and now former representative John Sweeney (R-NY), are of Armenian heritage and find their ethnicity to be personally important. Several respondents noted the Armenian congressional caucus is active and large, and dozens of members of Congress will attend Armenian American functions to show their support of the lobby.

In addition to the prowess of the Armenian lobby, other policymakers argued that potential grassroots opponents to the lobby, such as the Turkish American and Azeri American lobbies, are much smaller and are no match for the Armenian lobby. That is not to say that there are no rivals to the Armenian lobby: respondents noted the Pentagon and presidential administrations support strong relations with Turkey; the US oil and gas industry opposes Armenian American efforts to sanction Azerbaijan; and the Turkish government spends millions of dollars on professional lobbyists, such as former representative Bob Livingston (R-LA). Still, none of these challengers provides grassroots opposition to the Armenian lobby. One congressional staffer stated this lack of grassroots opposition does have an effect: "Many members of Congress ask, 'What does Turkey have to do with anything?' We have Armenians in our district."

As evidence of the influence of the Armenian lobby, many policymakers cited the size of US foreign aid to Armenia, which these respondents found quite large in terms of per capita aid, or in comparison to foreign aid distributed to similar countries like Georgia. Other policymakers noted the efforts by the lobby to influence US relations with Turkey and Azerbaijan, the latter a country with which presidential administrations would prefer to have stronger relations because of its petroleum deposits and strategic location. For example, the Armenian lobby is credited with securing Section 907 of the 1992 Freedom Support Act, which specifically banned Azerbaijan from receiving aid (Shain 1994).[4] However, the most frequently mentioned example was the attempts by the Armenian lobby to persuade the executive branch to officially recognize the 1915 Armenian genocide, an issue discussed by 36.6 percent of policymakers. One senior policymaker stated, "With the Armenian genocide issue, Armenian American groups will come by 12 times a year." Others noted the ability of Armenian Americans to frame recognition of the genocide as a human rights issue. According to a number of respondents, the genocide controversy cost John M. Evans, the US ambassador to Armenia from 2004 to 2006, his job because he stated in 2005 that the massacres constituted a genocide.[5] Armenian American activists then worked to prevent the confirmation of the next nominee to the post, Richard E. Hoagland, unless he also acknowledged the killings as a genocide (Abraham 2006; Doyle 2006). Hoagland refused, instead deferring to the official US position, and his nomination stalled in the US Senate (Reynolds 2007; Richter 2007).[6] The White House withdrew the nomination of Hoagland in August 2007, and for several respondents, the ability of some Armenian activists to scuttle the Hoagland nomination was evidence of the lobby's influence.

Although respondents were not asked about the genocide specifically, many discussed the US position, and policymakers themselves were split regarding whether the United States should recognize the events of 1915 as a genocide. Many respondents work within the State Department, some of whom quoted directly the official White House position, and others on Capitol Hill resist changing the official US position. In contrast, other Capitol Hill policymakers believe there is little doubt the "tragic events of 1915" do indeed constitute a genocide. For example, one committee staffer commented that Ambassador Evans was fired for "having the audacity to say something that was true: that there was a genocide."

Nonetheless, while respondents did in general view the Armenian lobby as quite influential, many policymakers offered evidence that the lobby is not unstoppable. Other policymakers noted that, despite their very active and well-organized campaign, the Armenian American lobby has failed to change US policy and achieve its top priority: the US government still does not recognize the genocide. Other policymakers, who see the Armenian lobby as influential, argued that the lobby only has an effect on issues related to Armenia. For example, one State Department careerist noted: "Armenian Americans have lots of sway with issues connected to Armenia, but with nothing else." Finally, although the Armenian lobby has traditionally enjoyed an asymmetrical grassroots lobbying advantage, the growing relationship between Turkey and Israel, and the subsequent efforts on the part of some Jewish Americans to provide grassroots support for Turkey, may supply a mechanism to offer a countervailing grassroots force to Armenian American organizations (Ambrosio 2002b).

The Hispanic American Lobby

Although it was ranked fairly high in the survey results, several policymakers expressed doubt regarding the idea that a Hispanic American lobby that seeks to influence foreign policy even exists. For example, a committee staffer asserted that there "isn't much of a Hispanic American lobby in terms of foreign policy. [The lobby is] concerned about immigration, but more about health care and other domestic issues," a sentiment echoed by others who see the Hispanic lobby as much more interested in domestic issues than foreign policy. Another policymaker called the Hispanic lobby "too diffuse," while a committee staffer stated: "They are all over the map and hard to put together as a functional group. They are not all in the same place over . . . immigration or country specific issues."

Nonetheless, no respondent indicated the influence of the Hispanic lobby is slipping, and several policymakers believe the Hispanic lobby is growing more influential, in part because of demographic trends. One congressional staffer noted that Hispanic Americans are now becoming an increasingly large voting bloc in many congressional districts, while another staffer contended that Latino groups are becoming increasingly important in presidential elections. A third staffer remarked that Hispanic groups are an important source of campaign contributions for Democrats. One committee staffer argued that the lobby is "hugely powerful and important, but they are getting slammed this election cycle. . . . I think in the long term, they will show their power much more."

A number of policymakers reported that the Hispanic lobby is active regarding immigration, but several of these policymakers also went on to say that Irish Americans have more influence regarding immigration than Hispanic Americans do. Indeed, the Irish lobby was cited by almost twice as many policymakers regarding immigration and visas as the Hispanic lobby. Several policymakers also spoke of Hispanic groups being active in the debate regarding CAFTA. However, aside from immigration and trade, respondents did not identify any other foreign or intermestic policy realms in which the pan-Hispanic lobby is active.

Policymakers were somewhat divided regarding the effect of the 2006 immigration protests, which were largely associated with Hispanic groups. While some of those interviewed indicated the protests and rallies were a sign of the emerging strength of Hispanics, most who expressed an opinion were doubtful that the protests and rallies would help achieve the desired ends. Some expressed the belief that the protests did more to mobilize latent opposition to immigration reform than to enlarge the base of support for the pro-immigration movement. One bureaucrat stated: "I think the campaign by Hispanic Americans and immigrants is going to be counterproductive. In some ways, they've made people more angry with them." A staffer remarked that, in regard to the pro-immigration rallies, it is "yet to be seen if it failed or if it will help, but I don't think it is going well."

Others labeled the efforts by Hispanic groups to reform immigration and provide a mechanism for undocumented workers to become citizens a failure. Several policymakers noted that Hispanic organizations also failed in their efforts to oppose CAFTA. One staffer noted that the Hispanic lobby had not achieved its goal of immigration reform, which is significant, given the size of the Latino population in the United States. The policymaker went on to note two factors that hinder the success of the lobby: many Hispanic Americans are not US citizens, and many are at the lower end of the socioeconomic scale and thereby face barriers to organizing and having political influence. Still other policymakers asserted that Hispanic and other ethnic groups are by no means alone in the policymaking process: Anglos, nativist, and nonethnic Americans are active in immigration policy, and one bureaucrat argued that members of Congress are "attuned to what American citizens want as opposed to legal residents."

The Taiwanese American Lobby

Taiwanese Americans are perceived by policymakers as being very interested in foreign policy because of the volatile relationship between Taiwan and the People's Republic of China. In the words of one senior policymaker, Taiwanese Americans are "much more aware that there are 800 missiles pointed across the Strait of Taiwan from China, much more than the average American." The lobby is described as very active and organized, maintains an active presence on Capitol Hill, and can mobilize Taiwanese Americans to contact their members of Congress. Another senior policymaker said, "the Taiwanese work tirelessly, and irk the dickens out of mainland China every time." The lobby is also seen as a strong presence on Capitol Hill, and a number of important members of Congress are seen as champions of the lobby. The Taiwanese congressional caucus is the second largest ethnic caucus, evidence that there is widespread support of the lobby among legislators. Respondents also reported that the lobby works to develop strong relations with staffers, and the lobby will pay for fact-finding trips to Taiwan.

Several policymakers discussed the Taiwanese lobby's efforts to influence US policies toward both Taiwan and China, including US military and security policy, as well as bring attention to human rights issues in China. The lobby was also credited with pressing the Bush administration to ease restrictions on the travel of Taiwan's president, Chen Shui-bian, within the United States in 2001, after the Clinton administration sequestered Chen at his hotel when he stayed in Los Angeles in 2000 (Landler 2001). Several policymakers believe Taiwanese Americans were helpful in pushing the Bush administration to embrace building a closer relationship between the United States and Taiwan, including convincing the administration to support Taiwan's admission to the World Health Organization (WHO). One of these policymakers also noted that Taiwanese Americans also successfully lobbied Congress to pass a resolution supporting Taiwan's entry into the WHO.

Nonetheless, the Taiwanese lobby has not achieved its main goals. Several policymakers noted that attempts to change the US "One China Policy" have been, in the words of one bureaucrat, "completely unsuccessful . . . any attempts to recognize Taiwan have been totally unsuccessful." Respondents noted that President Bush reaffirmed US opposition to Taiwanese independence in 2004 (Ross 2006), and the lobby has failed to stop the Bush administration from creating stronger military ties with China (Cody 2006). Finally, one policymaker argued the Taiwanese American lobby is ineffective while the Taiwanese government is a very effective lobby, pointing out that relationship is "backwards from most cases." Another policymaker agreed that of the two, the Taiwanese government is more effective than the Taiwanese American lobby.

The African American Lobby

In contrast to the Hispanic lobby, several respondents indicated African Americans can be motivated by foreign policy concerns. One committee staffer stated:

> It's possible to get African Americans motivated to call us about African issues, even though many or most cannot trace their ancestry to a single country. They are motivated by the continent. With Hispanic and Asian Americans, there is not the same sense of motivation: either they are motivated by a country, or there is no motivation.

Still, several policymakers stated that the African lobby is much more influential in terms of domestic issues, and a few policymakers who deal with African foreign policy issues reported little contact with groups that represent the African American community. Nonetheless, other policymakers stated the African American lobby has brought attention to humanitarian issues in Africa, helped to increase funding for HIV/AIDS work in Africa, provided significant leadership regarding the crisis in Darfur, and promoted the Jubilee Act[7] and debt relief. Policymakers also acknowledged the efforts by the African American lobby to end apartheid in South Africa, which one committee staffer labeled as "extremely important." In addition, respondents noted that the African American lobby has influenced US policies toward Haiti and the Caribbean.

The Greek American Lobby

Among policymakers, the Greek American community is widely regarded as highly organized and active in foreign policy, with an ability to mobilize constituents in many congressional districts, especially key districts. Respondents on Capitol Hill and in the State Department remarked that Greek Americans contact them on at least a weekly or even daily basis about Cyprus, and some respondents spoke of apparently coordinated efforts between the Greek embassy and grassroots campaigns by Greek American groups. In terms of effectiveness, some policymakers view the level of US aid to Cyprus as evidence of the influence of the Greek lobby. For example, one policymaker stated: "Look at the $15–20 million in aid to Cyprus. There are 750,000 people [in Cyprus]. They have a middle-Europe standard of living. I think this is an example of ethnic group influence, because it is a level of assistance that is the same as Egypt. It happens because Greek Americans want Congress" to be involved in setting the level of foreign aid. The same respondent also contended the Greek American community has exhibited "tremendous influence" in US relations with Greece, especially in the context of the conflict between Greece and Turkey. The policymaker asserted that "Greece has no trade importance, no strategic importance, no geopolitical importance. If it wasn't for Greek Americans," US aid to Greece would be far lower. While a number of respondents labeled the Greek American community as the second or third most organized ethnic lobby, a few respondents remarked that the influence of the Greek lobby appears to be "slipping." Others noted that, while the Greek lobby is highly organized, the lobby has failed to achieve a number of its goals. For example, in 2004 the Bush administration officially recognized the former Yugoslav Republic of Macedonia as simply the Republic of Macedonia (Carassava 2004), despite strong opposition from Greek Americans and some members of Congress (Greenhouse 1994, 1995). More importantly, policymakers noted that the United States still maintains good relations with Turkey despite decades of lobbying by Greek Americans.

The Indian American Lobby

In contrast to the Greek community, a number of respondents indicated that the Indian American community is waxing. One respondent stated that there are now four "I's" of ethnic politics, with the Indians joining the Israelis, Irish, and Italians. While it is clear that more second-generation Indian Americans are becoming part of the policymaking process, not all respondents believe that this generation cares about US-India relations as much as domestic issues, such as jobs, discrimination, and racism. Nonetheless, many policymakers stated that the Indian American community is active and organized in the foreign policy–making process. In addition, Indian Americans have emerged as one of the more important ethnic groups in terms of campaign contributions for candidates of both political parties, and a number of members of Congress have emerged as champions of issues important to the Indian community. Although respondents by and large did not indicate that congressional caucuses are central to policymaking, a number of policymakers stated as fact that the Indian caucus is now the largest on Capitol Hill, and these respondents saw this as a sign of the increased prowess of the Indian lobby. In addition to being very active in supporting the US-India Civil Nuclear Agreement, policymakers noted the Indian lobby promotes trade with India (including removing barriers to outsourcing), increasing the number of visas for skilled workers and students, and stronger US relations with India, including a more broad military-to-military relationship. While there is broad consensus among policymakers that the Indian American community is now actively trying to influence the foreign policy–making process and, in the words of one bureaucrat at the State Department, "starting to flex their muscles more," few policymakers believe the Indian lobby is too powerful. While several policymakers stated the grassroots campaign by Indian Americans to lobby members of Congress to support the US-India Civilian Nuclear Agreement was critical to gain legislative approval, other policymakers openly wished the Indian lobby was more influential, so that the nuclear pact might have been passed more quickly. One policymaker stated that the Indian Americans "tend to get most of what they want. But they don't tend to ask for a whole lot." Another policymaker noted that some Indian Americans tried to block the 2006 proposal by the Bush administration to sell 36 F-16 fighter jets to Pakistan for $5 billion. "They did not succeed. But in the process, they solidified their own cohesion, and made a name for themselves."

Other Ethnic American Lobbies

The most discussed ethnic lobby that was not ranked highly in terms of influence was the Arab American lobby. Many policymakers stated that Arab American organizations are more politically active than a decade ago, and Arab Americans (and Muslim Americans) appeared to become more active in the wake of September 11. One committee staffer observed, "Arab and Muslim Americans . . . reach[ed] out to policymakers to let them know that they are not radicals waiting to blow up buildings."[8] Several policymakers stated that, despite the increased efforts by Arab Americans, the lobby suffers from a harsh political and social environment exacerbated by prejudice. Because of this, the lobby is largely unable to achieve any of its foreign policy goals. A typical statement was offered by a congressional staffer, who said, "Arab Americans are mostly preoccupied with things going on here [in the United States]. For a long time, they focused on Israel-Palestinian relations, now they focus on civil rights, but they are not effective for change in their home countries." Another committee staffer stated that Arab Americans "try a lot more. People are much more sensitized, but most of what they do is damage control. They are trying to minimize the amount of harm the US is perceived as doing to their interests." After being asked to repeat the last sentence, the staffer said, "I tried to put that as objectively as possible. I agree with them, that the US is doing a lot of damage." Respondents often compared the influence of Arab Americans to the influence of the Israeli lobby, and a typical comparison was offered by a State Department employee: "In terms of influence, Israeli Americans are at 10, and Arab Americans are at 0." While policymakers noted that

Arab Americans are interested in foreign policy, the Arab lobby is a pan-lobby, and the lobby is hindered by divisions within the Arab community.

Many respondents spoke of the changing nature of ethnic influence in the United States, with some communities declining in influence while other communities are becoming more organized and mobilized by ethnicity. Several respondents discussed the declining influence of Central and Eastern European lobbies. Many of these ethnic groups, such as Polish Americans and Central and Eastern European Americans, were considered very influential by journalists and scholars during and immediately after the Cold War. However, since their successful efforts to lobby for enlarging NATO, many respondents feel their influence has faded in terms of foreign policy. Likewise, several policymakers noted that the Italian lobby, once considered an influential force in foreign policy, is slipping in terms of sway, largely because it lacks issues on which to focus. For example, one bureaucrat stated the Italian lobby has "some influence, but [doesn't] have that much to say to us," while a committee staffer asked, "what would the[ir] issues be?"

Largely because of the arguments made by Alexander DeConde, the Anglo American lobby was included in the survey. However, the consensus among policymakers was that no such formal lobby exists. When asked to gauge the influence of each ethnic lobby included in the study, 17.1 percent of policymakers stated that no formal Anglo lobby exists, and a typical response offered was: "Is there one? They don't need one. Hard to believe there is one, because it's the impulse of most Americans who aren't Irish to be pro-English." Others argued that Anglo Americans don't have a formal lobby because they are directly part of the policymaking process, while still others stated that the British embassy has enough sway that an Anglo lobby is unnecessary. For example, one committee staffer asked, "Don't they run everything anyway?" And a bureaucrat stated: "The British embassy has a lot of influence . . . I mean it's not like they need a lobby." A few policymakers offered that a UK-US caucus had recently been organized.

Others noted that some ethnic lobbies, such as the Estonian and Hmong lobbies, are very small in terms of the size of the ethnic communities: according to the 2000 census, there are approximately 25,000 Estonian Americans and 170,000 Hmong Americans. Given their small numbers, these respondents felt that these ethnic groups "hit above their weight" in terms of influencing US foreign policy.

Policymakers identified a number of ethnic communities that are increasingly engaged in the foreign policy–making process and becoming more influential as a result, including Eritrean, Ethiopian, and Somali Americans; Central and Latin American communities; Korean Americans; and Sri Lankans. Still, no respondents indicated that these emerging communities have significant influence in the policymaking process.

■ Factors Contributing to Ethnic Lobbies' Influence

Population

The study did provide evidence that the size and distribution of the ethnic group do affect its ability to influence foreign policy. Over and over again, individuals interviewed on Capitol Hill for this study described the ability of constituents to schedule meetings, express concerns, and potentially influence members of Congress. Several policymakers we interviewed stated that even small ethnic communities can influence members of Congress to take a position, join a caucus, sign a petition, or vote on a resolution when there exists no opposition within that congressional district: that is, as long as the ethnic community has members in the district who are active and there exists no countervailing lobby, then the member of Congress is likely to take the action. Simply put, larger ethnic groups should have greater opportunity to sway their representatives (and sway more representatives), and thus influence foreign policy.

Several of the ethnic communities often cited as the most influential have concentrated populations, and the communities have helped elect representatives who become champions of the groups. Jewish Americans are likely the best example of this: a number of members of Congress are strong supporters of Israel, and the list includes both Jews, such as Jane Harman (D-CA), Henry Waxman (D-CA), and Joe Lieberman (D-CT), and non-Jews, such as Steve Chabot (R-OH). Armenian Americans have significant populations in California and the Northeast, and the members of Congress who represent these districts are major champions of the issues important to Armenians. For example, in his successful 2000 bid to unseat James E. Rogan (R-CA), Adam Schiff charged that Rogan had not done enough to pass a congressional resolution acknowledging the 1915 Armenian genocide (Mufson 2000). According to policymakers interviewed for this project, New Jersey senator Robert Menendez placed a hold on the nomination of Hoagland as US ambassador to Armenia because the Armenian National Committee of America opposed the nomination.[9] Policymakers also reported that Irish Americans enjoy strong support from members of Congress who represent districts with large Irish populations: for example, the Massachusetts delegation has a tradition of supporting Irish American issues. Some respondents stated that the influence of Arab Americans should increase now that fairly large Arab communities have been established in Michigan and elsewhere. Even ethnic groups with relatively small populations can have an influence if there are enough members in a congressional district. For example, one respondent stated that Laotian Americans have established a voice in Congress because of their communities in Minnesota and in parts of the South.

Although concentrated populations have helped some ethnic groups elect members of Congress who share their ethnicity, even ethnic communities that do not have brethren in key policymaking positions still can garner representation. Since members of Congress desire to be reelected, many members of Congress will champion issues that are important to their district, even if they are not necessarily important to the ethnicity of the member. For instance, Senator Menendez, who placed the hold on the nomination of the Armenian ambassador, is not Armenian; he's Cuban. In all likelihood. Menendez placed the hold out of deference to the relatively large Armenian American community in New Jersey, and not because of his own ethnicity. In a similar fashion, then-president Bush's 1991 decision to recognize an independent Ukraine was seen by some as an opportunity to "score domestic political points" among Ukrainian Americans and other voters of Eastern European descent, a voting bloc that traditionally voted Democratic (Rosenthal 1991, 1).

There are likely other benefits for an ethnic group that has a concentrated population. A clustered ethnic population also may help ethnic elites use ethnicity as a mobilization tool and maintain the saliency of foreign policy for the ethnic community. For example, one policymaker argued that concentrated populations of Irish Americans, Italian Americans, and Jewish Americans in New York help maintain the influence of the groups. However, simply having a concentrated population does not necessarily mean that ethnicity remains a mobilizing force. For example, the policymaker contended that some ethnic enclaves, like Irish Americans in Chicago, are much more active in maintaining the importance of ethnicity than other enclaves, like Irish Americans in San Francisco.

However, a dispersed population also helps an ethnic group achieve influence. Several policymakers we interviewed argued that the strength of AIPAC is due to its ability to mobilize voters in all 535 congressional districts in the United States, an ability, according to these policymakers, that is unmatched among ethnic groups. Others remarked that the political clout of Indian Americans is increasing because practically every congressional district has a doctor, engineer, or entrepreneur who is an Indian American. What is truly remarkable about the Armenian lobby is the size of its support on Capitol Hill given the relatively small and concentrated population: while there are Armenian Americans in virtually every congressional district in the United States,[10] the 2000 census reported that 116 congressional districts had fewer than 100 Armenian Americans and 290 districts had fewer than 500 Armenians. Nonetheless, the Armenian congressional caucus is large, and policymakers reported that members of Congress line up to speak at Armenian American events. It is likely that even small numbers of Armenian Americans are influencing some members of Congress to join the Armenian caucus and support the Armenian genocide resolution. The same logic may also apply to the Taiwanese American lobby. For example, although the 2000 census reported that 255 congressional districts had fewer than 100 Taiwanese Americans, there were Taiwanese Americans in virtually every district in the United States in 2000: the only district in the United States without Taiwanese Americans was the Oklahoma 2nd. However, like the Armenian congressional caucus, the Taiwanese congressional caucus and the Senate Taiwan caucus are large: 180 representatives and senators are members of their chamber's Taiwanese caucus. Again, it is likely that even small numbers of Taiwanese Americans are helping to convince some members of Congress to take an interest in Taiwanese affairs. Indeed, the website for the Formosan Association for Public Affairs congratulates its Oklahoma chapter president for successfully recruiting the entire Oklahoma delegation to join the congressional Taiwan caucus.

Assimilation

It is logical that ethnic groups with larger populations have an increased probability that members of the ethnic community will become integrated into the policymaking process itself. The larger the group, the more likely it is to have members of the group run for office or be hired by the government. However, assimilation plays a role as well: as members of an ethnic group become assimilated into society, there is an increased likelihood of access into the political process, and access is the first step toward influence (Wright 2003). One policymaker argued that two ethnicities, Jewish Americans and Cuban Americans, have an unusual amount of access to the foreign policy–making process, in part because so many Jewish and Cuban Americans have obtained positions of influence in government, in both the legislative and executive branches.[11] At the beginning of the 109th Congress there were thirty-seven Jewish American and six Cuban American members of Congress, meaning that both ethnic groups enjoy significant overrepresentation in Congress. For example, about 2.2 percent of the US population is Jewish, while 6.9 percent of the 109th Congress was Jewish. Likewise, only one half of a percent of the US population is Cuban, yet Cubans made up 1.1 percent of the 109th Congress. Further, many of the Jewish and Cuban American representatives hold key foreign policy–making positions. For example, the chair of the House Committee on Foreign Affairs, Tom Lantos (D-CA), and the next highest-ranking Democrat on the committee, Brad Sherman (D-CA), are both Jewish. The ranking Republican on the committee is Ileana Ros-Lehtinen (R-FL), who left Cuba with her family in 1959. Other ethnicities, such as African Americans, have tremendous access to domestic policy in Congress but are largely absent from key foreign policy–making positions in the legislative branch.[12]

In other cases, ethnic groups are fully assimilated into powerful positions, but many members of these ethnic groups may be so assimilated that their heritage plays little role in influencing position stances. For example, many Americans are likely to consider themselves to be of Italian or Irish heritage rather than identify themselves as Italian Americans or Irish Americans. Many policymakers interviewed for this project stated that because they were so far removed from the immigration experience and had no interaction with their ethnic communities, they did not consider themselves to be ethnic Americans, even if they were aware of their ethnic heritage.

Because of this, there are limits to what an ethnic community can expect from a policymaker who shares the same ethnicity. While most Cuban American lawmakers appear to be quite expressive about their ethnicity and related foreign policy positions, other ethnic lawmakers have downplayed their ethnic heritage. For example, several individuals interviewed for this project indicated that Representative Bobby Jindal (R-LA) does not wear his Indian heritage on his sleeve. Other respondents spoke of how Serbian American groups were pleased with the elections of Representative Rod Blagojevich (D-IL) in 1996 and Senator George Voinovich (R-OH) in 1998, yet were disappointed that two leaders of Serbian descent showed little interest in championing the positions of the Serbian Unity Congress and other pro-Serbian organizations. One Irish American we interviewed stated that his/her closest allies in Congress were Jewish Americans and African Americans, and that many Irish American members of Congress shied away from championing Irish issues for fear of appearing to sympathize with the Irish Republican Army (IRA). Fundamentally, few members of Congress are willing to champion an issue that is personally important if that position is unpopular with the district.

Issue Salience

Nearly all of the most influential ethnic lobbies find US relations with their ancestral homeland to be important. For example, the connection between many Jewish Americans and Israel is well documented: it is estimated that 41 percent of Jewish Americans have visited Israel, and 45 percent believe that being Jewish involves caring about Israel "a lot" (Ament 2005). It is clear from the interviews of policymakers that other ethnic communities, such as Greek, Armenian, and Taiwanese Americans, also desire to maintain strong bonds between the governments of their homelands and the United States. A top priority for Indian Americans is to strengthen military and trade relations between India and the United States. The Hispanic and African American lobbies, the two pan-ethnic lobbies rated as having the most influence, desire to increase US attention to problems in the Americas and Africa, respectively.

Indeed, the decline of influence of the Italian American lobby is likely due in part to the strong ties between the United States and Italy: several respondents stated that the Italian American lobby has little for which to lobby, since relations between the United States and Italy are so strong. The same could be said of the Anglo American lobby. Of the most influential ethnic lobbies, only Cuban Americans do not desire to increase US ties to their homeland.

The collapse of the Soviet Union appears to have had differing effects on the issue saliency of foreign policy for different ethnic Americans. According to some interviewed for this study, the independence of Armenia greatly increased the opportunity for advocacy; before the collapse of the Soviet Union, an independent state of Armenia was inspirational, where it is now practical. For Armenian Americans, independence did not dim the saliency of foreign policy, since independence allowed the suppressed conflict between Armenia and Azerbaijan over the enclave of Nagorno-Karabakh to resurface. Armenian organizations responded to these events, refocusing their efforts to mobilize Armenian Americans on the conflict in Nagorno-Karabakh, as well as on foreign aid for the fledgling state, recognition of the 1915 genocide, the broader Armenian-Azerbaijan conflict, and the 1988 Spitak Earthquake. For other ethnic Americans whose ancestral homelands were controlled by the Soviet Union, there were issues for mobilization after the fall of the Soviet empire, but many of those focal points have faded. Initially, Baltic Americans and Central and Eastern European Americans focused on providing US foreign aid for their homelands. Then, these Americans helped encourage the enlargement of NATO. Now, according to many policymakers interviewed for this study, triggers for mobilization have faded.

We found evidence that enemies do influence ethnic groups. Again, a major focus of AIPAC is Iran, and some policymakers interviewed for this study indicated that the US invasion of Iraq was in part motivated by a desire to topple an enemy of Israel (see, also, Mearsheimer and Walt 2006). Many policymakers discussed the importance of Fidel Castro for mobilizing Cuban Americans, at least for older Cuban Americans. Of the remaining influential ethnic lobbies, at least the Armenian, Greek, and Taiwanese American communities are concerned with the prospect of stronger ties between the traditional enemies of their homelands and the United States. For the Armenians and Greeks, the concern is with stronger relations between the United States and Turkey, while Taiwanese Americans are wary about US affairs with China. The same may be true with Indian Americans in terms of US relations with Pakistan. For the Irish American community, the enemy does not threaten the Republic of Ireland, but instead threatens Catholics who live in Northern Ireland. As the violence in Northern Ireland has declined, Northern Ireland has become less of a motivating factor for Irish Americans, so much so that Irish American organizations are in danger of losing the ability to mobilize Irish Americans politically (Thompson and Rudolph 1987).

Resources

The Armenian, Cuban, Greek, and Jewish communities all have sophisticated, well-funded, multifaceted organizations with decades of experience dedicated to foreign policy concerns. With the emergence of USINPAC, the Indian American community now has a similar, albeit nascent, foreign policy organization. In contrast, no multifaceted organization represents Irish Americans. Instead, there are three main Irish organizations interested in foreign policy, and each has a slightly different focus: the Irish American Unity Conference is a grassroots organization; the Irish National Caucus is essentially a one-person advocacy organization; and the Irish American Democrats is a partisan political action committee. The main African American and Hispanic American organizations that concentrate on foreign policy are not-for-profit, which limits their ability to lobby members of Congress. The main Italian organization, the National Italian American Foundation, is focused more on cultural heritage than on foreign policy.

It is no coincidence that most of the remaining ethnicities included in the study are not associated with multifaceted organizations dedicated to foreign policy. Indeed, outside of the ethnicities ranked in the top ten of influence, only a handful of comprehensive ethnic organizations exist that focus a substantial amount of energy on foreign policy, including the American-Arab Anti-Discrimination Committee, the Arab American Institute, the Joint Baltic American National Committee, and the American Task Force for Lebanon. Other sophisticated ethnic-based organizations exist, but these groups do not focus primarily on foreign policy. There are other organizations that do concentrate on foreign policy, such as the Albanian American Civil League and the American Kurdish Information Network, but many of these organizations are primarily one-person shows.

Much of the strength of the Israeli, Cuban, and Armenian lobbies is derived from their grassroots strength. All three of these lobbies have successful, long-term grassroots mobilization operations. The African American community has produced similar campaigns in the past, most notably the domestic civil rights movement, but also in regard to US policies toward South Africa and apartheid. The Greek lobby also has a history of strong grassroots mobilization. However, other lobbies do not. For example, the Hispanic lobby has not produced a long-term grassroots campaign targeting a foreign or intermestic policy yet. It is not yet clear if the grassroots efforts by the Hispanic lobby from 2005 to 2007 will develop into a sustainable mobilization instrument that can convert the potential of the nation's largest minority group into a political force that influences the foreign policy–making process.

▪ Multivariate Analysis

In order to help determine which factors are most important in determining the influence of ethnic American groups, several ordinary least squares (OLS) regression models were developed. The dependent variable in these models is the mean influence rating for each of the lobbies included in the policymaker survey. A number of independent variables were used in the models to help capture the effects of population, resources, assimilation, and issue salience. First, several variables were created to help gauge the effects of the size of the ethnic group, including *Population,* which measures the overall population of the ethnic group, and *Population concentration,* which measures the geographical concentration of ethnic groups using the Gini Index presented earlier in Table 4.2. In addition, another set of population variables was created in order to help capture the effects of concentrated population, and these variables counted the number of congressional districts in which each ethnic group composed 1 percent (*1% of CD*), 2.5 percent (*2.5% of CD*), 5 percent (*5% of CD*), 10 percent (*10% of CD*), 25 percent (*25% of CD*), and 50 percent (*50% of CD*) of the district's population. However, aside from *Population concentration,* all of these measures of population are highly correlated with one another, and therefore cannot be included in the same model.[13] Because of this, separate models were developed to examine the effects of these population measures.

Three measures of assimilation were included in the analysis: *Foreign-born* measures the percentage of the ethnic group that was born outside of the United States, *Non-English* measures the percentage of the ethnic group that speaks a language other than English at home, and *Congressional delegation* counts the number of members of the 109th Congress who belong to the ethnic group.[14] *Congressional delegation* is highly correlated with the population measures, and it cannot be included in models that feature the population variables. Because the variables *Foreign-born* and *Non-English* are highly correlated ($r = .919$), separate models were created to examine the effects of each. In addition, these two assimilation variables are correlated strongly with the Gini Index and cannot be included in models that feature the variable *Population concentration.*[15]

Several measures of resources were also included in the analysis. *Income* measures the median household income of the ethnic group, while *PAC contributions* measures the amount of donations made by brethren PACs from 1998 to 2006 to federal candidates. The variable *Organizational strength* is a four-point scale comprised of several factors that help speak toward an ethnic group's organizational prowess, including the presence of dedicated foreign policy organizations, evidence of grassroots mobilization, and evidence that organizations have access to the foreign policy–making process.

The saliency of foreign policy is difficult to operationalize, especially since surveys are not available that measure the importance of foreign policy across the thirty-eight ethnic groups included in the study. In order to capture the importance of foreign policy to each ethnic group, the variable *Saliency* was created to categorize the degree to which organizations that represent each ethnic group focus on foreign policy versus other policy concerns. Four categories were used: foreign policy is the central purpose of the organization; foreign policy is a major purpose of the organization; foreign policy is a minor purpose of the organization; and there was no evidence that foreign policy is of concern to the organization. If multiple organizations exist that represent an ethnic group, then all organizations identified were analyzed, and the organizations most dedicated to foreign policy were used for the coding. Although organizations were used in the coding, *Saliency* is not a measure of organizational strength or resources, and it is distinct from those measures. For example, we found evidence that foreign policy is very salient to Ukrainian Americans: the Ukrainian Congress Committee of America (UCCA) is very focused on foreign aid for Ukraine and helping Ukraine develop stable democratic institutions. Because of this, the Ukrainian lobby was placed in the same category as Armenian, Cuban, and Greek lobbies. However, in terms of organizational resources, the Ukrainian lobby is not in the same league as these other lobbies: the UCCA has no Washington office, its website is largely inactive, and its ability to pull Ukrainian Americans into the political process pales in comparison to other ethnic lobbies. Likewise, both the Iranian lobby and Pakistani lobby were coded as belonging to the second highest category of foreign policy salience. Both lobbies appear to focus first on brethren promotion, yet both lobbies also appear to find foreign policy to be a major concern. However, the Iranian lobby has a much greater organizational presence in Washington, while the Pakistani organizations appear to be largely inactive since 2005. While they are distinct variables, *Organizational strength* and *Saliency* are highly correlated ($r = .761$) and therefore must be included in separate models.

Two other saliency variables were created. The variable *Enemy* is designed to capture the effects that an enemy of the ancestral homeland might have on group mobilization and, ultimately, influence. The variable *Historical trauma* is designed to capture the impact of a historical trauma on a group's influence. Both are dummy variables, and both were coded by examining the websites of ethnic organizations and journalistic accounts to determine if either factor was used in an ethnic group's rhetoric, action alerts, or mobilization efforts. It is important to note that the use of an enemy or historical trauma had to be identified in our research, and the coding process did not rely on historical examples of enemies or traumas. For example, while China was an enemy of Japan in World War II, we found no evidence that Japanese American organizations use China as a mobilization tool.

Finally, the variable *Status quo* captures the effects of an ethnic group championing policies that seek to alter or protect existing US policies. This variable was created by examining the most salient issues for each ethnic group and coding the degree to which the policy positions of the ethnic group converge or diverge from existing US policies (see Appendix D for coding information). The result is a scale ranging from 1 to 5, with 1 indicating the positions of the ethnic group would require a significant shift of the status quo, and a score of 5 indicating that the positions of the ethnic group involve protecting existing U.S. policies.

▓ Multivariate Analysis Results

Table 5.2 presents the OLS models that include the variables *Population, Income,* and *PAC contributions.* Models 1–4 include *Non-English,* while Models 5–8 include *Foreign-born.* Because *Saliency, Enemy, Trauma,* and *Organizational strength* are all highly correlated, each was placed in a separate model. The results indicate that an ethnic group's overall population has a significant and positive influence on the ethnic group's influence in foreign policy making: the coefficient for *Population* is significant and positive across all eight models. The results also indicate that a group's resources

Table 5.2 Predictors of Ethnic Group Influence

Variable	Model 1	Model 2	Model 3	Model 4	Model 5	Model 6	Model 7	Model 8
Population	.084**	.082**	.094**	.077**	.085**	.083**	.098**	.076**
	(.016)	(.016)	(.019)	(.015)	(.017)	(.017)	(.022)	(.017)
Household	.557*	.551**	.714**	.506**	.520**	.520**	.689**	.453*
income	(.173)	(.175)	(.203)	(.169)	(.181)	(.182)	(.219)	(.178)
PAC	.357**	.374**	.395**	.371**	.365**	.364**	.385**	.361**
contributions	(.072)	.073	(.074)	(.071)	(.074)	(.075)	(.077)	(.074)
Non-English	14.45*	14.0*	18.56**	14.2*				
at home	(5.7)	(5.76)	(6.44)	(5.59)				
Foreign-born					13.69	13.53	19.07*	12.34*
					(6.96)	(7.0)	(8.17)	(6.85)
Saliency	4.05*				4.13*			
	(1.49)				(1.55)			
Enemy		8.10*				8.45*		
		(3.19)				(3.3)		
Trauma			8.91*				9.1	
			(4.29)				(4.62)	
Organizational				4.33**				4.24**
strength				(1.45)				(1.51)
Constant	−15.0	−10.3	−23.6	−12.3	−11.66	−7.55	−21.26	−7.36
	(11.9)	(11.6)	(15.13)	(11.2)	(12.6)	(12.2)	(16.26)	(11.93)
R-square	.663	.654	.634	.676	.639	.634	.606	.646
F	12.6**	12.1**	11.1**	13.3**	11.3**	11.08**	9.85**	11.68**
N	38	38	38	38	38	38	38	38

Note: Cell entries are ordinary least squares estimates with standard errors in parentheses. *p < .05; **p < .01.

have a significant and positive effect on the group's influence: the coefficients for *Income* and *PAC contributions* are significant across all eight models, and the coefficients for *Organizational strength* are significant in Model 4 and Model 8.

There is evidence that assimilation, especially in terms of retaining linguistic heritage, plays a significant role in affecting ethnic group influence. Models 1 through 4 demonstrate that the percentage of ethnic brethren who speak a language other than English at home has a significant influence on the ethnic group's influence. In contrast, the coefficient for *Foreign-born* is significant in only one of the four models in which it was included. The analysis indicates that ethnic groups that retain their linguistic heritage have greater influence in foreign policy making.

Issue saliency also appears to play an important role in determining ethnic group influence. The coefficient for *Saliency* is large in both Model 1 and Model 5, suggesting that saliency of foreign policy has a significant effect on ethnic group influence. Likewise, the analysis of Model 2 and Model 6 suggests that the presence of an enemy increases foreign policy influence for ethnic groups. In contrast, the coefficient for *Trauma* is significant in Model 7, but only marginally significant in Model 3.

Table 5.3 presents Models 9 through 16, which substitute the variable *Congressional delegation* for *Population*. The coefficients for *Congressional delegation* are large and positive for all eight models, indicating that a larger congressional delegation increases ethnic group influence. The other results are similar to those found in Models 1 through 8, especially in terms of group resources: *Income, PAC contributions,* and *Organizational strength* all have a significant and positive effect on ethnic group influence. In terms of assimilation, the coefficients for *Non-English* are significant in Models 9–12, but *Foreign-born* is only marginally significant in Models 13–16. None of the saliency measures were significant predictors of ethnic groups' influence in these models, although *Saliency* was marginally significant in Model 9.

Table 5.4 presents the models that examine the effects of a concentrated ethnic group population. Since *Population concentration* is highly correlated with *Non-English* ($r = .729$), the latter variable was not included in Models 17 through 20. Surprisingly, the coefficients for *Population concentration* are not significant in any of the models, indicating that the size of an ethnic group is of more importance than the degree to which it is concentrated into congressional districts, at least as captured by the Gini Index. Another way of testing the effects of a concentrated population is by replacing *Population concentration* with the variables that measure the number of congressional districts in which ethnic groups compose a certain percentage of the population. Table 5.5 shows the effects of the variables that count the number of congressional districts in which each ethnic group

Table 5.3 Predictors of Ethnic Group Influence, Including Congressional Delegation

Variable	Model 9	Model 10	Model 11	Model 12	Model 13	Model 14	Model 15	Model 16
Congressional delegation	.822**	.805**	.859**	.784**	.765**	.751**	.784**	.720**
	(.158)	(.161)	(.174)	(.151)	(.178)	(.179)	(.197)	(.173)
Household income	.548**	.541**	.610**	.516**	.450*	.448*	.489*	.411*
	(.176)	(.179)	(.195)	(.169)	(.188)	(.189)	(.208)	(.183)
PAC contributions	.212*	.217*	.219*	.212**	.207*	.210*	.218*	.208*
	(.080)	(.081)	(.083)	(.076)	(.086)	(.087)	(.090)	(.083)
Non-English at home	19.4**	18.7**	21.05*	19.74**				
	(6.39)	(6.48)	(7.02)	(6.11)				
Foreign-born					15.07	14.56	16.1	14.69
					(7.82)	(7.87)	(8.59)	(7.58)
Saliency	2.63				2.52			
	(1.59)				(1.67)			
Enemy		4.39				4.62		
		(3.21)				(3.43)		
Trauma			3.61				2.27	
			(3.97)				(4.27)	
Organizational strength				3.76*				3.50*
				(1.53)				(1.67)
Constant	−14.04	−10.06	−15.3	−14.8	−4.82	−1.65	−3.68	−4.50
	(12.19)	(11.9)	(14.5)	(11.5)	(12.9)	(12.58)	(15.37)	(12.25)
R-square	.659	.648	.637	.688	.605	.599	.579	.628
F	12.0**	11.4**	10.87**	13.68**	9.5**	9.26**	8.53**	10.48**
N	37	37	37	37	37	37	37	37

Note: Cell entries are ordinary least squares estimates with standard errors in parentheses. *p < .05; **p < .01.

composes a certain percentage of the population. All of these variables that measure district population thresholds are significant, although Model 21 and Model 22, which include the 1 percent and 2.5 percent thresholds, are better at explaining the variance in the dependent variable, as captured by the R-square measures. That is, while the coefficients for the higher thresholds, such as 25 percent and 50 percent of the district's population, are significant, the models that include these variables do a poorer job of explaining ethnic group influence. This may be evidence that it is more important for an ethnic group to obtain a lower threshold of the population across a number of districts in order to have an influence in the policymaking process.

Finally, Table 5.6 presents the models that include the *Status quo* variable. In each of the four models, the coefficient for the *Status quo* variable is positive and significant, indicating that defending established policies leads to substantially greater influence. These findings may help explain why a number of Central and Eastern European ethnic groups that were reported to be influential in the 1980s and 1990s were not ranked especially high in Table 5.1. Their efforts to expand the Visa Waiver Program to include Poland,

Table 5.4 Predictors of Ethnic Group Influence, Including Ethnic Group Concentration

Variable	Model 17	Model 18	Model 19	Model 20
Population	.084**	.083**	.089**	.074**
	(.020)	(.020)	(.025)	(.019)
Household income	.520*	.537*	.629*	.448*
	(.216)	(.217)	(.264)	(.210)
PAC contributions	.317**	.313**	.328**	.317**
	(.078)	(.078)	(.084)	(.076)
Population concentration	.223	.239	.272	.195
	(.169)	(.171)	(.197)	(.165)
Saliency	4.15*			
	(1.61)			
Enemy		8.77*		
		(3.44)		
Trauma			6.94	
			(4.78)	
Organizational strength				4.33**
				(1.56)
Constant	−19.4	−17.45	−24.62	−13.76
	(21.3)	(22.1)	(26.4)	(20.4)
R-square	.616	.615	.565	.626
F	10.26**	10.21**	8.31**	10.72**
N	38	38	38	38

Note: Cell entries are ordinary least squares estimates with standard errors in parentheses. *p < .05; **p < .01.

the Czech Republic, and the Baltic states represent a substantial shift of the status quo, especially given the fact that requirements for countries to participate in the Visa Waiver Program are being tightened and not loosened.

Conclusions

The analysis presented in this chapter reinforces the hypotheses and research of other scholars. Across all measures, the overall size of the ethnic group does affect its influence, and when controlling for other factors, larger ethnic groups command more influence in the foreign policy–making process. It is also clear that resources are an important source of ethnic group influence. Greater monetary resources may be used to establish and fund PACs, which can be an important means of gaining access to the policymaking process. Perhaps more importantly, ethnic groups with higher levels of monetary resources have a greater ability to establish viable organizations that engage in and monitor the policymaking process. These organizations can also be instrumental in developing and maintaining grassroots political movements,

Table 5.5 Predictors of Ethnic Group Influence, Including Size of Ethnic Population in Congressional Districts

Variable	Model 21	Model 22	Model 23	Model 24	Model 25	Model 26
Household	.364	.441*	.455*	.484*	.521*	.483*
income	(.190)	(.192)	(.194)	(.193)	(.214)	(.219)
PAC	.383**	.399**	.413**	.418**	.382**	.391**
contributions	(.083)	(.081)	(.082)	(.080)	(.084)	(.087)
Non-English	13.0	15.2*	14.9*	14.08*	5.96	5.23
at home	(6.81)	(6.90)	(6.89)	(6.61)	(6.23)	(6.38)
1 percent	.046**					
of district	(.013)					
2.5 percent		.062**				
of district		(.016)				
5 percent			.077**			
of district			(.02)			
10 percent				.133**		
of district				(.033)		
25 percent					.448**	
of district					(.136)	
50 percent						1.07**
of district						(.368)
Constant	4.42	−.078	−.129	−.930	3.02	5.77
	(12.4)	(12.6)	(12.7)	(12.46)	(13.04)	(13.29)
R-square	.527	.545	.542	.556	.506	.477
F	9.20**	9.88**	9.77**	10.33**	8.44**	7.52**
N	38	38	38	38	38	38

Note: Cell entries are ordinary least squares estimates with standard errors in parentheses. *p < .05; **p < .01.

which can be critical in influencing the policymaking process, especially at the congressional level.

Assimilation also appears to play an important role in affecting ethnic group influence. The quantitative analysis indicates that ethnic groups that continue to speak their ancestral language at home have greater influence in the foreign policy–making process. Speaking a language other than English at home may represent that the ethnic group is relatively new to the United States, and thus still becoming assimilated. Alternatively, it may capture the conscious choice to retain the cultural heritage of the ethnic group. Perhaps because of that, this measure appears to play a greater role in determining ethnic group influence than simply accounting for the percentage of the ethnic group that was born outside of the United States.

Both the qualitative and quantitative analyses indicate that issue salience plays an important role in determining ethnic group influence. This conclusion would almost certainly be stronger if this project had included a larger sample of ethnic groups that are only marginally interested in foreign policy. The existence of salient foreign policy issues appears to play a significant

Table 5.6 Predictors of Ethnic Group Influence, Including Status Quo

Variable	Model 27	Model 28	Model 29	Model 30
Population	.080*	.078**	.090**	.071**
	(.014)	(.015)	(.018)	(.013)
Household	.497**	.497**	.649**	.437**
income	(.157)	(.166)	(.190)	(.150)
PAC	.307**	.319**	.333**	.299**
contributions	(.068)	(.072)	(.073)	(.066)
Non-English	14.99**	13.84*	18.41**	15.09**
at home	(5.21)	(5.46)	(6.12)	(4.99)
Status quo	5.17**	4.35*	4.71*	5.42**
	(1.68)	(1.77)	(1.80)	(1.62)
Saliency	-4.35**			
	(1.40)			
Enemy		7.19*		
		(3.02)		
Trauma			8.46*	
			(4.06)	
Organizational				4.92**
strength				(1.36)
Constant	−27.51*	−19.22	−33.18*	−25.91*
	(11.56)	(11.50)	(14.76)	(10.79)
R-square	.744	.715	.704	.764
F	14.53**	12.56**	11.89**	16.21**
N	37	37	37	37

Note: Cell entries are ordinary least squares estimates with standard errors in parentheses. *p < .05; **p < .01.

role in increasing an ethnic group's influence. There is also evidence that the existence of an enemy or historical trauma may increase the influence of an ethnic group, probably because those factors help increase mobilization.

Finally, the analysis suggests that championing established policies—that is, protecting the status quo—leads to greater influence, at least as perceived by policymakers. The analysis supports the hypothesis that ethnic groups that champion the status quo enjoy a strategic advantage that translates into greater influence.

The findings presented in this chapter help predict which ethnic lobbies are likely to see their influence increase or wane in the future. A number of factors are contributing to the declining influence of some European lobbies. Most of the European ethnic groups are very assimilated into US society, and there exist few issues that can prompt mobilization. The Italian lobby's influence in foreign policy is almost certainly declining, and there appears little that would reverse the decay of its sway. With the collapse of the Soviet empire, many Central and Eastern European ethnic lobbies now lack a salient issue that can stimulate political participation within the ethnic community. Coupled with the fact that some of these Central and Eastern

European ethnic groups have been very assimilated into US society, it is increasingly likely that many of these ethnic groups will cease to be influential in the policymaking process. For example, the major Polish immigration to the United States began a century ago. By 2005, fewer than 6 percent of Polish Americans were born outside the United States, and less than 9 percent spoke a language other than English at home. Unless a significant issue emerges that energizes the Polish American community, the Polish lobby may soon cease to have any significance in terms of foreign policy. The same holds true for the Czech and Ukrainian lobbies. The existence of strong organizations helps retard the decay of the Polish, Italian, and Baltic lobbies, but these lobbies are likely to decline in foreign policy influence as they lose their ability to mobilize their ethnic brethren to participate in the foreign policy–making process. Finally, these lobbies have shifted their goals from preserving the status quo (mainly, taking a hard line against the Soviet Union) to seeking to change existing policies (expanding the Visa Waiver Program).

In contrast, foreign policy concerns may help mobilize ethnic groups that have more significant numbers of recent immigrants to the United States. Cuban Americans are an excellent example of an ethnic group having an important influence on foreign policy within a generation of arriving in the United States, and clearly issue saliency played a significant role in driving Cuban American political activism. China's attempts to expand its political influence may mobilize Japanese, Korean, Vietnamese, Filipino, and especially Taiwanese Americans to become more active in foreign affairs. As noted earlier in this chapter, Korean Americans and Vietnamese Americans now have populations of greater than 1 million, and Korean Americans mounted a strong grassroots campaign in support of the Comfort Women Resolution. Finally, Indian Americans, as an ethnic group, may not be as energized by foreign policy as, say, Cuban Americans, but Indian Americans are certainly poised to become more influential in the foreign policy–making process. Again, Indian Americans are now the wealthiest ethnic group in America, they now number almost 2 million, and they are establishing an organized presence in Washington. All of this means that if an event, such as a confrontation between India and Pakistan, were to mobilize Indian Americans further, their influence would likely increase.

◼ Notes

1. Although its status is legendary, there is little evidence on the CANF's website that the organization encourages grassroots mobilization. There is no "take action" or similar link from the website, and there is no link to government officials. While policymakers reported that the organization does engage in grassroots mobilization with its members, CANF does not provide a mechanism to mobilize nonmembers via their website.

2. However, some of these same policymakers acknowledged that many Americans also identify with Great Britain.

3. In comparison, the Hispanic American lobby was discussed by 14.6 percent of policymakers as having a substantial influence on immigration policy.

4. In 2001, Congress amended the act to allow the president to waive the ban if Azerbaijan met certain conditions. While President Bush has waived the sanctions annually since 2002, critics charge that Section 907 damages US relations with Azerbaijan.

5. Ambassador Evans stated at an appearance at the University of California–Berkeley that it was "unbecoming of us as Americans to play word games here. I will today call it the Armenian genocide" (as quoted in Cornwell 2006). Evans was recalled as ambassador in May 2006, a move many believe was in response to his genocide comments (Abraham 2006; Doyle 2006).

6. According to several policymakers interviewed for this study, Richard Hoagland's nomination was torpedoed by the ANCA. While the Armenian Assembly of America pressured Hoagland to acknowledge the genocide in 2006, the group eventually supported the nomination (Reynolds 2007).

7. Proponents of the Jubilee Act state that it "cancels impoverished country debt; removes economic conditionalities from the cancellation process; mandates transparency and accountability from governments and international financial institutions; and moves forward with more responsible lending practices" (Jubilee USA 2007).

8. A few policymakers disagreed that Arab American groups are more politically active, instead arguing that the Arab American lobby lacks organization and visibility.

9. Senator Menendez stated he placed a hold on the confirmation in "response to the Bush administration's refusal to recognize the Armenian genocide," and because the nomination was not in the "best interest of Armenia and her Diaspora" (Menendez 2006).

10. The US Census reported that the only congressional district in the United States in 2000 without Armenian Americans was the New York 16th, located in the Bronx.

11. However, the same policymaker, who is of neither Cuban nor Jewish descent, argued that neither ethnicity has *too* much influence. While both ethnicities have great access, that access does not necessarily translate into getting everything the lobbies desire.

12. That may change in the future. Of the forty-eight representatives on the Committee on Foreign Affairs for the 110th Congress, five are African American, two are non-Cuban Hispanic American, and one is Asian American.

13. For example, the least-correlated variables were *Population* and *50% of CD* ($r = .734$). The highest correlation was found between *2.5% of CD* and *5% of CD* ($r = .978$).

14. We found it impossible to determine the number of members of Congress who are Anglo Americans.

15. A potential concern is that *Foreign-born* and *Non-English* could have a nonlinear effect on the dependent variable. For example, ethnic groups that include a large number of individuals who do not speak English at home have little influence on foreign policy, while groups that are very assimilated (and thus have little interest in foreign policy) also have very little influence. However, scatter plots of each of these variables with the dependent measure (*Influence*) do not indicate this to be the case.

6

The Comparative Influence of Ethnic Groups

The previous chapter established which ethnic groups are the most influential in the foreign policy–making process, and most of the results are not surprising: the Israeli American lobby was rated by far the most powerful ethnic lobby, and the Cuban American lobby was viewed as the second most influential (see Table 5.1). Seven other ethnic lobbies were ranked as having a moderate degree of influence, including four established lobbies (the Irish American, Greek American, Armenian American, and Taiwanese American lobbies), one emerging ethnic lobby (the Indian American lobby), and two pan-ethnic lobbies (the Hispanic American and African American lobbies). Chapter 4 also confirmed that a number of factors explain the influence of these lobbies, including financial and organizational resources, the saliency of foreign policy issues to the ethnic group, and the degree to which ethnic groups maintain their ethnic heritage.

While we now know which ethnic groups are most influential and what factors help explain their influence, key questions remain: How does the power of ethnic lobbies compare to other actors in the foreign policy–making process? In other words, are ethnic lobbies more influential than other domestic sources of foreign policy making, such as business groups, the media, and public opinion? By better understanding the comparative influence of ethnic groups, we may be better able to answer another key question: Are ethnic groups too influential in the foreign policy–making process? This chapter seeks to better understand the comparative role that ethnic groups play in the foreign policy–making process, where they are one player among many.

Ethnic Groups: One Voice Among Many

Traditionally, scholars studying foreign policy making focused almost entirely upon elites, dismissing the idea that the American public could or should affect foreign policy. Part of the normative rationale for the elitist perspective of foreign policy making was based on the belief that Americans paid little attention to foreign policy, and public opinion on issues of foreign policy was usually depicted as being "particularly shallow and without meaningful content" (Erikson and Tedin 2005; see also Almond 1960; Uslaner 1991). Further, some argued that when American public opinion did impose itself upon foreign policy decisions, the results were often contrary to the national interest. For example, in rather terse language, Walter Lippmann wrote: "The unhappy truth is that the prevailing public opinion has been destructively wrong at the critical junctures. . . . It has shown itself to be a dangerous master of decisions when the stakes are life and death" (1955, 20).

However, while still acknowledging that the American public is not always interested in foreign affairs, more recent scholarship suggests that "the 'know-nothingist' portrayal found in much of the literature on public opinion and foreign policy" is misplaced (Jentleson 1992, 72). For example, Richard Herrmann, Philip Tetlock, and Penny Visser demonstrate that individuals utilize a "relatively thoughtful process . . . moderated by political knowledge" when developing opinions about using US military forces abroad (1999, 567; see also Shapiro and Page 1988; Jentleson and Britton 1998). Other evidence suggests that the effect of public opinion on foreign policy is "usually complex, variable, and interactive rather than simple, constant, and unidirectional" (Holsti 2004, 308; see, also, Graham 1994; Page and Shapiro 1983; Jacobs and Page 2005). In other words, the public can and does influence foreign policy, even if the link between public opinion and foreign policy making may not be transparent and always direct.

One such way this may occur is through the electoral process. Although the public may ignore foreign policy much of the time, foreign policy may still influence elections. Since elected officials desire to be reelected, politicians are compelled to consider public sentiments because the public could eventually find foreign policy to be salient. Former congressman Charles Whalen (R-OH) argues that low levels of information and infrequent interest in foreign affairs can result in incumbents being vulnerable to attacks by challengers (Hastedt 2006). Foreign policy issues are often complex and multifaceted, allowing challengers to mount aggressive, and at times misleading, campaigns based on an incumbent's voting records. While foreign policy may not be important to voters in every election, it has the potential to become a salient campaign issue, thus affecting the policymaking process as elected officials weigh what public sentiments might be if an issue rises to prominence.

Fundamentally, ethnic groups compose a segment of public opinion, a segment that may find foreign policy to be more salient than the general public does. Because of this, ethnic groups are often examples of *issue publics,* or groups of people who find a policy realm to be personally important and who develop stable attitudes relevant to the issue domain (Converse 1964; Krosnick 1990).[1] According to Jon Krosnick, an individual may find an issue to be especially salient because of perceived self-interest, because of social identification with reference groups or individuals, or because the individual finds the policy to be "relevant to his or her basic social and personal values" (1990, 73). As a result of both personal attachments to an ethnic identity and the use of ethnic mobilization, ethnic communities can develop into issue publics. Of course, ethnic communities can also develop into issue publics that are focused on domestic issues, like civil rights, job opportunities, and community services. Indeed, most ethnic organizations identified for this project are focused much more on domestic concerns than on foreign affairs. However, there is no shortage of examples of ethnic American groups behaving very much like issue publics in their attempts to influence US foreign policy: Jewish Americans supporting US aid to Israel, Greek Americans opposing Turkey's occupation of parts of Cyprus, Armenian Americans supporting the US recognition of the 1915 Armenian genocide, and the list goes on.

Yet, ethnic groups are not the only organized interests that aspire to influence foreign policy. First and foremost, scholars have chronicled efforts by business groups to influence foreign policy, energy policy, and trade policies for decades (Keohane 1984; Frieden 1996; Huntington 1997). For example, Samuel Huntington asserts that, in the absence of a clear national interest to guide foreign policy, commercial interests impel foreign policy significantly. As another example, Stephen Weissman chronicles how business and agriculture groups can "exert a disproportionate influence over Congress" on issues of foreign and trade policies, overwhelming other interests such as human rights groups or ethnic organizations (1995, 70).

Further, and apart from those representing business, other organized interests also attempt to shape public policy. For example, foreign governments, foreign political parties, non-US businesses, and other foreign principals conduct lobbying and public relations campaigns to influence US policies, although these actors are forbidden from making campaign contributions.[2] While elected policymakers do not represent foreign principals (i.e., foreign principals are not constituents), and since foreign individuals and groups cannot donate to political campaigns, they are fundamentally different from other types of interest groups. Nonetheless, foreign lobbies conduct expensive lobbying campaigns, some of which are headed by former members of Congress (Albert 2001; Rothstein 2006), and some scholars assert that foreign entities can influence US foreign policy (Hrebenar and Thomas 1995; Hula 1995). In addition, there are other issue publics (ideological groups, religious organizations, human rights, environment, and labor) that strive to influence foreign affairs. Finally, nonelected elites, such as think tank associates, academics, and other knowledge-based experts, may influence policy debates and policymakers through technical reports, expert testimony, and scholarly publications (Haas 1992; Jacobs and Page 2005). Nonelected elites also may influence the public dialogue because the "news media increasingly depend on experts from Washington-based think tanks" (Mearsheimer and Walt 2007, 175).

Thus, there are a number of reasons why ethnic groups may not have undue power in the foreign policy–making process. An ethnic lobby that desires to influence foreign policy is likely to be only one voice in the decisionmaking process, as business groups, ideological organizations, human rights groups, unions, and even other ethnic lobbies may try to influence policy outcomes. In addition, ethnic lobbies face significant financial and organizational disadvantages compared to business organizations (Schlozman and Tierney 1986; Berry 1997). Further, foreign policy making is still dominated by the executive branch (Weissman 1995), a branch that is far more difficult for ethnic groups to access than Congress. For these reasons, it is hypothesized that ethnic groups, as a class of interest groups, do not dominate the foreign policy process or enjoy greater influence than other domestic actors, like business groups. Indeed, as noted in Chapter 1, only a handful of ethnic lobbies are routinely cited by policy analysts as having a disproportionate amount of political sway: usually, the Israeli, Cuban, Armenian, Greek, Irish, and Eastern European lobbies.

Further, only two ethnic-based *interest groups* (as opposed to ethnic lobbies) are routinely cited as having a great deal of influence: the American Israel Public Affairs Committee (AIPAC) and the Cuban American National Foundation (CANF). Again, no ethnic or country-specific interest group garners more attention than AIPAC, and it is perceived as being among the most effective lobbying organizations in Washington. Glenn Frankel states that AIPAC "gained a reputation as the National Rifle Association of foreign policy. . . . But in some ways it was even stronger. The NRA's support was largely confined to right-wing Republicans and rural Democrats. But AIPAC made inroads in both parties and both ends of the ideological spectrum" (2006, 17–24). Tony Smith states that AIPAC played a leading role in numerous Middle East policies, including placing sanctions on Russia if it aided Iran's efforts to improve missile technology. John Mearsheimer and Stephen Walt summarize the influence of AIPAC by stating that "of all the groups that make up the [Israel] lobby, it is AIPAC that holds the key to influence in Congress, a fact that is widely acknowledged by politicians from both parties" (2007, 153). Indeed, Mearsheimer and Walt claim that AIPAC is so influential that it helps mute criticisms of Israel not only among members of Congress, but also within the media, because many newspapers are "afraid" of the organization (2007, 174).

Among ethnic lobbies, only CANF approaches AIPAC's status: indeed, CANF was explicitly structured after AIPAC (see Haney and Vanderbush

1999; Brenner and Landau 1990). Patrick Haney and Walt Vanderbush assert that CANF played the role of "near co-executor" of US policy toward Cuba for years (1999, 341), and the organization played a significant role in establishing funding for, and subsequent management of, Radio and TV Martí. Smith contends that "CANF demonstrated real power over American foreign policy" in the ratification of the 1996 Helms-Burton Bill and other legislation related to Cuba (2000, 69). John Newhouse argues that CANF became "one of the country's most powerful political-action groups," and the group assumed a great deal of control over Radio Martí and processing Cuban immigrants from third countries (1992, 76–77). Weissman contends that CANF also played a significant role in shaping US policy toward unrest in Africa because the group wanted to humiliate the Cuban military contingent in Angola (1995, 130).

Because of the unique position of the Jewish and Cuban lobbies, as well as the organizational prowess of their leading interest groups, it is hypothesized that of the ethnic American lobbies, only the Israeli and Cuban American lobbies are perceived as being too influential in foreign policy making. Although other ethnic lobbies do exhibit the characteristics of issue publics, there is greater congruence between the positions of the Jewish and Cuban lobbies and official US positions than with other ethnic lobbies, so that the Jewish and Cuban lobbies enjoy a strategic advantage of defending the status quo rather than trying to change it. Other ethnic lobbies simply do not always enjoy such a strategic advantage. For example, Armenian Americans desire the United States to recognize the 1915 Armenian genocide, which the Department of State opposes. Further, the Jewish and Cuban lobbies have concentrated populations that have helped elect to Congress substantial numbers of ethnic brethren concerned with foreign policy. In contrast, other ethnicities, such as African and Hispanic Americans, have substantial representation in Congress, but elites from these ethnicities tend to focus on domestic issues and not foreign policy (Jones-Correa 2002; Scott and Osman 2002, 75).

Data and Methods

To gauge the relative influence of different actors on foreign policy, we interviewed fifty-three Washington insiders. A total of eighteen different entities were included in the survey instrument. From the above discussion, there may be numerous actors from outside the government that may influence the formulation of foreign policy: the constituents for members of Congress; mass public opinion; business groups; foreign lobbies (foreign governments and embassies, foreign nationals, non-US companies, and their agents, which are required to register under the Foreign Agents Registration Act); international organizations (such as the UN, the International Monetary Fund, and the World Health Organization); nonelected elites (such as think tanks, academics, and opinion leaders); nongovernmental organizations (such as the International Red Cross, Human Rights Watch, and labor unions);[3] national party leaders (such as former Republican National Committee chair Ken Mehlman and Democratic National Committee chair Howard Dean); and ethnic interest groups. In addition, elected policymakers, such as the president and members of Congress, and their agents (White House staffers, including the National Security Council [NSC], personal staffers for members of Congress, congressional staffers assigned to relevant committees, and congressional caucuses) are instrumental in developing foreign policy.[4] Executive agencies, most notably the Departments of State and Defense, will affect foreign policy as well.

Specifically, respondents were asked: "Please tell us the degree to which each of the following actors affects US foreign policy by ranking the influence of each on a scale of 0–100 (with 0 meaning no influence and 100 meaning a great deal of influence)."[5] In addition to the quantitative ratings, many respondents explained the rationale for their answers or otherwise commented on the relative influence of the actors.

In addition, policymakers (but not ethnic group leaders) were asked to rate the degree to which ethnic American groups influence US foreign policy making, as well as six policy realms (foreign aid, oil and energy, human rights, trade, military and security, and immigration) on a five-point scale. Policymakers were then asked if they strongly agree, somewhat agree, neither agree nor disagree, somewhat disagree, or strongly disagree with a series of normative questions designed to gauge the influence of ethnic groups (see Appendix A). Finally, policymakers and ethnic group leaders were asked to rate the influence of thirty-eight ethnic lobbies, as presented in Chapter 4. After the results were tabulated, follow-up interviews were conducted to ask respondents if they believed the most influential of those ethnic groups were too powerful.

We recognize that the scores are not "true" measures of influence, but are instead measures of perceived influence. Nonetheless, perceived influence matters a great deal: other actors may be more likely to respond to an actor that is perceived as being influential, while they may ignore an actor who is perceived as being ineffective. In addition, the elites interviewed for the project are experts involved deeply in the policymaking process, and research has demonstrated that, when aggregated, individual perceptions can provide a very good measure of reality (Surowiecki 2004). Although there was at times variance among the individuals we interviewed about the relative influence of actors, taken as a whole, these data are a very valuable measure of the comparative influence of those who seek to affect the policymaking process.

▦ Results

Table 6.1 presents the results of the elite survey, with the mean for each actor indicating the average amount of influence according to the experts we interviewed. However, individual respondents may have different beliefs on what "influence" means or how actors should be placed on the scale of 0 to 100. For instance, the highest score given by one respondent could be 40, while other respondents might rate all 18 actors as having influence scores of more than 40. Because of the variation across respondents regarding the range of their scores, the mean influence score was calculated for each respondent and this mean score was used to compute a relative influence score for all eighteen foreign policy actors. This relative influence score was computed by calculating the average influence score for each respondent, and then dividing the score given by the respondent's figure for each foreign policy actor by the respondent's average score. Doing so helps create a more standard scoring across all respondents for all eighteen actors. Table 6.1 also presents this computed relative influence score for each actor, and scores above 1.0 indicate the actor has an above average amount of influence, while scores below 1.0 indicate the actor has a below average amount of influence.

Clearly, internal actors were perceived as having greater influence on foreign policy than those outside the government. It is of little surprise that the president is perceived as having the greatest influence over foreign policy: Article II of the US Constitution outlines the president's role as commander-in-chief and discusses the president's authority to make treaties. The president was rated as having the most influence by nearly all of the respondents, often receiving a score of 100. One State Department bureaucrat stated that "no one person has more influence" over foreign policy, while another bureaucrat remarked, "whatever the president says, goes." Another stated flatly: "He makes the final decisions. It's his policy: he owns it." Other bureaucrats indicated that the president affects foreign policy through political appointees, who then shape the direction of agencies, even agencies that are nominally independent from political pressures.

Still others, while acknowledging the president's strong influence over foreign policy, indicated that the president's ability to shape policymaking does have limits. One bureaucrat asserted that the president, because of time and resource constraints, can only influence about 20 percent of foreign policy, meaning that "80 percent of foreign policy does not change depending on the administration, both in terms of issues or the US positions." Several respondents, both on Capitol Hill and at the State Department, made similar appraisals, asserting that the president's influence is very high "when he is focused on something," but presidents have too many issues on which to

Table 6.1 Influence of Actors on Foreign Policy Making

Actor	Mean Rating	Standard Deviation	N
President	89.96	10.4	51
White House staffers	74.40	18.9	50
Department of Defense officials	72.25	14.1	50
State Department bureaucrats	67.55	18.7	50
Members of Congress	64.19	22.4	49
Committee staffers	59.83	22.0	50
Business groups	55.97	20.5	49
News media	55.34	19.1	51
Ethnic American groups	52.39	18.7	47
Nonelected elites	49.02	19.5	46
Mass public opinion	48.27	17.9	49
Personal congressional staffers	46.94	25.6	51
Constituents of members of Congress	46.45	21.2	50
Nongovernmental organizations	44.53	20.6	31
Congressional caucuses	43.16	20.0	49
International organizations	41.91	20.8	47
National party leaders	40.99	23.1	48
Foreign lobbies	39.72	17.9	48

Note: Respondents rated the influence of each actor on a scale of 0 to 100.

Actor	Relative Mean Rating	Standard Deviation	N
President	1.69	.36	51
White House staffers	1.37	.38	50
Department of Defense officials	1.35	.31	50
State Department bureaucrats	1.23	.37	50
Members of Congress	1.17	.42	49
Committee staffers	1.06	.33	50
News media	0.99	.24	51
Business groups	0.98	.29	49
Ethnic American groups	0.92	.24	47
Mass public opinion	0.87	.26	49
Constituents of members of Congress	0.85	.38	50
Nonelected elites	0.85	.27	46
Personal congressional staffers	0.82	.38	51
Nongovernmental organizations	0.80	.26	31
Congressional caucuses	0.76	.28	49
International organizations	0.74	.33	47
National party leaders	0.73	.40	48
Foreign lobbies	0.70	.25	48

Note: Relative rating calculated by dividing the respondent's rating for each actor by the respondent's mean rating for all eighteen actors.

concentrate. In addition, others we interviewed argued that public opinion can affect the president's ability to implement a policy if a significant majority of the public opposes it.

Finally, some administrative-specific trends emerged. Several congressional staffers argued that Congress had allowed the president great latitude in foreign policy for much of this president's first term, but, in the words of one staffer, "Congress started seizing power back" when President George W. Bush's approval rating declined in 2005 and 2006. While these staffers still rated the president as having the greatest single influence on foreign policy, they contended that the president's power in determining foreign policy had declined relative to the influence of other actors, namely members of Congress. Finally, a few respondents indicated that while the presidency has a strong effect on foreign affairs, President Bush relies on his advisors more than previous presidents to formulate his foreign policy. For example, one committee staffer asserted that Vice President Dick Cheney has a larger role in developing foreign policy than vice presidents have had in previous administrations. In a similar fashion, an ethnic group leader who rated the president as having by far the greatest impact on foreign policy stated, "but this president is dependent on others like Rice, Rumsfeld, [and] Wolfowitz." Nonetheless, respondents as a whole rated the presidency as having a tremendous impact on foreign policy, far higher than any other actors. The US-India Civilian Nuclear Agreement, to be discussed later in the conclusion of this book, is an excellent example of the influence of the president.

The next three sets of actors ranked as having the most influence over foreign policy (White House staffers, Department of Defense officials, and bureaucrats at the Department of State) all are located within the executive branch as well.[6] Many respondents stated that White House staffers[7] are influential because of their close proximity to the actor with the greatest influence over foreign policy: the president. One congressional staffer argued that, as the presidency has assumed more power over the past fifty years because of the increased importance of foreign affairs, White House staffers have increased their influence, most notably at the expense of personal staffers for members of Congress. Other policymakers contended that White House staffers shape the foreign policy objectives of the president, thus influencing foreign policy making as a whole. Finally, some respondents indicated that because the president has so many matters to attend to, the influence of White House staffers is quite high. Nonetheless, not all respondents agreed with this assessment. Several congressional staffers argued the power of White House staffers was overstated, and "they just carry out what the president wants to do."[8] Nonetheless, White House staffers were seen as having the second greatest influence over foreign policy.

Department of Defense officials were ranked as having the third greatest amount of influence over foreign policy, and some respondents contended Defense Department officials had greater sway in the current Bush administration than they enjoyed with previous presidents.[9] One bureaucrat posited that much of the enhanced influence of the Defense Department was due to former defense secretary Donald Rumsfeld, who was more interested in foreign policy than previous secretaries of Defense. However, several respondents, while acknowledging Defense officials do influence foreign policy, contended that much of their foreign policy role involves implementing the policy decisions made by others. One bureaucrat stated the influence of Defense officials "depends on the issue. On many issues, they look to State and civilians to make policy, and then they carry it out." A few respondents noted that the Defense Department officials also bring domestic concerns to the policymaking process, such as military bases and jobs. One committee staffer argued that "with Defense officials, it's not just the abstract foreign policy world. It brings in the military-defense complex and the districts they are located in. We're talking about bases[, too.]"

Bureaucrats at the Department of State were also rated as having an above average amount of influence. Several respondents indicated that part of the influence of State Department careerists is derived from the fact that the president's time is finite, and foreign policy making upon which the president does not have the time to concentrate becomes institutionalized within the State Department. While some respondents asserted that the sway of State Department bureaucrats is lower in the Bush administration than in previous presidential administrations, others argued that such sentiments were off the mark. One ethnic group leader asserted that the influence of career bureaucrats depended on the presidential administration as well as "how the Secretary [of State] organizes his or her structures." As with Department of Defense officials, some congressional staffers offered that State Department bureaucrats affect the implementation of policies developed by Congress and the president, thereby increasing the influence of State careerists. Several respondents expressed discontent that State careerists have a substantial effect on foreign policy. One committee staffer bemoaned the ability of State Department bureaucrats to protect institutionalized policies and thwart the desire of Congress to develop new approaches to foreign policy. One ethnic group leader confided that career bureaucrats at State have "much more [influence] than we like," although another asserted that it isn't the careerists who are influential in the State Department, but the presidential appointees who are "in the driver's seat."

Of the remaining actors included in the survey, only members of Congress and committee staffers were rated as having an above average amount of influence over foreign policy. A major theme to emerge from the interviews was that the influence of members of Congress varied greatly, in part because most members of Congress do not focus on foreign policy. While some members are very interested in foreign affairs, other members, in the words of one policymaker, "don't have a passport, and state publicly that they will never have a passport," and have virtually no interest in affecting foreign policy. An ethnic group leader agreed, adding, "committee assignments compel some members to deal with foreign policy, but that leaves 400 who don't have to." Respondents indicated that members who serve on relevant committees, who have established themselves as policy experts, or who have demonstrated a long-term interest in a foreign policy issue, have the greatest ability to influence foreign policy making. Nonetheless, several bureaucrats rated the influence of members of Congress as being quite high, and a third of the bureaucrats interviewed commented on the fact that Congress controls the appropriation process, which increases the power of members of Congress. As a result, executive agencies "pay attention" to representatives and senators, even junior representatives who don't serve on important committees. Several congressional staffers discussed the means used by interested members of Congress to influence foreign policy. One staffer stated:

> Even if a particular piece of legislation is not adopted, the mere process— the notification procedures, the disbursement of funds, oversight—means that members do directly affect the issue. Sometimes it is individual members. Sometimes it is members using the committee process. Members may hold or delay disbursement of funds by requiring greater information. They may secure enough support to block or push forward a particular program. Through the general authorization process, there are departments in State that have originated because of one individual member of Congress who felt strongly about an issue.

One policymaker also asserted that the Senate's advice and consent role in approving ambassador appointments increases the influence of the Congress as a whole.

Committee staffers assist the legislative process through a host of functions, including policy analysis, drafting legislation, and recruiting witnesses for hearings. Committee staffers differ from personal staffers because the former are assigned to specific committees, while the latter work directly for an individual member of Congress. Respondents for this project rated committee staffers as having almost as much sway as individual members of Congress.[10] In the words of one careerist at the State Department, committee staffers are "not as influential as members, but these are key staffers of key members we care a lot about. They're players because their member is a player, but they are also players in their own right." According to this bureaucrat, because committee staffers work for some of the most powerful members of Congress, "even deputy assistant secretaries (in State) are deferential and polite to committee staffers." The bureaucrat went on to state that some committee staffers have a great deal of expertise, and some have been working in foreign policy for twenty years. Other respondents agreed that committee staffers tend to possess the experience and expertise that imbue influence. Several Capitol Hill policymakers asserted that while the level of influence of committee staffers may depend in part on the level of discretion given to them by the member of Congress to whom they are assigned, "committee staffers are policy experts and help set the tone" for the committee or subcommittee work. Several personal and committee staffers argued that because committee staffers are more central to the legislative process, they have a significant influence. One staffer stated that committee staffers "shape the legislative process through scheduling hearings, selecting topics, picking witnesses, drafting legislation, framing the legislative debate, and picking amendments. Of course, this is all dependent on the Members," but the committee staffers have a great deal of influence over the process. "In terms of drafting legislation, members don't write this stuff, [committee] staffers do." Members read the proposed legislation, and then accept it, give feedback and make changes, or reject it. Several Capitol Hill policymakers gave the example of the delay in the vote on selling F-16s to Pakistan as a symbolic example of the ability of committee staffers to influence the policymaking process.

All of the remaining actors, including ethnic groups, were rated as having a moderate to below average effect on foreign policy. A group of mostly domestic nongovernmental actors, including the media, business groups, ethnic American groups, nonelected elites, personal staffers, public opinion, and congressional constituents, were appraised as having a moderate influence.[11] Interviewees noted the ability of the media to call attention to events, particularly tragedies and potential controversies. One ethnic group leader stated that "a *Post* article, or a *New York Times* editorial, can be more important than twenty members of Congress or ten Senators. [The Supreme Court nomination of] Harriet Miers was not a foreign policy issue, but the media played an important role in derailing that. The Dubai [port management] issue . . . is similar," and the press drove a lot of that issue. One careerist at the State Department contended that "the media helps affect how ordinary Americans react to events, especially negative events." Another bureaucrat agreed, arguing that the media's influence is more pronounced when they highlight the tragedy with photos or video. Several respondents stated that the media was critical in influencing US policies toward Bosnia in the early to mid-1990s. Respondents also indicated that political leaders understand the importance of the media and work to influence the "fourth estate."

Business groups were rated as having the most influence of any organized domestic interest. Respondents indicated that the influence of business groups varied across issue realms and over time. Trade policy was the most commonly cited foreign policy realm that business could affect, but visa waivers, outsourcing, oil and energy, and defense policies were also named as areas business could shape. Although the impact on trade was labeled by some as substantial, some respondents argued business's overall influence on foreign policy was fairly limited. For example, one staffer remarked that business interests often are not driving foreign policy but only "enter the fray after the issue is already moving forward."

In terms of influencing US foreign policy, ethnic groups in general were rated as having a modest impact. Perhaps the single greatest theme to emerge from the study was that the influence of ethnic American groups varies substantially across ethnic groups and lobbies. Nearly all respondents who gave qualitative answers offered that the influence of ethnic groups differs greatly, from group to group and from issue to issue. A typical response was offered by a committee staffer: "[That's] difficult to answer. It varies, frankly, with the ability of different groups. Some are very organized, very focused, so they know how to get their message across to members. Others are diffuse, are not organized, and don't have an impact." Most respondents indicated that only a few ethnic groups are quite influential, while most ethnic groups and lobbies are not. In the words of one bureaucrat, "Sometimes, [ethnic] groups are quite strong. However, across the board, their influence is relatively low." A subtheme to emerge was that ethnic groups derive their power from grassroots lobbying and organizational prowess, which can mobilize group members in a large number of congressional districts, and respondents argued that only five or six ethnic lobbies have this mobilization ability. Still others noted that some ethnic groups enjoy a "coincidence of interests" between the United States and their ancestral homeland. Such groups, such as Jewish Americans and Cuban Americans, appear to be influential because US policies already favor their goals, evidence that groups that promote status quo policies have greater influence.

Nonelected elites, such as think tanks, academics, and other nongovernmental experts, were viewed as enhancing the policymaking process, especially in terms of providing new information to the policymaking process. Several respondents asserted that nonelected elites are active and provide useful information, but the policymakers were uncertain how much nongovernmental elites affected decisionmakers. One senior congressional staffer offered that he attends their briefings, but that think tanks often fail to "take into account . . . political circumstances" when making policy recommendations. Still, this policymaker found the briefings useful.

Although personal staffers assigned to foreign affairs—legislative assistants and senior legislative aides who are charged with the foreign policy portfolios for individual members of Congress—enjoy access to members of Congress, they were rated as having a below average influence over foreign policy making. Several respondents indicated that many personal staffers ostensibly designated as the office's expert on international or foreign affairs really spend little time or energy on these issues. One bureaucrat stated that, on the whole, "they're generally inexpert, rarely engaged in foreign policy." One senior congressional staffer asserted that the influence of personal staffers varies greatly depending on their level of knowledge, experience, and expertise, as well as the level of discretion afforded to them by their members. Still other respondents gave personal staffers higher influence ratings. One bureaucrat stated: "To a good extent [they have influence]. They're the ones who get down in the weeds in a way that members don't." One committee staffer offered that the influence of personal staffers really "depends on the member [of Congress they work for]. Certain staffers *are* the foreign policy decision makers for their offices." Still, personal staffers were rated as having the lowest influence of any governmental actor (aside from congressional caucuses) in the study.

The influence of public opinion was rated as significantly lower than the sway of the media. Still, one congressional staffer asserted that "the president argues he doesn't listen to the public, [that] he does what he thinks is right. But, the Dubai port deal shows the public can affect foreign policy." Other respondents agreed, stating that every president is influenced by public opinion to some degree. Many of those interviewed argued that the role of public opinion varies greatly across issues, and several asserted that the impact of public opinion grows greater the longer the issue is salient to the public. One member of Congress stated: "Over time it does. On a day-by-day basis, it's not as much . . . but it [the influence of mass opinion] goes higher the longer a foreign policy situation is on the front page of the paper." Other respondents concurred with this assessment, but only a few issues, most notably immigration, high gas prices, Israel, and terrorism, were cited as being salient to the public. Beyond those issues, many respondents felt that the broader public was fairly ignorant of foreign affairs, although a subset of the public follows foreign affairs broadly and attentive publics do exist that follow specific issues. One bureaucrat stated: "The public is not interested in foreign policy a lot. Issues like Iraq do interest the public, but on a sustained basis, it is rare that foreign policy becomes a wedge issue." Nonetheless, several respondents indicated that public opinion that is organized by a group can affect members of Congress, and public sentiments may be operationalized every two years via elections. One committee staffer, echoing the views of several respondents, stated that "when it's organized, it forces members to reconsider and evaluate a particular policy. It causes a pause. It may not alter the policy, but it may start the process that will alter the policy. Come election day, there may be a shift in policy." The influence of constituents of members of Congress, a second way of gauging the importance of public sentiments on foreign policy, was rated as somewhat lower than overall public opinion. The experts we interviewed acknowledged that constituent groups can influence the process, and these groups can be ethnic, religious, business, or ideological in nature. However, respondents noted there is wide variation in the effectiveness of such constituents.

The remaining actors, including congressional caucuses, national party leaders, NGOs, international organizations, and foreign lobbies, were ranked as having the least power to influence foreign policy. Many respondents noted that while some congressional caucuses are important, numerous congressional caucuses are inactive, don't have budgets or staffs, and exist largely to appease constituents. Several staffers noted that their members join caucuses when asked to do so by constituents, while one staffer stated the representative "doesn't join caucuses that much. A lot are not very active. It seems disingenuous to join if you know the caucus isn't going to do anything." Two State Department careerists observed that they had not been contacted by a congressional caucus in years.

There was little consensus on the influence of national party leaders, with a few policymakers giving party leaders scores that indicated very little or no influence over foreign policy. Several respondents argued that party leaders can be influential, but they, for the most part, do not focus on issues of foreign affairs and therefore do not exert a great deal of influence over foreign policy. The one exception for these respondents is the continuing war in Iraq. Others disagreed, asserting that Republican party leaders have the ear of the president and, thus, a great deal of influence.

In many respects, the comments about NGOs were similar to the feedback given for nonelected elites: they provide information that may be helpful to policymakers. Indeed, one committee staffer argued that NGOs fall into the same classification as think tanks and academics. A typical response was offered by a committee staffer who said that "NGOs are info providers. They do, from time to time, provide language that can be used to make policy statements." Other policymakers felt that the influence of NGOs is due to their ability to bring attention to issues and crises on which the public and policymakers were not focused. One committee staffer stated that NGOs played an important role in bringing attention to the crisis in Darfur.

Many respondents indicated that many policymakers have little esteem for international organizations (IOs), and, in the words of one bureaucrat, their influence is "pretty low . . . these days." An ethnic leader remarked, "there is widespread contempt for IOs in the Congress and this White House," a sentiment reinforced by a committee staffer who stated: "We tell them to go to hell a lot because they want us to do stupid things that go against the national interest." One bureaucrat observed that while the United States does work with the UN, "I don't know how much influence the UN has on US foreign policy."

Finally, foreign lobbies were rated as having the least influence on foreign policy of any of the actors included in the study. Some ethnic leaders asserted that foreign lobbies can and do influence US foreign policy, since many hire former members of Congress to lobby on their behalf.[12] One ethnic leader argued: "They can have considerable influence. It depends who the lobbyists are. Former members of Congress can go places that others can't go," because former members of Congress enjoy many of the same privileges as serving members.[13] Nonetheless, most policymakers (and a few ethnic leaders) argued the power of foreign lobbies was overstated, and the influence between lobbies can vary dramatically. One bureaucrat stated, "There are a few that are influential, and a lot that are really not." A senior policymaker remarked that the influence of foreign lobbies was "not as much as people think," while a staffer observed, "Some have very good PR campaigns. [However, I'm] not sure that we believe them." One committee staffer asserted: "I throw them [lobbyists for foreign states] out of my office."

In summary, when compared to other actors, ethnic groups in general were gauged as having a decidedly modest effect on the foreign policy–making process. As we might expect, many policymakers were rated as having much greater influence than ethnic groups, and the media and business groups were both viewed as having more sway in foreign policy making. The next section measures much more directly policymaker perceptions regarding whether ethnic groups do have too much influence.

■ Perceptions of Ethnic Group Influence

Policymakers, but not ethnic group leaders, were asked an additional series of questions to better gauge the influence of ethnic lobbies. It is clear from the interviews with policymakers that ethnic groups are quite active in the policymaking process, at least in terms of targeting some congressional offices and bureaus at the Department of State. For example, 77.8 percent of policymakers reported being contacted by ethnic groups on a daily (25 percent) or weekly basis (52.8 percent). In addition, 91.9 percent of policymakers agreed that one or more ethnic groups had tried to persuade them through direct lobbying. However, some congressional offices and some State Department officials reported that they seldom heard from ethnic groups or individuals about ethnic concerns. Surprisingly, given the importance of grassroots lobbying to ethnic groups, only 44.4 percent of Capitol Hill policymakers agreed (33.3 percent disagreed) that an ethnic group had tried to persuade them through a grassroots lobbying campaign. Further, only 20.1 percent of Capitol Hill policymakers agreed, while 42.1 percent disagreed, that an ethnic group had tried to affect at least one of their elections.

Overall, policymakers did not agree that the terrorist attacks of September 11, 2001, decreased lobbying activities of ethnic groups. For example, 62.5 percent of policymakers stated that attempts by interest groups to contact them had remained about the same since September 11, while 31.3 percent believed ethnic groups were more active since 2001. Some policymakers indicated that ethnic group activities declined in the immediate aftermath of September 11, but that ethnic group lobbying soon returned to its previous levels. A number of policymakers noted that Indian American groups became more active after the terrorist attacks, but none of the policymakers believed the increased activity was due primarily to September 11. Others noted that Arab American and Muslim American groups became more active, although some policymakers believed these groups had begun their increased political activism prior to 2001.

It is possible that the terrorist attacks of September 11 galvanized the foreign policy objectives of the United States, creating a consensus that the national interest is to defeat terrorism. Such a consensus could very well reduce the influence of ethnic groups, since ethnic groups would find it harder to advance parochial interests in an environment focused so much on achieving the national interest. Among policymakers, however, there was no consensus that September 11 did decrease the influence of ethnic lobbies compared to the influence of other actors in the foreign policy–making process. A plurality (40.5 percent) did agree that the terrorist attacks decreased the influence of ethnic lobbies, while 32.4 percent disagreed with the statement, and 27 percent neither agreed nor disagreed. Several policymakers noted that the terrorist attacks likely increased the influence of some ethnic lobbies, while decreasing the influence of others. While some analysts predicted that the Israeli lobby might see its influence decrease after September 11, some policymakers argued that the opposite actually occurred. For example, one committee staffer stated that September 11 "increased the influence of the Israel lobby. It's not as if we went into Iraq because of the Israel lobby, but they did a good job selling to the [Bush] administration that there was no divergence of interests between Israel and the US." Another committee staffer noted that "the world has changed. We are all over the place." And, as the scope of US policy has expanded, ethnic groups whose ancestral homelands are affected by the United States are becoming more involved in the foreign policy–making process. Other policymakers argued that the politics of foreign policy have remained the same: what September 11 changed was the actors involved in those politics.

So, if the politics are the same, just how effective are ethnic lobbies? The results of the questions measuring the influence of ethnic groups across different issue realms are presented in Table 6.2. In terms of the overall foreign policy–making process, the mean rating was 2.80, indicating that policymakers believe ethnic groups have a moderate influence on foreign policy making. Examination of the breakdown of responses reveals a similar conclusion: 43.6 percent of respondents agreed that ethnic groups have a "moderate" influence on foreign policy making, 23.1 percent believed the influence is "significant," and 33.3 percent of respondents said that ethnic groups had "somewhat" or "slight" influence (see Figure 6.1). Again, a major trend to emerge from the interviews was that policymakers believe influence differs substantially from group to group, and even from issue to issue: one bureaucrat noted that "ethnic groups can be extremely strong, or next to nothing."

In terms of specific policy domains, respondents gauged the influence of ethnic groups to be most pronounced in the realms of foreign aid, immigration, and human rights (see Figure 6.2). In a number of interviews, policymakers cited the ability of ethnic groups to affect foreign aid appropriations as the best evidence of ethnic group influence. Aid to Israel, Cyprus,

Table 6.2 Ethnic Group Influence by Policy Realms

	Mean	Standard Deviation	N
Overall foreign policy	2.80	0.92	39
Foreign aid policy	2.95	1.00	37
Immigration policy	2.82	0.93	36
Human rights policy	2.77	1.13	37
Military and security policy	2.12	1.09	37
Trade policy	1.99	0.93	36
Oil and energy policy	1.29	1.05	35

Note: Respondent rated the influence of ethnic groups on each issue realm using a scale of 0 to 4. 4 = significant influence; 3 = moderate influence; 2 = somewhat influence; 1 = slight influence; 0 = no influence.

Figure 6.1 Influence of Ethnic Groups on US Policymaking

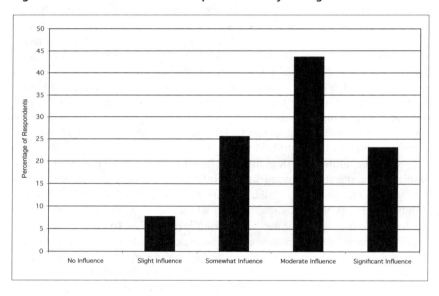

and Armenia was the most often cited example of ethnic groups affecting foreign aid. For example, one official at the State Department offered that "some groups like AIPAC obviously are a crucial factor in the level of foreign assistance we give Israel," and a number of policymakers stated that Jewish Americans help mobilize support for aid to both Israel and Egypt. Another State Department bureaucrat stated: "Look at the $15–20 million in aid to Cyprus. There are 750,000 people. They have a middle-Europe standard of living. . . . It happens because Greek Americans want Congress"

Figure 6.2 Influence of Ethic Groups on Foreign Aid, Human Rights, and Immigration Policies

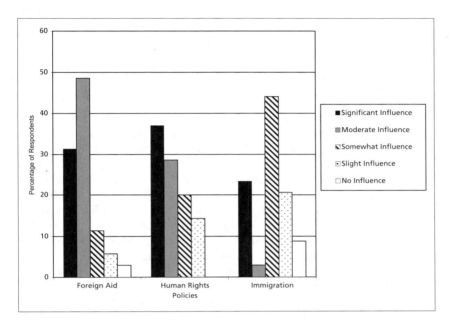

to increase the aid. A committee staffer argued that "Armenian Americans have the greatest influence with foreign aid. It's quite disproportionate to the aid we provide to Armenia's neighbors, like Georgia." Others noted that African American and Jewish American groups have helped to increase aid to Africa for HIV/AIDS and other humanitarian relief.

Immigration reform dominated the headlines at times during the study, and immigration policy was discussed a great deal by policymakers. Some policymakers noted that, despite the protests around the country, not all members of Congress were inundated regarding immigration, with members of Congress from Texas, California, and elsewhere in the Southwest hearing more from constituents than other parts of the country. In addition, senators tended to receive more pressure about immigration than members of the House because the Senate represents larger districts than the House. Still, policymakers gauged that ethnic groups had the second greatest influence in terms of immigration policy, and policymakers stated they receive a great deal of feedback from ethnic groups regarding immigration. Policymakers noted that much of the immigration debate from 2005 to 2007 centered on Hispanics, in part because Central and South American ethnic groups played such a large role in immigration patterns over the past twenty years. Many of these groups find immigration policy to be extremely salient, and they favor policies that reunite families. There are also country-specific issues, such as Hondurans seeking to retain Temporary Protected Status. Hispanic groups are not alone in the immigration debate; many Asian groups also favor family reunification policies, and Irish groups are also active in the issue of immigration and amnesty. In addition, policymakers noted that ethnic groups are by no means given a free pass in terms of immigration, and they face strong countervailing pressure from Anglos and nativists. For example, one State Department official stated that policymakers are "attuned to what American citizens want as opposed to legal residents."

In general, policymakers viewed ethnic groups as having a moderate influence on human rights policy. A number of policymakers contended that ethnic groups provide valuable information regarding human rights abuses in their ancestral homeland, and by doing so, inform members of Congress about abuses that otherwise might be ignored. This effect is maximized when ethnic groups can make direct contact with individual members of Congress through meetings with constituents. Other policymakers noted that some ethnic groups are only concerned about human rights as they pertain directly to their ancestral homeland or even to certain individuals. Still other policymakers asserted that some ethnic groups frame issues as involving "human rights abuses" when the group actually has a much wider agenda in mind. For example, many Cuban Americans would not be satisfied if Castro's record on human rights was improved: they want a regime change. Finally, one policymaker argued that ethnic groups can help ensure that some states are given a "free pass" regarding human rights abuses.

The influence of ethnic groups slips in terms of military and security policy and trade policy, where the mean ratings indicate that respondents assessed ethnic groups to have "somewhat" influence in the issue realms (see Figure 6.3). Many policymakers noted that a number of ethnic groups are involved significantly in trying to affect military and security policy, but, in the words of one bureaucrat, "significant and effective can be two different things." That is, while ethnic groups may be a significant part of the discussion, it doesn't necessarily mean that they have an effect on policy. However, nearly all of the policymakers who offered feedback about ethnic group involvement in military policy stated that Jewish American groups have significantly influenced US military policy toward Israel. Taiwanese Americans and Indian Americans were also cited as attempting to influence US military policies.

In general, most respondents did not view ethnic groups as having a substantial interest in, or effect on, trade policy. One committee staffer stated flatly that "business, not ethnic, groups influence trade policy," while another staffer offered: "Most trade issues are fought between labor and chamber folks, or the business roundtable and environmental groups." Even if ethnic groups are involved in trade issues, many policymakers indicated that the

Figure 6.3 Influence of Ethic Groups on Military and Security, Trade, and Oil and Energy Policies

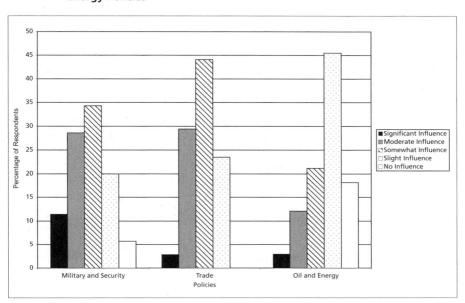

ethnic groups have little effect. One bureaucrat stated: "Economic considerations usually trump ethnic lobbies. Concern over trade with Latin America is usually more important than what Salvadoran Americans or Mexican Americans want." The most commonly cited examples of ethnic group involvement in trade policies centered on concern over free trade agreements, Cuban American groups opposing trade with Cuba, and Indian American groups supporting increased trade with India.

Finally, the effect of ethnic groups falls further when considering the issue of oil and energy policy, where the mean rating indicates that respondents believe ethnic groups have only a slight influence in this area. A majority of policymakers asserted that ethnic groups have, in the words of one staffer, "practically no influence" in this policy realm. One bureaucrat noted, "Most, but not all, of the time, concerns over money and trade outweigh ethnic concerns. Witness our relationship with Saudi Arabia, despite Israel's concerns." A few policymakers did assert that Jewish and pro-Israel groups have an influence on oil policy. For example, one bureaucrat stated, "the Israeli lobby has a fascinating impact on oil and energy policy that we don't usually think about," while a committee staffer stated, "Jewish groups are much more sensitive to the fact that our energy policy is forcing our foreign policy to get into areas that we are in because they have oil."

Speaking more broadly about ethnic group influence in terms of overall policymaking, there is little evidence that policymakers believe that, in general, ethnic groups exert undue influence. For example, only 17.9 percent of respondents agreed with the statement "Ethnic interest groups have too much power in the policymaking process," while 66.7 percent of policymakers disagreed with the statement (see Table 6.3). In addition, there was little support for the proposition that the interests of ethnic lobbies are increasingly superseding the national interest. Only 10.5 percent of policymakers agreed with the statement "Increasingly, US foreign policy reflects ethnic interests and not national interests," while 71.1 percent of respondents somewhat or strongly disagreed with the statement. For example, one bureaucrat asserted, "I think if there has been any movement, it is a slight decrease in the influence of narrow ethnic lobbies, and a slight increase in the influence of broader lobbies." A committee staffer contended that "there are some issues, even cases, where we are making policy based on an ethnic group, but most [decision makers] believe it is in the national interest." Another committee staffer gave a more qualified response, after disagreeing that US foreign policy reflects ethnic interests: "If you asked about American policy in the Middle East, you'd get a different answer." Further, although policymakers acknowledged that specific ethnic groups do have a great deal of influence, 74.4 percent of policymakers agreed that "ethnic interest groups are no more powerful than other domestic groups," while only 7.7 percent of policymakers disagreed with the statement. Business groups were identified by several respondents as being more influential than ethnic groups. One committee

Table 6.3 Perceptions of Policymakers About the Influence of Ethnic Groups

Statement	Mean	Standard Deviation	N
Increasingly, US foreign policy reflects ethnic interests and not national interests.	1.00	1.01	38
Increasingly, ethnic interest groups are influencing congressional elections.	2.34	0.99	38
Ethnic interest groups affect congressional elections no more than other organized groups.	2.68	1.06	37
Increasingly, ethnic interest groups are influencing presidential elections.	2.42	0.89	38
Ethnic interest groups make positive contributions to the policymaking process.	3.18	0.68	39
Ethnic interest groups are no more powerful than other domestic groups.	2.87	0.92	39
Ethnic interest groups have too much power in the policymaking process.	1.31	1.00	39

Note: Respondent responded to each statement using a scale of 0 to 4. 4 = strongly agree; 3 = somewhat agree; 2 = neither agree nor disagree; 1 = somewhat disagree; 0 = strongly disagree.

staffer stated: "On a case-by-case basis, with some issues, ethnic groups are more powerful. But in the aggregate, business is much more powerful than ethnic groups."

A majority (60.5 percent) of policymakers did agree that "increasingly, ethnic interest groups are influencing congressional elections," although nearly all of the policymakers who offered qualitative feedback about this issue believed ethnic group involvement in congressional elections has not increased. Instead, ethnic groups have been players in congressional elections for decades, and what has changed is the mix of ethnic groups that are involved in electioneering. Several policymakers noted that Hispanic groups were "taking a beating" in 2006, but they believed the Hispanic vote is becoming a more important voting bloc. An even larger majority (73.0 percent) supported the statement that "ethnic interest groups affect congressional elections no more than other organized groups." One committee staffer stated ethnic groups probably have less influence than others: "Business interests are more powerful. So are social conservatives on many issues. I can think of four or five interests more powerful than ethnic groups." Another committee staffer noted that "ethnic groups are no stronger than other domestic groups, like the AARP."

There was large support among policymakers for the idea that ethnic groups enrich the policy debate: 84.6 percent of policymakers agreed with the statement that "ethnic interest groups make positive contributions to the policymaking process." Several policymakers stated that ethnic groups help champion issues, especially human rights, that would otherwise be ignored by the policy process. In a similar fashion, others cited the importance of ethnic groups in providing a countervailing voice against other interests, such as business or even other ethnic communities, entrenched in the political process.

■ Too Much Influence? The Follow-Up Study

Despite recognizing the positive contributions of ethnic groups, many respondents indicated that, while they believe ethnic groups in general do not possess too much influence, they do believe that a few ethnic lobbies and groups are too powerful. For example, one committee staffer stated: "There are a few issues that [ethnic] groups have tremendous influence, and a lot where they have none. In terms of Israel policy, on a scale of 0 to 4, ethnic interest groups are a 10. In terms of Rwanda policy and Sudan policy, ethnic groups have zero influence." In order to better ascertain if this is correct, policymakers were reinterviewed in late 2006 and early 2007 and read a statement about each lobby rated as being one of the ten most influential in the original survey.[14] Because there is disagreement among some individuals about the correct term, respondents were first asked about the *Jewish Amer-ican* lobby, and then queried using the term *Israeli American* lobby. The results are presented in Table 6.4 and Figure 6.4, which indicate that most policymakers believe the Cuban American, Israeli American, and Jewish American lobbies have too much influence in the foreign policy–making process: 71.5 percent of policymakers agreed that the Israeli American lobby has too much power; 69.6 percent agreed that the Cuban American lobby is too influential; and 60.9 percent agreed that the Jewish American lobby is too powerful. Of the remaining lobbies, only the Armenian American lobby was perceived as being too powerful by over half of the respondents, with 56.5 percent agreeing with the statement.

Many respondents asserted that the Israeli American lobby is more influential because it affects policies for the entire Middle East. Indeed, several policymakers cited foreign aid to Egypt, US policies toward Iran, and the war in Iraq as issues influenced by the Israeli American lobby. Despite the fact that the term "AIPAC" was not used in the survey, 39 per-cent of policymakers spoke of AIPAC as having a significant influence on foreign policy making. One policymaker declared:

> AIPAC is the 800 pound gorilla. If your survey were not anonymous, no one would mention AIPAC. If word were to leak out, they [those who mentioned AIPAC] would be looking for a new career. No one says any-thing bad about AIPAC. Other lobbies try to emulate AIPAC. The Cuba émigré lobby in Miami has a far disproportionate amount of power, but only over Cuba policy. The Armenian lobby has power over Armenia. But, it is not the same thing as with AIPAC. You can have an honest debate about Cuba, about Armenia. You're not going to get an honest debate over

Table 6.4 Perceptions That Ethnic Lobbies Have Too Much Power

Lobby	Mean Rating	Standard Deviation	N
Cuban American	3.04	1.17	25
Israeli American	3.00	1.16	22
Jewish American	2.84	1.03	25
Armenian American	2.16	1.25	25
Greek American	2.00	0.95	21
Taiwanese American	1.92	0.97	24
Irish American	1.64	1.11	25
Indian (Indo) American	1.50	1.18	24
Hispanic American	1.09	0.85	23
African American	0.88	0.93	25
Italian American	0.67	0.70	24

Note: Policymakers were asked if each of the lobbies has too much power in the foreign policy–making process using a scale of 0 to 4. 4 = strongly agree; 3 = somewhat agree; 2 = neither agree nor disagree; 1 = somewhat disagree; 0 = strongly disagree.

Figure 6.4 Most Influential Ethnic Lobbies: Are the Lobbies Too Powerful?

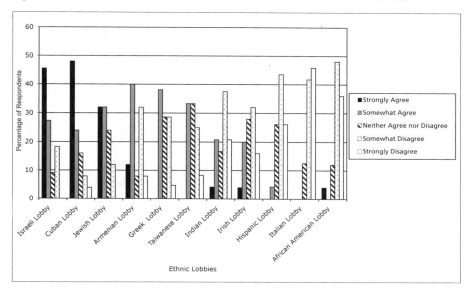

Israel and Palestine and the Middle East. It would be an interesting debate to have members of Congress write their own speeches, without AIPAC's talking points in front of them, and give them in anonymity. On the CSPAN debate, the faces of the members would be blurred. It would not resemble any debate we see in Congress.

Other respondents agreed with the assertion that it is difficult to have an open debate on Middle East policies, indicating that the influence of the Israeli lobby involves agenda control (see Bachrach and Baratz 1962 for discussion of agenda control and power). Several respondents cited the sheer amount of foreign aid given to Israel as evidence that the Israeli American lobby has too much influence.[15]

Like the above policymaker, several other respondents agreed that other ethnic lobbies have tried to emulate AIPAC, but that these other lobbies do not have the same sort of influence. Several stated that while they believe the Cuban American lobby has far too much power, the influence of the lobby is fairly limited only to policies related to Cuba (and electoral politics in southern Florida). In a similar fashion, respondents argued that the influence of the Armenian American lobby is limited to foreign aid to Armenia, US relations with Turkey and Azerbaijan, and the recognition of the Armenian genocide.

A minority of policymakers did not agree that the Cuban, Jewish, and Israeli lobbies have too much power. Most of these respondents reasoned that the policymaking process is pluralistic in nature and, in the words of one interviewee, "Those who speak, speak. Those who don't, don't." Some of these respondents asserted that the Israeli American lobby does not get everything it wants,[16] even when dealing with a friendly administration like the current Bush administration (Stolberg 2006). A few argued that the appearance of too much influence by the lobbies identified as being most powerful is actually a result of flaws of the US political system. For example, one respondent argued that the Cuban American lobby appears powerful because of the importance of Florida in the electoral college: if presidential elections were decided by popular vote instead of the electoral college, Cuban Americans would not exert so much influence on US policies toward Cuba.

Finally, as noted before, some policymakers spoke of the "coincidence of interest between" the United States and the ethnic homeland as exacerbating the influence of the ethnic lobby. Indeed, the two ethnic lobbies cited as being the most powerful, the Israeli and Cuban lobbies, are protecting current US policies and positions, a strategic advantage that may help explain their appearance of influence.[17] In contrast, the Armenian lobby is fighting the status quo by seeking for the United States to formally recognize the 1915 Armenian genocide. To date, the lobby has been extremely vocal but unsuccessful in swaying the executive branch.

■ Conclusion

There is no shortage of examples of ethnic interest groups attempting to influence foreign policy. At times, many Americans don't realize how many foreign policy issues are of interest to at least one ethnic group. For example, before a prominent Hmong American was arrested for plotting to overthrow a foreign government, few Americans likely knew that many Hmong Americans would like to see the United States institute a policy of regime change in Laos (Davey 2007). Other examples, like Hispanic Americans protesting in favor of immigration reform, can dominate the headlines. However, simply because ethnic groups attempt to influence foreign policy does not mean that the groups have their desired effect. Aside from concerns that the Israeli, Cuban, and Armenian American lobbies are too powerful, we found little evidence that ethnic groups, in general, exert too much influence on foreign policy. A large majority of respondents argued that, overall, ethnic groups are just one domestic actor within a pluralistic universe, and other domestic actors, such as business groups and the media, have a greater effect on foreign policy than do ethnic lobbies. As a result, we agree with the findings of Thomas Ambrosio, who writes: "Although in some cases ethnic identity groups may have a disproportionate level of influence over specific policies, it is important not to exaggerate their power. Only in rare circumstances is the influence of a particular ethnic lobby the lone factor in determining policy" (2002c, 212).

As a case in point, consider the 1999 expansion of NATO discussed at the beginning of this book. In-depth analysis of the decisionmaking process by the Clinton administration to push for expansion provides little evidence that the impetus for the policy was securing the votes of ethnic Americans. Rather, there was "the need for the Clinton administration to demonstrate that a Democratic president could conduct foreign and defense policy effectively," especially after the failures absorbed by the administration regarding Bosnia (Goldgeier 1999, 77). For example, Clinton was motivated to seem strong in the face of Russian opposition to NATO expansion. Goldgeier concludes that ethnic politics played more of a role in deciding how to pursue congressional approval of the policy of expansion than in developing the administration's policy toward enlargement. As another example, in the interviews conducted for this project, similar sentiments were echoed about the 2006 US-India Civilian Nuclear Agreement. President Bush was motivated to strike the deal because of nonethnic interests, such as opening Indian markets to US trade and rewarding India's record on nonproliferation. The Bush administration and allies in Congress worked with Indian American groups, but also a host of business and trade organizations, to help secure the passage of the agreement, but not to develop the policy itself.

▦ Notes

1. The theory of issue publics posits that most individuals do not focus their lives on politics and can only devote time and energy to a few issues; the costs associated with following more than a few issues are too high for most individuals; and individuals do not need to be "especially cognitively sophisticated in order for attitudes toward government policies to become personally important" (Krosnick 1990, 72; see also Converse 1964).

2. Foreign entities also must register with the US Department of Justice in order to comply with the Foreign Agents Registration Act (FARA) of 1938 and its subsequent amendments. However, because foreign principals may lobby policymakers directly, FARA has made only a "marginal impact on everyday lobbying operations in Washington" (Schlozman and Tierney 1986, 54).

3. In pretesting of the survey instrument, several respondents stated that labor unions should be included in the broader category of nongovernmental organizations.

4. Further, some foreign policy officials consider the opinions of members of Congress to be a measure of public opinion (Cohen 1973; Powlick 1991).

5. Questions were worded broadly to inquire about the influence of institutions more than individuals. For example, respondents were asked, "On a scale of 0–100, how much does the president affect US foreign policy?" and not "On a scale of 0–100, how much does President George W. Bush affect US foreign policy?" Despite this, some respondents gave examples relating to the current Bush administration. Nonetheless, we believe the data are valuable, since they help gauge the relative influence of actors, providing a yardstick for future studies.

6. The means for White House staffers and Department of Defense officials are statistically indistinguishable, while the mean for State Department bureaucrats is significantly lower than the mean for White House staffers ($t = 2.56$, $p = .014$) and Defense officials ($t = 2.36$, $p = .023$). The mean for State Department bureaucrats is statistically indistinguishable from that for members of Congress.

7. The term *White House staffers* includes the NSC and other staffers who serve in the executive office of the president.

8. One committee staffer gave an administrative-specific critique that since 2003 or so, the NSC is no longer empowered to coordinate and direct the foreign policy decisionmaking process and instead "the career bureaucrats [at State] are driving policy. You can't get the White House's and president's position. If you call, NSC refers the matter to State, and the career bureaucrats give the position."

9. Many of these same respondents expressed reservations over this trend. For example, one senior Republican policymaker stated that Department of Defense officials had more influence "than I would like" over foreign policy.

10. Personal and committee staffers as a whole did not inflate their own influence in the survey: staffers rated personal staffers and committee staffers as having less influence than did other respondents. Among nonstaffers, the mean influence score for committee staffers was 61.9, while staffers rated committee staffers as having a score of 57.4. Among nonstaffers, the mean influence score for personal staffers was 53.1. In contrast, staffers rated personal staffers as having an influence score of 39.5.

11. Most of the mean ratings for this cluster are statistically indistinguishable, although the mean ratings for business groups and the news media were significantly higher than the means for nonelected elites, public opinion, personal staffers, and congressional constituents.

12. For example, Bob Livingston (R-LA) formed the Livingston Group after resigning from Congress in 1999. By 2001, the lobbying firm's single biggest client was the government of Turkey (Albert 2001). The firm's website lists six "senior counselors" who served in the US House of Representatives.

13. Former members can "roam freely on the House and Senate floors, in the House gym and in areas of the Capitol that are otherwise 'members only'" (Birnbaum 2005, A19).

14. We were able to contact twenty-six of the original forty-one policymakers for a follow-up interview.

15. Most respondents who made this argument provided one of two comparative justifications for their statement: either Israel has a fairly small population, or Israelis enjoy a fairly high standard of living. Some respondents made both arguments.

16. For example, the 1996 Iran-Libya Sanctions Act, which extended a commercial ban on Iran and sanctioned foreign companies that invested in Iran, was authored in part by AIPAC. However, the legislation only dealt with Iran originally, and AIPAC opposed adding Libya to the bill. AIPAC was unable to prevent Libya from being included in the act (Lancaster 2000).

17. It is arguable that these lobbies did help establish the status quo. DeConde (1992) and others assert that Jewish Americans and other friends of Israel helped sway US policy toward Israel beginning in the 1940s. Likewise, Haney and Vanderbush (1999) and others contend that Cuban Americans influenced US policies toward Cuba. Ironically, these examples occurred *during* the Cold War, when many scholars posit that ethnic groups had *less* influence over foreign policy because the United States had a clearly defined national interest. Thus, the two lobbies, which many policymakers believe have too much influence, achieved their strategic advantage during a period that, in theory, should have retarded their ability to exert undue influence.

7

Reassessing the Power
of Ethnic American Lobbies

The perceived expansion of ethnic group influence in foreign policy has led some to worry that ethnic groups now have too much power to determine national policies. In short, critics worry that parochial interests can and do override the national interest. Are these assessments accurate? To help address these concerns, this book sought to address two main and inter-related questions: First, which ethnic lobbies are most powerful, and why? Second, how does the power of ethnic lobbies compare with business, labor, elites, and public opinion? This chapter summarizes the findings of the book, as well as how these findings speak to the controversies regarding the role that ethnic groups play in determining foreign affairs.

▨ Which Groups Have Influence?

The greatest theme to emerge from the study was that the influence of ethnic American groups varies substantially across ethnic organizations, ethnic lobbies, and even across issue realms. The survey of policymakers and Washington insiders provides a useful benchmark for gauging the relative influence of thirty-eight ethnic lobbies. While there may be some disagreement on the proper terminology, the Jewish or Israeli lobby was rated by far as the most powerful ethnic lobby in terms of overall influence in the foreign policy–making process. This is due to a number of factors. There is no doubt that many Jewish Americans find foreign policy to be an important issue, and significant events, such as the Six Day War, help maintain the saliency of US-Israel relations for many Jewish Americans. Policymakers interviewed for this project made it clear that the Jewish lobby is the best organized ethnic lobby, and it is represented by several sophisticated organizations that understand the policymaking process extremely well. Those organizations tap into, and help maintain, a remarkable network that is adept at grassroots lobbying. Further, Jewish Americans participate at very high levels in politics: estimates of voter turnout rates among Jewish Americans are extremely high, Jewish Americans are active in electoral politics, and Jewish Americans are represented extremely well in Congress. Although data are not available regarding individual contributions to federal candidates for all ethnic groups, we do know that Jewish and pro-Israel PACs dominate the ethnic PAC contributions, even if pro-Israel PACs constitute a modest role in the overall PAC universe.

The Cuban American lobby was ranked as the second most influential lobby. Many Cuban Americans find foreign policy to be very salient, and Cuban Americans are well organized. Cuban Americans also have strong representation in Congress, and the Cuban American delegation is focused on preserving the policy of isolating the Castro regime. Is the Cuban lobby's influence declining? The signs are mixed. On the one hand, Cuban American organizations have not reported lobbying expenditures since 2001, and some respondents stated that the influence of CANF has slipped. And while foreign policy is still salient to many Cuban Americans, there is growing evidence of a generational divide, in which younger Cuban Americans do not give the same importance to regime change as older Cuban Americans.[1] On the other hand, a new Cuban American PAC has emerged that supports continuing the trade embargo, contributing $214,000 to federal candidates in 2004 and almost $570,000 in 2006, a sign that the hard-line Cuban lobby is very much alive. It is important to remember that Cuban Americans are a smaller and more concentrated ethnic group than Jewish Americans, so the overall grassroots potential of the Cuban lobby is lower than that of the Jewish lobby. However, since many Cuban Americans desire to maintain the status quo, the lobby is in an influential position. It must maintain veto points, which it can do by electing brethren and ideologically like-minded candidates to key congressional positions. If the Cuban lobby was faced with the opposite task, passing new legislation to impose an embargo, then the lobby would almost certainly fail. Other groups, most notably business groups, would be able to use veto points to kill the legislation.

The next seven lobbies rated by respondents as being the most influential—the Irish, Armenian, Hispanic, Taiwanese, African, Greek, and Indian American lobbies—all received fairly indistinguishable mean influence scores. Each of these lobbies has significant organizational resources, the ability to initiate grassroots campaigns, and the capacity to raise substantial campaign contributions. Yet each of these lobbies has a limitation. The Armenian, Taiwanese, and Greek lobbies are promoting policies—recognizing the Armenian genocide, ending the One China Policy and formally recognizing Taiwan, and weakening relations with Turkey—that are changes to the status quo, thus placing the lobbies at a strategic disadvantage. The other lobbies—most notably the Hispanic lobby, but also the Irish, African, and Indian lobbies—represent ethnic communities that do not find foreign policy to be as salient as Jewish, Cuban, and Armenian Americans. For these reasons, all of these seven lobbies have achieved some influence in foreign policy, yet none of these lobbies rises to the influence of the Jewish or Cuban American lobbies.

The remaining lobbies included in the survey may at times influence foreign affairs, but their overall impact on foreign affairs appears to range from modest to marginal. Each of the remaining lobbies has a significant impediment to success, whether it be a lack of organizational or other resources, low levels of salience toward foreign policy, and/or seeking goals that represent a significant shift of the status quo.

Key Findings About the Factors That Contribute to Influence

The size of an ethnic group is an important source of political influence, since a large grassroots network can be instrumental in influencing Congress. While the statistical analysis does demonstrate that larger ethnic groups do have more influence, there are ample examples of small groups with strong grassroots organizations, such as Armenian Americans, having a significant influence on policymaking. In other words, having a large population is not a necessary precondition for influence, because groups do not need large numbers to gain access to policymakers. Our interviews with members of Congress and congressional staffers showed that the offices of members of Congress were open to their constituents, regardless of the size of the ethnic community in the district. Indeed, we found that group members could live in nearby districts within the same state and still gain access to members of Congress. This example points to the power of a well-organized ethnic group to identify members of their ethnic community throughout the United States to mount grassroots lobbying campaigns.

Larger groups may enjoy greater sway once they have access, forcing a member of Congress to weigh the pros and cons of pleasing or alienating a sizeable minority of his or her constituency. Larger groups may also benefit from having members of their ethnic community living throughout the United States, thereby increasing the odds that the ethnic group can gain access to more offices on Capitol Hill. We found that groups that have organized communities within a congressional district do appear to have ready access to their representatives. Some members of Congress are seen as champions of certain ethnic groups, and this is often due in part to the sizeable ethnic communities that populate their districts. However, in several cases, this advocacy on the part of some members of Congress may be due more to their own personal values than to the work of ethnic groups. For example, the intolerance for the Castro regime displayed by Representatives Lincoln Diaz-Balart (R-FL) and Mario Diaz-Balart (R-FL) is in large part due to their own life experiences (Goodnough 2006). We doubt their support of the embargo on Cuba would be any lower if they represented districts in other states. Nonetheless, the Cuban American communities in their districts do provide political support for their policy stances, allowing these members of Congress to take a very hard line, which almost certainly irritates some constituents who would benefit from trade with Cuba.

In addition, organizational resources play a critical role in explaining ethnic group influence. Not only were organizational resources found to be significant in the statistical analysis, but policymakers often explicitly discussed the most influential ethnic groups in terms of their organizational prowess. Strong organizations are critical for monitoring the policymaking process, producing policy briefs, building ties with policymakers and the media, and organizing grassroots campaigns. It is telling that eight of the nine ethnicities rated as being the most influential are represented by organizations that are dedicated to foreign policy concerns. The analysis presented in Chapter 5 also demonstrated that financial resources—both household income and PAC contributions—play a significant role in the influence of ethnic lobbies, even when controlling for other factors such as the population, issue saliency, and organizational strength. It is likely that monetary resources help facilitate political participation, which in turn increases the influence of the ethnic group.

Likewise, both the qualitative and quantitative analyses indicate that issue salience plays an important role in determining ethnic group influence. Policymakers interviewed for this project stated that ethnic groups are frequently able to persuade members of Congress to support the group's position because the issue is important to constituents and there exists little reason for the representatives to oppose the group's stance. In the absence of another set of constituents who strongly object to the position, a member of Congress will often choose to support the vocal minority because the group feels fervently about the issue. The existence of an enemy or historical trauma may increase the influence of an ethnic group, probably because those factors help increase mobilization. Assimilation may play a role as well, as the statistical analysis indicated that the retention of linguistic heritage is a significant predictor of influence. It is possible that ethnic groups that retain their linguistic heritage may find foreign policy concerns to be more salient. Further research should examine if these two factors are indeed interconnected. Finally, the analysis suggests that championing established policies is a significant predictor of influence. The analysis supports the hypothesis that ethnic groups that defend the status quo do enjoy a strategic advantage that translates into greater influence.

In interviews with policymakers, we found two factors that diminish the effectiveness of ethnic communities. First, ethnic communities that are divided will have a much harder time influencing the policymaking process. Indeed, competing groups from the same ethnicity provide countervailing effects within their own communities. Policymakers stated that the Eritrean and Iranian communities are good examples of this. Second, ethnic groups that lobby in support of a foreign leader whose own policies are repugnant are not likely to have a great deal of influence in the policymaking process, at least in the post–Cold War era. For example, one policymaker contended that Eritrean Americans who support Isaias Afewerki "almost have a negative influence [because] the Eritrea government is behaving so badly." Likewise, another policymaker argued that during the Balkan conflict in the early 1990s, "Serbian Americans absolutely failed miserably to influence foreign policy. . . . [They] kept focusing on the idea that Serbia was under attack, and could never get through their heads the larger American and Serbian interest in getting Milosevic out of there."

Some ethnic groups are united in their desire to remove the leader or regime of their ancestral homeland. These communities may model themselves after Cuban Americans, who have achieved a great deal of perceived and real influence. However, at least until 2003, the United States generally did not advocate regime change as a policy. Because of this, groups like Ethiopian Americans and Hmong Americans that advocate a policy of forcing regime change, instead of the more traditional (and, hence, closer to the status quo) policies of using diplomatic, economic, and other avenues to influence foreign states, are less likely to enjoy influence than other ethnic groups. The 2003 preemptive invasion of Iraq may provide some hope to such American communities that the United States will take more aggressive positions toward the regimes that rule their ancestral homeland, but we believe such instances will be rare.

In contrast, ethnic American groups that enjoy a good relationship with the leaders of their ancestral homelands do, in general, enjoy greater influence in the policymaking process. For example, the Jewish American, Armenian American, Greek American, and, now, Indian American lobbies enjoy a great deal of influence, at least among the ethnic American lobbies. This is likely due in part to the strategic advantage of having both the ethnic American groups and their foreign counterparts advocating for the same policies.

Key Findings About Ethnic Group Formation and Maintenance

Our research underscores the role that entrepreneurs play in ethnic interest groups. In several cases, the groups formed because of a single individual who overcame the collective action problem personally. For example, Father Sean McManus reported that he formed the Irish National Caucus because he found no formal Irish advocacy organization in Washington, DC, in the early 1970s. Other groups were resurrected because of a new leader. In some cases, the entrepreneur *is* the interest group and even the entire lobby. For example, it is likely that the Kurdish lobby would cease to exist if Kani Xulam quit his advocacy work. Broader human rights groups might continue to advocate for the Kurds, but the American Kurdish Information Network and the broader sense of a Kurdish American lobby are dependent upon Xulam. That fact helps show the weakness of the Kurdish lobby and others like it whose institutional capacities are severely limited. In the absence of a key individual, these lobbies would disappear.

Others seem to wither when a leader dies or leaves the organization. To help prevent this from happening, the stronger organizations become institutions, so that their leader is not as critical to their success, and their power does not ebb and flow as much as noninstitutionalized organizations. The Polish American Congress, once considered a powerhouse of an ethnic lobby, was also described as "literally a mom-and-pop shop" consisting of Casimir and Myra Lenard (Longworth 1998). However, for much of the study, we found little evidence that the Polish American Congress was engaging in the policymaking process; only since February 2007 did the organization again start issuing action alerts to mobilize Polish Americans. By relying too heavily on one individual (just Casmir Lenard until his death in 2007; Myra Lenard died in 2000), the PAC risked ceasing to have any organized presence in the foreign policy–making process. To give another example, Ethiopian Americans will likely need to evolve beyond individual leaders and form institutional organizations in order to become a more lasting, effective voice in the policymaking process.

This study lends evidence to support Tony Smith's hypothesis (2000) that the threshold for an ethnic interest group to gain access to and have the opportunity to affect the policymaking process is a budget of approximately $1 million and 250,000 voters across a few congressional districts. Several organizations studied here are relatively small outfits, operating with a few paid employees and relatively modest budgets. However, by being well organized and forging both short-term and long-term alliances and relationships with other ethnic and nonethnic organizations, the entities studied here are able to leverage their resources and, at times, achieve impressive results. Undoubtedly, technological advancements have aided these small organizations, as desktop publishing programs let groups produce professional and specialized publications, cell phones enable scarce employees to multitask and conduct business for the organization even while traveling or commuting, e-mail allows groups to contact their members both quickly and inexpensively, and the Internet enables organizations to champion issues, publicize issue positions, and distribute information and persuasive arguments to a very wide audience. These technological innovations help large organizations as well, but modernization is likely to be more important to small organizations, allowing them to better compete with bigger and better-financed shops.

◼ Comparing Ethnic Group Influence to Other Actors

While the policymaking experts interviewed did assert that ethnic interest groups do have influence in the foreign policy–making process, the findings indicate that the impact of ethnic groups is similar to that of other domestic actors that are not part of the government, such as the media, business groups, and nonelected elites. Indeed, the media and business groups were both rated as having more influence than ethnic groups, and the mean relative influence of the media (nearly 1.00) was significantly greater than the mean relative influence of ethnic groups (nearly .92).[2] In most cases, policymakers such as the president, State Department bureaucrats, members of Congress, and committee staffers were credited with much greater influence than ethnic groups or other nongovernmental actors. These findings are supported by other research which demonstrates that presidents have a much greater sway on foreign policy than members of Congress (who might be unduly affected by ethnic interest groups), foreign policy is often influenced by business interests more than ethnic interests, and ideological considerations have as great as or a larger effect on foreign policy than ethnic considerations (Weissman 1995).

It is possible that the true influence of ethnic groups is actually greater, since these groups can affect actors who are embedded in the government, such as members of Congress and congressional staffers. However, it is worth noting that the actors identified as having the greatest effect on foreign policy are the very actors that are *most immune to ethnic group influence because they are the most difficult for ethnic groups to access.*[3] While ethnic groups can arrange appointments with their elected representatives in Congress fairly easily, meetings with the president, White House staffers, and Department of Defense officials are much more difficult to obtain. And while ethnic groups can and do contact Department of State careerists, the ability of ethnic groups to influence bureaucrats, such as State Department officials, is more difficult than, say, congressional staffers. Because the Department of State reports to the president, and because State Department careerists do not stand for election, State Department bureaucrats and officials have greater ability to rebuff proposed changes to established foreign policy proposed by ethnic (and other) interest groups.

A good example of this is the recognition of the Armenian genocide of 1915, an issue championed a great deal by Armenian American groups. A large number of congressional offices may support recognizing the genocide officially, but a resolution to recognize the Armenian genocide has been stalled consistently in Congress. Even when elections were potentially at stake, House leaders have refused to allow a floor vote on a genocide resolution. For example, in October 2000, Speaker of the House Dennis Hastert (R-IL) canceled a floor vote on a genocide resolution after intense lobbying by President Bill Clinton, despite the fact that Hastert had promised fellow Republican James Rogan that a floor vote would be allowed. With the change of partisan control of Congress after the 2006 midterm elections, many Armenians hoped that Speaker of the House Nancy Pelosi (D-CA), a longtime supporter of the genocide resolution, would allow a floor vote as soon as April 2007 (Arsu and Knowlton 2007). However, the Bush administration and the government of Turkey argue strongly that a floor vote would severely damage US-Turkey relations, and it is not clear that a floor vote will ever occur. Just as a Republican-controlled Congress acquiesced to a Democratic president's concern over the effects of the Armenian genocide resolution in 2000, the 110th Congress also appears to be bowing to considerable pressure not to pass the resolution because it could significantly harm the national interest. After the US House Foreign Affairs Committee approved the Armenian Genocide Resolution on October 10, 2007, and it appeared to be headed for a floor vote, President Bush and Turkey increased their efforts to squash the resolution. Citing that US-Turkey relations would be harmed by a floor vote, seventeen representatives withdrew their support for the legislation, enough to kill the measure. It is now very doubtful that the resolution will be brought to the floor anytime soon.

Even if Congress were to pass a resolution "calling on the President to ensure that the foreign policy of the United States reflects appropriate understanding and sensitivity concerning issues related to human rights, ethnic cleansing, and genocide documented in the United States record relating to the Armenian Genocide," the president would not be required to use the word *genocide*, and both Democratic and Republican presidential administrations have refused to do so. As a result, State Department bureaucrats and officials will not use the term *genocide* to label the mass killings of 1915. For example, one State employee, when asked to give examples of how ethnic groups try to influence the foreign policy–making process, answered that a good example of ethnic group activism is the efforts by Armenian American groups to pass resolutions condemning the "quote and unquote Armenian genocide." When asked why the respondent put quotation marks around the term *Armenian genocide*, the official answered: "That is an historical judgment. Clearly something terrible happened, but I don't like to throw around the term 'genocide,' so I'll leave that to the historians." Others interviewed at State gave similar answers. Another State bureaucrat directed us to the official White House position on the subject, which refers to "terrible and tragic events" but does not use the term *genocide*.

The effort by Armenian Americans to get the United States to recognize the Armenian genocide was the second most cited example of ethnic group activity in this study, behind only the efforts of AIPAC and other pro-Israeli groups to promote strong ties between the United States and Israel. Nonetheless, the influence of the Armenian American lobby was not ranked as second by respondents; it was ranked as fourth. While the Armenian lobby is widely recognized by policymakers as being very active, skillfully organized, and well funded, the lobby has been unsuccessful in achieving one of its biggest goals: official recognition of the Armenian genocide by the US government. In part, the inability of Armenian Americans and others to achieve this goal is due to the fact that existing US policy is not to recognize the genocide. Recognition of the genocide represents a significant shift of the status quo, and Armenian Americans have, to date, been unable to overcome that significant hurdle.

The failure to achieve the goal is also due in large part to the insular nature of the executive branch. While Armenian American groups are successful in achieving goals that are largely decided by Congress, such as maintaining parity of military assistance funding between Armenia and Azerbaijan, the Armenian American lobby has far less sway over the executive. Several experts interviewed for this project attributed this to the ability of Armenian Americans to gain wide access to the offices of members of Congress, while having much less success in gaining access to the White House. In interviews conducted with leaders of Armenian American groups, the ethnic group leaders acknowledged a frustration with their lack of access to the White House. Thus, the Armenian genocide example illustrates the limits to ethnic group influence in the foreign policy–making process. Ethnic groups can and do enjoy access to the legislative branch, but their influence is largely limited to the branch of government that is *not* the institution with the greatest foreign policy power. While ethnic groups may find they are pushing on an open door on Capitol Hill, many are pushing against a closed door at the White House. Access is the key to influence in a pluralistic society, and most ethnic groups don't have access to the White House.

Assessing the Role of Ethnic Contributions to Candidates

In general, we found little support for the idea that ethnic PACs are dangerous to the electoral system. Many ethnic organizations purposely eschew PACs so as not to violate their nonprofit status. Others gave more practical reasons for not partaking in campaign financing: they want to remain bipartisan and avoid alienating candidates and officeholders, or group leaders believe the paperwork associated with running a PAC is not worth the effort.

Although four dozen or so ethnic PACs do exist, their contributions to federal campaigns are modest as a whole, since PACs can only give $10,000 per election cycle to any given candidate.

Of greater concern are the individual contributions by members of an ethnic lobby to federal candidates, which can easily outpace PAC contributions. The Center for Responsive Politics (CRP) reports that pro-Israel individual contributions can be double the amount given by pro-Israel PACs, although the ratio of individual contributions to PAC contributions has averaged 1.45:1. In its report on the Cuban lobby, CRP reported that the ratio of individual contributions to PAC contributions was 4.58:1 from 1982 to 2000. If the figures released from Armenian National Committee of America (2005) are correct, then the ratio of individual contributions to PAC contributions by Armenians was an astonishing 32.5:1. According to the ANCA report, in the 2004 election Armenian Americans gave more to federal candidates and parties ($3.9 million) than individuals associated with the pro-Israel lobby ($2.9 million).

Likewise, other research has indicated that Jewish Americans contribute more than the Center for Responsive Politics is able to capture in its calculations. For example, one study estimated that Jewish Americans contributed at least $13 million to Democratic presidential candidates Al Gore and Bill Bradley and $3.75 million to Republican presidential candidates in 2000 (Edsall 2002). In contrast, the CRP reports that the pro-Israel lobby gave $3.9 million in individual contributions to all federal candidates in 2000. Future research could center on the degree to which individual-based ethnic contributions are fueling congressional and presidential races.

The ANCA report begs the question: Are Armenian Americans buying members of Congress? The 2005 ANCA report listed the members of Congress who received the greatest levels of contributions by Armenians: Representative Frank Pallone (D-NJ), Representative Joe Knollenberg (R-MI), Senator Mitch McConnell (R-KY), Representative Adam Schiff (D-CA), and Representative George Radanovich (R-CA). Representatives Schiff and Radanovich have large Armenian American enclaves in their districts, and Representative Knollenberg also has a sizeable Armenian population in his district, so one can argue that these members of Congress are responding to important constituent groups. Indeed, that is what members of Congress are supposed to do: represent local interests at the national level. In contrast, Representative Pallone and Senator McConnell do not have sizeable Armenian populations in their districts, so it is more difficult to argue that they are responding to constituent groups. While New Jersey does have a sizeable Armenian population, most Armenians live in other districts in the state. Nonetheless, Pallone has long championed recognizing the Armenian genocide, and he was a cofounder of the Armenian congressional caucus in 1995 (Auerbach 1995). We contacted Pallone's office and spoke to staffer Tiffany

Guarascio to inquire about what caused Pallone to become a champion of recognizing the Armenian genocide. She gave three reasons: Pallone lives across the street from an Armenian church and he has close contact with the community; one of Pallone's first staffers was an Armenian American who was very passionate about the issue; and Pallone is interested in international affairs and is fascinated by that region of the world and its history. We then contacted the former staffer, Rosalie Chorbajian. Chorbajian was a congressional staffer for Pallone's predecessor, Representative James Howard, who died in office in 1988. When Pallone was elected to fill the vacant seat, Chorbajian continued as a staffer for Pallone until her retirement in 1995. I asked Chorbajian why Armenian Americans were so supportive of Pallone. She replied that, as with Representative Howard, she had told Pallone about her family's experience, specifically that her father's family was massacred during the Armenian genocide, and her father only escaped because he was not at home at the time. She gave Pallone information on the issue, including that opponents of the genocide call the events a civil war. Pallone became a champion of recognizing the genocide, and Armenian Americans were very grateful for his support. So, while Armenian Americans have clearly rewarded Pallone with campaign contributions, it does not appear that Pallone's legislative behavior was driven by the promise of large donations from Armenian Americans. Indeed, the opposite appears much more likely: Pallone championed the issue after being elected, which led Armenian Americans to contribute to his campaigns.[4]

■ Assessing the Influence of Individual Lobbies

Again, the major theme to emerge from the study was that ethnic groups, in general, do not have undue influence on foreign policy. Instead, the influence of ethnic American groups varies substantially across ethnic lobbies, organizations, and issues, and it is possible that individual ethnic lobbies may exert tremendous influence on the policymaking process.

The Israel lobby was clearly ranked as the most influential ethnic lobby. Can we better conceptualize the influence of Jewish Americans, as opposed to the Israel lobby, on US foreign policy? One potential way of doing this is to imagine what US foreign policy might be, to paraphrase President Dwight Eisenhower, if there were not one Jewish person in America. At one time, the absence of Jewish Americans might have slowed US support for Israel. Perhaps Harry Truman would not have so quickly recognized Israel in 1948 if he lacked Jewish American advisors, although the horrors of the Holocaust did contribute to support among Americans for a Jewish state. Perhaps John F. Kennedy would not have sold US military hardware to Israel in 1963 if Jewish Americans were not an important part of his electoral base. But much of the support for Israel during the Cold War was based not just upon religious affinity but also upon ideology and pragmatism, and the United States needed an ally in the region to help fight the spread of communism. Through this lens, US support of Israel was seen as a way to damage "Moscow's reputation as an ally while enhancing U.S. prestige," and Israel provided important military intelligence to the United States, including access to Soviet equipment (Mearsheimer and Walt 2007, 52).

Even with the end of the Cold War, a great deal of the support in the United States for Israel comes from neoconservatives such as former US ambassador to the UN John Bolton and columnist George Will (Mearsheimer and Walt 2007). For example, Will argued widely that Israel should conduct a short war, which should eliminate Palestinian infrastructure, "including all newspaper and broadcasting facilities," and then build a tall wall that should include all of Jerusalem (2001, A23). Other support comes from evangelical Christians and Christian Zionists who developed a significant grassroots network to support Israel and who "have access to the White House and strong support within Congress" (Lampman 2004, 15). Supporters outside of Congress include Republican strategist Ralph Reed, and advocates for Israel in Congress included former House majority leader Tom DeLay (R-TX), who stated in a visit to the Middle East, "I don't see occupied territory; I see Israel," and Senator James Inhofe (R-OK), who says Israel has a right to the occupied territories "because God said so" (Lampman 2004). Of course, US defense contractors support selling their goods to Israel. Thus, even without ethnoracial grassroots support for Israel coming from American Jews, there is considerable support for the state of Israel in the United States, and these supporters have a significant strategic advantage: they are fighting to preserve the status quo. Thus, while Jewish Americans add a substantial component to the pro-Israel lobby, especially in terms of grassroots and electoral support, US policies would likely support Israel even without the presence of the Jewish American lobby. The question is what the degree of that support would be without a Jewish American lobby, and that is very difficult to measure.

To be sure, Jewish Americans became a potent political force in the late 1960s, and a number of factors contributed to the increased influence of the American Jewry: American Jews had a long tradition of philanthropy, were relatively wealthy and well educated, and already had high rates of political participation; a campaign against anti-Semitism "helped remove lingering discriminatory barriers"; and the Six Day War galvanized American Jews and helped instill a new sense of Jewish pride (Mearsheimer and Walt 2007, 118). The evidence is strong that Jewish Americans did influence US policy toward Israel, but it is unclear what US policy toward Israel would be in the absence of the Jewish American lobby.

The Jewish American lobby is not invincible, and it can and does lose battles. For example, in 1991 Israel embarked on a massive housing program in order to address home shortages caused by large waves of immigration from the former Soviet Union. Israel asked for $10 billion in US loan guarantees, but President George H. W. Bush wanted assurances that new housing settlements would not be built in the West Bank or Gaza Strip. Israeli prime minister Yitzhak Shamir refused, and according to some journalists, Shamir "instructed AIPAC to get the guarantees through Congress over the administration's objections" (Frankel 2006, 24). When President Bush refused to offer the loan guarantees, 500 to 1,000 citizen lobbyists came to Capitol Hill to rally lawmakers to support the loan guarantees. In a news conference, Bush portrayed "himself as a David tussling against Goliath. 'There were something like a thousand lobbyists on the Hill working the other side of the question,' Bush said. . . . 'We've got one lonely little guy down here doing it.'" (Frisby 1991, 1). Support in Congress for the loan guarantees dropped quickly, and AIPAC backed down. While the Jewish lobby has very strong support in Congress, a president who opposes the lobby will diminish its effectiveness.

It is easier to see the influence of Cuban Americans on US policies. While the United States has opened trade with other communist states, granting permanent most-favored-nation trading status to China in 2000 and Vietnam in 2006, the United States continues to isolate the Castro regime. Because of the steps the United States has taken to open trade with other communist states and former enemies, it is very difficult to imagine that it would maintain an economic embargo on Cuba if the Cuban American lobby did not exist, and this speaks directly to the power of the Cuban lobby.

In the follow-up interviews, the Armenian lobby emerged as the only remaining ethnic group to be rated as having too much influence. That is likely due to two factors. First, of those nine ethnic groups included in the follow-up study, Armenian Americans are the smallest in terms of population. Indeed, the Armenian lobby received a mean influence score very similar to the Irish and Hispanic lobbies, two of the largest ethnic groups in the United States and each with populations approximately 100 times larger than the Armenian American population.[5] In terms of their ability to call attention to the Armenian genocide and compel members of Congress to at least consider the genocide resolution, the Armenian lobby has had a disproportionate influence in relation to the size of its population. Second, the follow-up surveys were conducted during a period when the ANCA stalled the confirmation of Richard E. Hoagland as US ambassador to Armenia. Although the difference in means was not significant, careerists were more likely than Capitol Hill policymakers to believe the Armenian lobby has too much influence, and this may be due to the ability of the ANCA to block the Hoagland confirmation.[6] The influence of the Armenian lobby is apparent if one considers what the foreign policy–making process would look like if the lobby did not exist. In the absence of an Armenian lobby, it is extremely doubtful that there would be an annual tussle over recognizing the Armenian genocide or controversy about presidential nominees for ambassador to Armenia. It is also extremely doubtful that Section 907 of the Freedom Support Act would exist. In short, the Armenian lobby does have influence, almost certainly disproportionate to the size of the Armenian American population.

Nonetheless, there are clear limits to the power of the Armenian lobby. Again, the lobby has, to date, been unable to secure even a floor vote, let alone passage, of a nonbinding resolution condemning the Armenian genocide, and unless the right candidate is elected president, it is doubtful that the executive branch will even use the term *genocide*. Further, Section 907 is now largely symbolic, since the president can and does now waive it annually.

It is also clear that the remaining ethnic lobbies that make up the top nine in the survey have influence in foreign policy as well. For example, if there were no Irish lobby, it is unlikely that visa waivers would be granted to some Irish visitors who the State Department feels are connected to terrorism. And, if the African American lobby did not exist, apartheid might still be a reality in South Africa. But for most of the remaining lobbies, their successes have been modest, and there is little evidence that the remaining lobbies have a disproportionate amount of influence. Further, there are numerous examples of how these ethnic lobbies have not been able to influence foreign policy to the degree to which they desire. For example, while the Taiwanese American lobby might, to quote one senior policymaker interviewed for this project, "irk the dickens" out of the Chinese government, the lobby has failed to get the United States to recognize Taiwan officially. Indeed, the United States barely allows the president of Taiwan to travel in the United States, and it forbids "Taiwan diplomats to fly their flag over their official building in Washington" (Dillin 2001). Perhaps more telling, for all of the activism by the Greek American lobby, it was unable to maintain the 7:10 ratio of foreign aid to Greece and Turkey, and it has failed to convince the United States to apply pressure on Turkey regarding Cyprus and the Aegean Sea dispute.

◼ Some Perspective on Ethnic Group Lobbying

If one believes that ethnic interest groups have too much influence, then the question of what to do about ethnic interest groups goes back to James Madison's dilemma. Fundamentally, attempts to limit the ability of ethnic groups to influence the policymaking process will infringe on the liberty of ethnic Americans, and efforts to insulate the policymaking process from ethnic interest groups will mean that the political system is insulated from other groups as well. While the ability of the Cuban American lobby to influence

US foreign policy toward Cuba may be considered troubling, policies developed when the opportunity structure of the policymaking process was much more elitist could also be found suspect. For example, much of US policy in Central America during the Cold War, which sacrificed human rights in the name of defeating communism, was questionable. Elites don't necessarily always get it right, and, at times, ethnic groups have played an important role in highlighting important issues ignored by the foreign policy–making establishment. As Paul Watanabe points out, "ethnic groups in many instances make strong, positive contributions to the formulation of rational, workable, and humane policies" (1984, xiv).

Ethnic groups do have access to policymakers, especially to members of Congress, staffers, and bureaucratic agencies. In many cases, ethnic communities have some degree of influence because sizeable segments of their community are concentrated in congressional districts. They lobby their members of Congress, present their points of view, and try to affect the political process. They lobby their members of Congress because these elected officials are supposed to represent them as constituents. However, nonethnic groups have the same access. Ethnic groups were rated as having less influence in foreign policy making than business groups. Nongovernmental organizations that are not ethnic based, such as environmental and human rights groups, can and do attempt to affect policymakers. Simply put, ethnic groups do not have a monopoly on access. Because of this, how can we tell members of Congress to ignore their ethnic communities while not telling members of Congress to ignore the AARP, the Chamber of Commerce, or the National Rifle Association? In most cases, ethnic groups pale in comparison to the influence of these lobbies. Only AIPAC has the policymaking prowess to rival organizations such as the Chamber of Commerce or the AARP.

One of the major critiques of ethnic lobbies is the imbalance they bring to the policymaking process. For example, R. C. Longworth (1998) asserts that there are no Turkish or Azeri lobbies to match the Armenian and Greek lobbies. Frank Greve (1995) contends that "many ethnic lobbies in Washington operate virtually unopposed," since there is little organization among Americans of English, Palestinian, or Turkish descent to counter the Irish, Jewish, Greek, and Armenian lobbies, and there is no pro-Beijing lobby to oppose the Taiwanese American lobby. Longworth also states that the Arab American lobby is no match for the Jewish American lobby, because the former is "notoriously ineffective," in part because it represents sixteen nationalities. These authors are correct: for all practical purposes, there are no English American organizations to counter Irish American groups, no pro-Beijing ethnic groups to oppose Taiwanese Americans, and little Turkish American opposition to the Greek and Armenian lobbies. Yet, it is not as if the organized ethnic communities dictate foreign policy carte blanche. There exists significant opposition to the policies advocated by the Armenian,

Greek, Irish, and Taiwanese lobbies by the State Department. Further, powerful elements of the business community—most notably the oil and defense industries—have opposed each of the named ethnic groups.

Finally, it is clear that different actors work together, which helps blur the lines of influence and causality. Many of the policymakers we interviewed volunteered that various policymaking actors work in conjunction with one another. For example, one policymaker stated that it was difficult to judge the influence of nonelected elites since think tanks are often created to help champion the goals of other actors, and think tanks often work directly with these actors and others. There is ample evidence that actors internal to the policymaking process work with actors outside the policymaking process to champion goals important to both sets of actors. Most recently, key members of Congress and the Bush administration worked with Indian American organizations and business groups to promote the US-India Civilian Nuclear Agreement.

Smith argues that ethnic groups take advantage of how open and porous the US political system is, and ethnic groups use those multiple entry points to affect the foreign policy process. There is no doubt that Smith is correct: the US policymaking process *is* quite open, and ethnic groups take advantage of the multiple entry points to try to shape foreign policy. Of course, a multitude of other groups—business, ideological, labor, and so on—also take advantage of the pluralistic nature of the US political system. Smith also contends that ethnic groups take advantage of the porous nature of US policymaking and affect foreign policy in a manner that may be contrary to the national interest.

The problem with this argument is that elected officials advocate the same goals that Smith implies are not in the national interest. President Ronald Reagan took a very hard line against the Castro regime, and his agents may have helped create the CANF to further that very goal. President George W. Bush takes a very hard line in support of Israel. For example, in March 2001, Bush told Israeli prime minister Ariel Sharon that the president would use force to protect Israel, a statement that surprised at least some of those in attendance, since it marked a significant departure in US policy (Stolberg 2006). To be consistent in applying Smith's argument, if one believes that current US policies toward Cuba and Israel are not in the US national interest, then both Reagan and Bush, it would seem, did not have the national interest in mind.

Many would shy away from that conclusion. After all, Reagan wasn't Cuban, and Bush isn't Jewish, so they weren't motivated by ethnic identities that might color their worldview. But both men were motivated by ideological identities that very much affected their worldview. Why is it that ideological identities are accepted as legitimate to influence foreign policy (and determine what is the national interest), but ethnic identities are not?

Until that question is answered better, arguing that ethnic groups do not have a legitimate place in the foreign policy process seems excessive. Instead, the focus should be placed on extremism, whether it be ethnic based, ideologically based, or based on some other worldview.

The research presented in this study does not indicate that ethnic groups, as a whole, have undue influence. Again, many policymakers qualified their responses by stating that a few ethnic groups did have too much power. Perhaps Tony Smith and other critics of ethnic politics paint using a broad brush in order to avoid accusations that they are racist or anti-Semitic. That does happen, and the response to John Mearsheimer and Stephen Walt's 2006 essay and 2007 book on the Israel lobby was swift, with several labeling their work as nothing short of anti-Semitism. For example, one scholar suggested the essay impugned the patriotism of Jewish Americans and was "merely, and unforgivably, bigotry" (Cohen 2006). While the research presented in this project supports the broader pluralistic ideal that ethnic groups can and should compete in the foreign policymaking process, it also confirms the need for critical analysis of the role and influence of ethnic groups in the pluralist universe.

Notes

1. See Goodnough (2005). A similar generational divide also appears to be present among Hmong Americans (Davey 2007).

2. For which $t = -2.06$.

3. Indeed, a central argument made by Mitchell Bard, a former editor of AIPAC's *Near East Report,* is that the president has the single greatest influence on foreign affairs, but that the president is also relatively isolated from interest group pressure. Nonetheless, Bard (1991) acknowledges that presidential candidates have great electoral incentives to be pro-Israel, presidents seeking reelection are "expected to support the Israeli lobby" (p. 19), and Jimmy Carter's stances on several Israeli issues contributed to his defeat in 1980 because of the "widespread defection of Jewish voters from the Democratic party" (p. 294).

4. It is much more difficult to argue that Senator McConnell was not influenced by Armenian contributions, since he was a leading critic of foreign aid in the 1990s but was championing aid to Armenia a decade later (Dobbs 2001). Perhaps it is not surprising that McConnell is also the leading critic of restrictions on political fundraising, and he believes that donating to campaigns is "as American as apple pie" (as quoted in Duncan and Nutting 1999, 546).

5. According to the 2000 census, there were 385,000 Armenian Americans, while there were 35.3 million Hispanic Americans and 30.5 million Irish Americans.

6. The mean Armenian power score was 2.00 for Capitol Hill policymakers, while it was 2.40 among careerists ($t = -1.49$).

Appendix A

Interview Questions

Exact Question Wording for the Policymaker Interviews Conducted in 2005 and 2006

I am going to ask you some questions about ethnic American groups. What I mean is that these groups of Americans share an ethnic identity. Please don't consider foreign nationals or governments when answering the next few questions.

1. Generally speaking, to what degree do ethnic American groups influence US foreign policymaking? 4) Significant influence; 3) Moderate influence; 2) Somewhat influence; 1) Slight influence; 0) No influence

2. To what degree do ethnic American groups influence US foreign aid policy? 4) Significant influence; 3) Moderate influence; 2) Somewhat influence; 1) Slight influence; 0) No influence

3. To what degree do ethnic American groups influence US oil and energy policy? 4) Significant influence; 3) Moderate influence; 2) Somewhat influence; 1) Slight influence; 0) No influence

4. To what degree do ethnic American groups influence US human rights policy? 4) Significant influence; 3) Moderate influence; 2) Somewhat influence; 1) Slight influence; 0) No influence

5. To what degree do ethnic American groups influence US trade policy? 4) Significant influence; 3) Moderate influence; 2) Somewhat influence; 1) Slight influence; 0) No influence

6. To what degree do ethnic American groups influence US military and security policy? 4) Significant influence; 3) Moderate influence; 2) Somewhat influence; 1) Slight influence; 0) No influence

7. To what degree do ethnic American groups influence US immigration policy? 4) Significant influence; 3) Moderate influence; 2) Somewhat influence; 1) Slight influence; 0) No influence

We will now ask some questions regarding influences of the foreign policy–making process. Please only consider foreign policy making, and not other policymaking realms.

8. Please tell us the degree to which each of the following actors affects US foreign policy by ranking the influence of each on a scale of 0–100 (with 0 meaning no influence and 100 meaning a great deal of influence).

A) On a scale of 0–100, how much do the issue positions of members of Congress affect US foreign policy? _____

B) On a scale of 0–100, how much do the constituents of members of Congress affect US foreign policy? _____

C) On a scale of 0–100, how much do the personal staffers of members of Congress affect US foreign policy? _____

D) On a scale of 0–100, how much do committee staffers affect US foreign policy? _____

E) On a scale of 0–100, how much do career bureaucrats in the State Department affect US foreign policy? _____

F) On a scale of 0–100, how much does the president affect US foreign policy? _____

G) On a scale of 0–100, how much do White House staffers affect US foreign policy? _____

H) On a scale of 0–100, how much do Department of Defense officials affect US foreign policy? _____

I) On a scale of 0–100, how much does the mass public affect US foreign policy? _____

J) On a scale of 0–100, how much do the news media affect US foreign policy? _____

K) On a scale of 0–100, how much do congressional caucuses affect US foreign policy? _____

L) On a scale of 0–100, how much do ethnic interest groups affect US foreign policy? _____

M) On a scale of 0–100, how much do business groups affect US foreign policy? _____

N) On a scale of 0–100, how much do foreign lobbies affect US foreign policy? _____

O) On a scale of 0–100, how much do nonelected elites (like think tanks, academics, and opinion leaders) affect US foreign policy? _____

P) On a scale of 0–100, how much do national party leaders (like Ken Mehlman and Howard Dean) affect US foreign policy? ____

Q) On a scale of 0–100, how much do international organizations (like the UN and the WTO) affect US foreign policy? ____

R) On a scale of 0–100, how much do nongovernmental organizations (like Human Rights Watch, environmental groups, and labor unions) affect US foreign policy? ____

9. Can you give examples of how ethnic interest groups have attempted to influence the foreign policy–making process?

   9a. Can you give examples of how ethnic interest groups have successfully influenced the foreign policy–making process?

   9b. Can you give examples of how ethnic interest groups have failed to influence the foreign policy–making process?

10. How often are you or your office contacted by ethnic interest groups? 4) Daily; 3) Once a week or more; 2) Once a month or more; 1) Less than once a month; 0) Never

11. Would you say that attempts by ethnic interest groups to contact you have increased, decreased, or remained about the same since September 11, 2001? 1) Increased; 2) Decreased; 3) Remained about the same

   11a. *If increased or decreased, ask:* "Would you say increased (decreased) a lot or some?" 1) a lot; 2) some

12. To what degree is foreign policy salient to your constituents? 4) Most of your constituents; 3) Many of your constituents; 2) Some of your constituents; 1) A few of your constituents; 0) None of your constituents

13. Are you a member of an ethnic caucus?

   13a. Why or why not?

We will now read you some statements, and we would like to know if you strongly agree, somewhat agree, somewhat disagree, or strongly disagree with the statements.

14. Increasingly, US foreign policy reflects ethnic interests and not national interests. 4) Strongly agree; 3) Somewhat agree; 2) Neither agree nor disagree; 1) Somewhat disagree; 0) Strongly disagree

15. The terrorist attacks on September 11, 2001, decreased the influence of ethnic lobbies compared to the influence of other actors in the foreign policy–making process. 4) Strongly agree; 3) Somewhat agree; 2) Neither agree nor disagree; 1) Somewhat disagree; 0) Strongly disagree

16. Increasingly, ethnic interest groups are influencing congressional elections. 4) Strongly agree; 3) Somewhat agree; 2) Neither agree nor disagree; 1) Somewhat disagree; 0) Strongly disagree

17. Ethnic interest groups affect congressional elections no more than other organized groups. 4) Strongly agree; 3) Somewhat agree; 2) Neither agree nor disagree; 1) Somewhat disagree; 0) Strongly disagree
18. Increasingly, ethnic interest groups are influencing presidential elections. 4) Strongly agree; 3) Somewhat agree; 2) Neither agree nor disagree; 1) Somewhat disagree; 0) Strongly disagree
19. One or more ethnic groups has tried to persuade me through direct lobbying. 4) Strongly agree; 3) Somewhat agree; 2) Neither agree nor disagree; 1) Somewhat disagree; 0) Strongly disagree
    19a. Which groups, and how did they attempt to persuade you?
20. I am less likely to meet an ethnic interest group than other types of interest groups. 4) Strongly agree; 3) Somewhat agree; 2) Neither agree nor disagree; 1) Somewhat disagree; 0) Strongly disagree
21. One or more ethnic groups has tried to affect one of my elections. 4) Strongly agree; 3) Somewhat agree; 2) Neither agree nor disagree; 1) Somewhat disagree; 0) Strongly disagree
    21a. Which groups, and how did they try to affect your election?
22. An ethnic interest group has conducted a grassroots lobbying campaign among my constituents. 4) Strongly agree; 3) Somewhat agree; 2) Neither agree nor disagree; 1) Somewhat disagree; 0) Strongly disagree
    22a. Which groups, and what was the campaign?
23. Ethnic interest groups make positive contributions to the policymaking process. 4) Strongly agree; 3) Somewhat agree; 2) Neither agree nor disagree; 1) Somewhat disagree; 0) Strongly disagree
24. Ethnic interest groups are no more powerful than other domestic groups. 4) Strongly agree; 3) Somewhat agree; 2) Neither agree nor disagree; 1) Somewhat disagree; 0) Strongly disagree
25. Ethnic interest groups have too much power in the policymaking process. 4) Strongly agree; 3) Somewhat agree; 2) Neither agree nor disagree; 1) Somewhat disagree; 0) Strongly disagree
26. Ethnic interest groups are an important source of campaign contributions for members of Congress. 4) Strongly agree; 3) Somewhat agree; 2) Neither agree nor disagree; 1) Somewhat disagree; 0) Strongly disagree
    26a. Which ethnic groups are important campaign contributors?
    26b. Which ethnic groups are important campaign contributors to Democrats?
    26c. Which ethnic groups are important campaign contributors to Republicans?

For the following questions, please tell us how influential each ethnic lobby is by using a scale of 0–100 (with 0 meaning no influence and 100 meaning a great deal of influence).
Note: The order of questions 27 through 64 was randomized.

27. On a scale of 0–100, how influential is the African American lobby?
28. On a scale of 0–100, how influential is the Albanian American lobby?
29. On a scale of 0–100, how influential is the Anglo American (British) lobby?
30. On a scale of 0–100, how influential is the Arab American lobby?
31. On a scale of 0–100, how influential is the Armenian American lobby?
32. On a scale of 0–100, how influential is the Asian American lobby?
33. On a scale of 0–100, how influential is the Baltic American lobby?
34. On a scale of 0–100, how influential is the Caribbean American lobby?
35. On a scale of 0–100, how influential is the Central/East European American lobby?
36. On a scale of 0–100, how influential is the Colombian American lobby?
37. On a scale of 0–100, how influential is the Croat American lobby?
38. On a scale of 0–100, how influential is the Cuban American lobby?
39. On a scale of 0–100, how influential is the Czech American lobby?
40. On a scale of 0–100, how influential is the Eritrean American lobby?
41. On a scale of 0–100, how influential is the Ethiopian American lobby?
42. On a scale of 0–100, how influential is the Filipino American lobby?
43. On a scale of 0–100, how influential is the Greek American (Hellenic) lobby?
44. On a scale of 0–100, how influential is the Hispanic American lobby?
45. On a scale of 0–100, how influential is the Indian American (not Native American) lobby?
46. On a scale of 0–100, how influential is the Iranian American lobby?
47. On a scale of 0–100, how influential is the Irish American lobby?
48. On a scale of 0–100, how influential is the Israeli American lobby?
49. On a scale of 0–100, how influential is the Italian American lobby?
50. On a scale of 0–100, how influential is the Japanese American lobby?
51. On a scale of 0–100, how influential is the Korean American lobby?
52. On a scale of 0–100, how influential is the Kurdish American lobby?
53. On a scale of 0–100, how influential is the Laotian/Hmong American lobby?
54. On a scale of 0–100, how influential is the Lebanese American lobby?
55. On a scale of 0–100, how influential is the Lithuanian American lobby?
56. On a scale of 0–100, how influential is the Mexican American lobby?

57. On a scale of 0–100, how influential is the Pakistani American lobby?
58. On a scale of 0–100, how influential is the Polish American lobby?
59. On a scale of 0–100, how influential is the Salvadoran American lobby?
60. On a scale of 0–100, how influential is the Serbian American lobby?
61. On a scale of 0–100, how influential is the Somali American lobby?
62. On a scale of 0–100, how influential is the Taiwanese American lobby?
63. On a scale of 0–100, how influential is the Turkish American lobby?
64. On a scale of 0–100, how influential is the Ukrainian American lobby?
65. How long have you worked in your current position?
66. How long have you worked on foreign policy?
67. Prior to this position, did you work or have some experience with foreign policy?
   67a. What was that experience?
68. Generally speaking, how would you describe your political views? 1) Extremely liberal; 2) Somewhat liberal; 3) Slightly liberal; 4) Moderate or middle-of-the-road; 5) Slightly conservative; 6) Somewhat conservative; 7) Extremely conservative

▦ Follow-Up Interviews for Policymakers

Our earlier research identified the following ten ethnic lobbies as having the most influence in the foreign policy–making process. I'd like to read you a statement regarding the influence of each, and I'd like you to tell me if you strongly agree, somewhat agree, neither agree nor disagree, somewhat disagree, or strongly disagree with each statement.

Note: Order of questions 1 through 10 was randomized.

1. The African American lobby has too much power in the foreign policy–making process. 4) Strongly agree; 3) Somewhat agree; 2) Neither agree nor disagree; 1) Somewhat disagree; 0) Strongly disagree
2. The Armenian American lobby has too much power in the foreign policy–making process. 4) Strongly agree; 3) Somewhat agree; 2) Neither agree nor disagree; 1) Somewhat disagree; 0) Strongly disagree
3. The Cuban American lobby has too much power in the foreign policy–making process. 4) Strongly agree; 3) Somewhat agree; 2)

Neither agree nor disagree; 1) Somewhat disagree; 0) Strongly disagree

4. The Greek American lobby has too much power in the foreign policy–making process. 4) Strongly agree; 3) Somewhat agree; 2) Neither agree nor disagree; 1) Somewhat disagree; 0) Strongly disagree

5. The Hispanic American lobby has too much power in the foreign policy–making process. 4) Strongly agree; 3) Somewhat agree; 2) Neither agree nor disagree; 1) Somewhat disagree; 0) Strongly disagree

6. The Indian American lobby has too much power in the foreign policy–making process. 4) Strongly agree; 3) Somewhat agree; 2) Neither agree nor disagree; 1) Somewhat disagree; 0) Strongly disagree

7. The Irish American lobby has too much power in the foreign policy–making process. 4) Strongly agree; 3) Somewhat agree; 2) Neither agree nor disagree; 1) Somewhat disagree; 0) Strongly disagree

8. The Italian American lobby has too much power in the foreign policy–making process. 4) Strongly agree; 3) Somewhat agree; 2) Neither agree nor disagree; 1) Somewhat disagree; 0) Strongly disagree

9. The Jewish American lobby has too much power in the foreign policy–making process. 4) Strongly agree; 3) Somewhat agree; 2) Neither agree nor disagree; 1) Somewhat disagree; 0) Strongly disagree

   9a. Some people disagree on whether the correct term should be "Jewish American lobby" or "Israel American lobby." What would your answer be if I stated: The Israel American lobby has too much power in the foreign policy–making process. 4) Strongly agree; 3) Somewhat agree; 2) Neither agree nor disagree; 1) Somewhat disagree; 0) Strongly disagree

10. The Taiwanese American lobby has too much power in the foreign policy–making process. 4) Strongly agree; 3) Somewhat agree; 2) Neither agree nor disagree; 1) Somewhat disagree; 0) Strongly disagree

Appendix B

Population Data Collection Information

When available, data were collected from US Census sources that included people with one or more ancestry categories reported. For most ethnic communities, data measuring the total population of the ethnicity, the number of foreign-born, the percentage of individuals speaking a language other than English at home, and median household income were collected from the 2005 American Community Survey (Table S0201. Selected Population Profile in the United States). Because of their small populations, data for Estonian Americans, Somali Americans, and Eritrean Americans are not available from the 2005 American Community Survey. As a result, data for Estonian Americans and Somali Americans were collected from the 2000 US Census Fact Sheets for a Race, Ethnic, or Ancestry Group. Data on Eritrean Americans are available by accessing the US Census data on individuals in the United States who are foreign-born (available at www.census.gov/population/www/socdemo/foreign/datatbls.html). The US Census estimated that in 2000 there were 17,520 individuals in the United States who were born in Eritrea. Based on this figure and the fact that 98.5 percent of Somali Americans in 2000 were foreign-born, we estimated that 17,787 Eritreans lived in the United States in 2000. Data for Kurdish Americans are not available from the 2000 census; however, Rajiv Chandrasekaran (2007) estimates there are 40,000 Kurds living in the United States, a figure confirmed by the American Kurdish Information Network.

Census data for Caribbean Americans include the West Indies, but exclude Cuban Americans. Figures for Anglo Americans were calculated using census data for English Americans. Figures for Central and Eastern European Americans were calculated using census data for the ancestries associated with the "Captive Nations" movement: Albanian, Bulgarian, Czech, Czechoslovakian, Estonian, Hungarian, Latvian, Lithuanian, Polish, Romanian, and Slovakian Americans

223

(Garrett 1978). Figures for Baltic Americans were calculated using census data for Estonian, Latvian, and Lithuanian Americans.

In 2000, the US Census reported that there were 293,568 individuals of Taiwanese ancestry in the United States. In 2005, the census reported that the figure was now 99,344. It is not clear why the number of Taiwanese Americans would plummet so much in five years. Since most estimates put the number of Taiwanese Americans at 500,000, the 2000 data were used for this analysis.

Because the US Census is forbidden from asking questions that detail religion, we relied on several studies to estimate the number of Jewish Americans. First, the United Jewish Communities conducted an in-depth survey of American Jews in 2000–2001, and the survey estimated that there were 5.2 million Jews in the United States in 2000 (United Jewish Communities 2003). Second, the Glenmary Research Center compiled data on religion in 2000 that estimate the number of Jews across the United States at the county level (Jones et al. 2002). The Jewish data were based on estimates provided by the Jewish Data Bank, which also conducts in-depth studies of American Jewish communities. Aggregating the data provided by the Glenmary database indicates there were 6.1 million Jews in the United States in 2000. Finally, a 2006 study by Ira Sheskin and Arnold Dashefsky estimates that there are 6.4 million Jews in the United States. Because the Glenmary data are county based, and were used in part to estimate the number of Jewish Americans in the 435 congressional districts, the figure of 6.1 million Jewish Americans was used in the analysis presented in this project.

The Glenmary county-level database provided a means to estimate the number of Jews in each congressional district. However, since congressional districts often cut across counties, and since American Jews tend to live in concentrated neighborhoods and communities, using county-level data to estimate Jewish populations within congressional districts is somewhat problematic. Because of this, we used ZIP code data provided by the Jewish Data Bank's community surveys to estimate the number of Jews living in a particular community's congressional districts whenever possible. ZIP code data were used to calculate the congressional districts representing New York City; South Florida; the Washington, DC, suburbs; Philadelphia; Atlanta; Baltimore; Las Vegas; and much of New Jersey. For other major Jewish communities, such as Los Angeles and Chicago, neighborhood data were used to refine the estimates made based on the Glenmary data set. These revised estimates were then compared to qualitative district analyses provided by *CQ's Politics in America: 2002* (Nutting and Stern, 2001) and other sources. The figures estimated by our methods match the district profiles very well.

Figures regarding Jewish American assimilation were based on a number of sources. First, United Jewish Communities estimates that the number of Jewish adults born outside the United States was 618,000 in 2000 (Ament 2004, 4). Determining the number of Jews in the United States who speak a language other than English at home was more difficult to gauge. Figures from the 2000 census indicate that 106,839 individuals consider themselves of Israeli heritage, and 66,209 of these individuals speak a language other than English at home, for a non-English percentage of 62 percent. The 2000 census also estimated that nearly 327,000 US residents speak Hebrew or Yiddish at home. A large influx of Jewish persons emigrated from the Soviet Union and its successor states from 1980 to 2000: over 327,000 Jews came to the United States during these two decades (NCSJ 2007), and a study from 2000 estimated that 227,000 Jews live in the United States who emigrated from the former Soviet Union since 1980 (Ament 2004). It is likely that most of those immigrants still speak Russian at home: for example, 48 percent of the interviews for the 2000 study were completed in Russian. Census data show that of the 2.6 million US residents who are of Russian ancestry, over 400,000 were born outside the United States, and 484,000 speak a language other than English at home. Given the number of US residents who speak Hebrew, Yiddish, or Russian at home, it was estimated that 600,000 Jews speak a language other than English at home.

Appendix C

Coding of Ethnic Websites

■ **Type of Organization**

There is wide variation in terms of the types of organizations that represent ethnic groups. As discussed in Chapter 3, we identified several prototypes for ethnic organizations.

Nonprofit Advocacy Model

The organization qualifies as tax-exempt under Section 501(c)(3) of the Internal Revenue Code. Contributions to such organizations may be tax-deductible. The organization cannot use monetary funds to lobby policy-makers, but it can use funds for the purpose of educating the public, the media, and policymakers.

PAC Model

The organization is registered as a political action committee with the Federal Elections Commission. The organization engages in electioneering, usually by collecting contributions from individuals and making contributions to federal and state candidates.

Lobbying Model

The organization is registered as a lobbying organization with the Clerk of the US House and the Secretary of the US Senate. While such organizations may be considered not-for-profit by the Internal Revenue Service, contributions to the organization are not tax-deductible.

AIPAC Model

The organization comprises several entities, with one entity being registered for lobbying purposes. Other organizational components usually include a 501(c)3 entity, a research department, and/or a PAC.

▓ Focus of Organization

There is also wide variation among ethnic organizations in terms of the degree to which the organization is focused on or devoted to foreign policy. Some organizations, like AIPAC and CANF, are clearly dedicated to influencing US foreign policy. Other organizations, which may attempt to influence foreign policy, are not necessarily dedicated exclusively to foreign policy issues, while still other organizations may have an entirely different focus, yet may also provide some leadership in terms of foreign policy.

In order to help determine the degree to which an ethnic group has an organization dedicated to foreign policy, we examined the websites of representative ethnic organizations. There are similarities across different organizations, and we used the following categories to code the focus of each representative organization.

Foreign Policy

Organization is dedicated to affecting US relations with foreign states. Includes promoting or maintaining strong relations between the United States and foreign states, encouraging the United States to take a hard line toward other states, and persuading the United States to address specific foreign policy issues.

Civil Liberties

Organization is dedicated to promoting civil liberties and civil rights of ethnic brethren within the United States, including opposing racial profiling, promoting legislation that targets hate crimes against ethnic brethren, and addressing issues of discrimination against ethnic brethren.

Human Rights

Organization is dedicated to promoting civil liberties, civil rights, and economic rights of ethnic brethren living outside the United States either in the ancestral homeland or elsewhere.

Immigration

Organization is dedicated to influencing US immigration policies.

Brethren Support and Promotion

Organization is dedicated to assisting ethnic brethren and promoting the accomplishments of ethnic brethren to the ethnic community and broader American society. Organization may facilitate networking among ethnic brethren and organizations, communicate accomplishments of ethnic brethren and organizations, promote the culture and heritage of the ethnicity, and oppose negative depictions of the ethnicity in the media. Organization may state its purpose involves bettering the economic standing of the ethnic community.

Political Participation

Organization is dedicated to encouraging political participation among ethnic brethren, including encouraging ethnic brethren to vote, become active in politics, run for office, or otherwise engage in the political process.

Appendix D

Coding of Issue Goals in Relation to the Status Quo

A five-point scale was used to measure the degree to which an ethnic group is protecting or opposing the status quo for specific issues. The scale is an adaptation of the scale of influence developed by David Goldberg (1990). The five-point scale is the following:

1. The ethnic interest group diametrically opposes the status quo. The ethnic group supports little, if any, aspect of the US position.
2. The ethnic interest group opposes the status quo. Although the ethnic group may support some elements of the existing policy, the ethnic group desires to enact major change of the status quo.
3. There are elements of the status quo that the ethnic group supports, while the group opposes other elements of the existing policy.
4. The ethnic interest group supports the status quo. The ethnic group may desire to change elements of the government's position, but the group largely supports the status quo.
5. The ethnic interest group wholly supports the status quo. The ethnic group's position is virtually identical to the position of the US government and its policies.

The status quo coding was based on US policies in 2005, and policies were determined by examining Congressional Research Service reports, as well as information from the State Department, USAID, and other sources. Table D.1 lists the policies associated with each ethnicity included in the status quo analysis, lists the status quo coding, and explains in the endnotes US policy and the rationale for the coding.

Table D.1 Status Quo Coding

Ethnicity	Most Salient Foreign Policy or Issues	Status Quo Coding
African	Global AIDS/HIV prevention and treatment	4[1]
	Stronger actions by United States to stop genocide in Darfur	3[2]
Albanian	Support of Kosovo independence	3[3]
Arab	Greater support for Palestinians in Arab-Israeli conflict	2[4]
Armenian	Recognition of the Armenian genocide	2[5]
	Section 907 of the Freedom Support Act	3[6]
	Foreign aid to Armenia	5[7]
Asian	Immigration: Family preference categories	3[8]
Baltic	US relations with the Baltic states	4[9]
	Concern over Russia's influence in region	2[10]
Caribbean	Economic development of the Caribbean	3[11]
Central and Eastern Europe	Visa Waiver Program	2[12]
Colombian	Socioeconomic development in Colombia	3[13]
Croat	Economic and democratic support for Croatia	3[14]
Cuban	Isolating Cuba and the Castro regime	5[15]
Czech	Visa Waiver Program	2[16]
Eritrean	Hard line against Ethiopia regarding border dispute	2[17]
Ethiopian	Human rights and democracy in Ethiopia	2[18]
	Opposition to the current regime	2[19]
Filipino	Full benefits for Filipino veterans of World War II	2[20]
	Immigration: Path to citizenship	2[21]
Greek	Withdrawal of Turkish forces from Cyprus	2[22]
	US-Greek relations	3[23]
	Aegean Sea boundary dispute with Turkey	3[24]
Hispanic	Immigration: Family preference categories	3
	Immigration: Path to citizenship	2
	Opposition to enacting CAFTA and expanding NAFTA	4[25]
Hmong	Greater protection of human rights for Hmong in Laos	2[26]
Indian	US-India relations	4[27]
	H-1B visas	3[28]
Iranian	Improved US-Iranian relations	1[29]
Irish	Reunification of Ireland	2[30]
	Civil rights in Northern Ireland	4[31]
	Immigration and visas	4[32]
Italian	US-Italian relations	5[33]
Japanese	US-Japanese relations	5[34]
Jewish	US-Israeli relations	5[35]
	Iranian nuclear program	4[36]
Korean	Reunification of Korea	2[37]
	Comfort Women Resolution	2[38]
Kurd	Greater protections for Kurds in Turkey	2[39]
Lebanese	US-Lebanese relations	3[40]
	Restrain Israel response to Hezbollah[a]	2[41]
	Ban of sale of cluster bombs to Israel[a]	3[42]
Lithuanian	US-Lithuanian relations	4[43]
	Growing Russian influence in region	2
Mexican	Immigration/family preference categories	3
	Immigration/path to citizenship	2
Pakistani	US-Pakistani relations	4[44]
Polish	Visa Waiver Program	2

(continues)

Table D.1 continued

Ethnicity	Most Salient Foreign Policy or Issues	Status Quo Coding
Salvadoran	Immigration/path to citizenship	2
	Opposition to enacting CAFTA and expanding of NAFTA	4
Serbian	Opposing UNMIK and preventing an independent Kosovo	3[45]
Somali	Ending Somali political unrest	2[46]
Taiwanese	Independent Taiwan	2[47]
	Easing travel restrictions for Taiwanese officials	3[48]
Turkish	US-Turkey relations	4[49]
	Opposition to US recognition of Armenian genocide	4[50]
Ukrainian	Foreign aid for Ukraine	3[51]
	Support for democracy in Ukraine	3

Notes: a. Arose as a salient issue during the study.

1. In 2003 President Bush signed legislation that provided $15 billion over five years to combat AIDS internationally. The NAACP supported that amount, but the organization appeared doubtful that the full $15 billion would be "actually appropriated and spent" (NAACP 2004).

2. In 2004 the Bush administration declared the atrocities in Darfur a genocide. Nonetheless, "the declaration of genocide" did not lead to "a major shift in policy nor a threat of intervention to end [the] genocide. Instead, Bush Administration officials continue to support a negotiated settlement between the rebels and the government of Sudan" (Dagne and Everett 2004, 14). NAACP and others called for tougher sanctions and other measures against Sudan (Dagne 2005). President Bush did not impose new sanctions until May 2007. NAACP called for the United States to use greater diplomatic and financial pressure to "ensure the rapid deployment of peacekeepers."

3. Albanian Americans supported the status quo of autonomy for Kosovo, but also argued that Kosovars had the "right to self-determination" and believed Kosovo should be "an independent, sovereign country" (National Albanian American Council 2004). In 2004 NAAC called for an expedited "timeline to resolve the final status of Kosovo." At least until 2004, the official Bush administration policy supported "autonomy for Kosovo within Serbia . . . but not independence," and the administration opposed reaching "an 'immediate' decision on Kosovo's status" (Woehrel 2003). The latter position changed in 2005, as the United States began working to accelerate a resolution to the issue, although the United States stated it did not endorse independence or "conditional independence" in both 2005 and 2006 (Woehrel 2006a). However, US policy appeared to shift in 2006, and by 2007 the United States officially supported Kosovo independence (Woehrel 2007).

4. While President Bush stated in 2002 that he envisioned a two-state solution to the conflict, he refused to meet with Palestinian president Yasir Arafat, although Bush did meet with Palestinian prime minister Mahmud Abbas in 2003. President Bush is viewed as pro-Israel: Bush supports Israel's unilateral actions in Gaza and the West Bank and believes Israel's settlements in the Occupied Territories should be recognized in any final borders (Mark 2004). Arab American groups opposed the series of walls to seal the West Bank and Israel retaining sovereignty over Jewish settlements in the West Bank; Bush endorsed the Israel plan on April 14, 2004.

5. The White House refuses to use the term *genocide*. However, President Bush calls it "one of the great tragedies of history: the forced exile and annihilation of approximately 1.5 million Armenians in the closing years of the Ottoman Empire." Since the status quo does acknowledge that "terrible events" did occur, this is not a situation where the ethnic group diametrically opposes the status quo.

6. Armenian Americans strongly support Section 907, which was enacted in 1992 and bans US aid to Azerbaijan and pressures Baku to lift its blockades of Armenia and Karabakh. However, subsequent legislation passed in 2002 modified the ban, allowing the president to waive Section 907, effectively neutralizing the effect of the original legislation.

(continues)

Table D.1 continued

7. Aid to Armenia is high, especially by per capita measures. Although US aid to Armenia dipped slightly to $95.6 million in 2005, it jumped to $326.7 million in 2006 because of $235.6 million in aid from the Millennium Challenge Corporation.

8. Asian and Hispanic organizations support the existing structure of family preference categories for allocating immigrant visas. However, these organizations strongly assert that the number of visas allocated annually (480,000) is too low given the demand for family immigration visas. The result is a significant backlog of visa applications, especially for relatives of lawful permanent residents. These groups also oppose the cap on visas from specific countries: in most cases, the maximum number of individuals allowed visas from any one country is approximately 25,600.

9. US relations with the Baltic states are strong, although Baltic American organizations seek to make relations even stronger. For example, Baltic organizations opposed drops in aid to the Baltic states (which declined by a third between 2003 and 2006), opposed cuts in funding Radio Free Europe/Radio Liberty in broadcasts in Baltic languages (the last Baltic broadcasts were made in 2004), and support expanding the Visa Waiver Program to include the Baltic nations.

10. The United States has largely ignored concerns raised by Baltic Americans, Czech Americans, and others regarding Russia's attempts to increase its influence over Central and Eastern Europe. The United States did criticize Russia's move to cut off natural gas to Ukraine.

11. While the United States supports economic and social development in the Caribbean, the proposed US foreign assistance to the Caribbean for fiscal year 2007 represented the lowest levels (in terms of constant dollars) in more than forty years (Sullivan et al. 2007). The Bush administration requested $198 million for Haitian assistance for fiscal year 2007, compared to the $223.7 million in aid distributed in 2005 (USAID 2007). The fiscal year 2007 Bush administration budget proposed reducing funds allocated for child survival and health, as well as development assistance.

12. Central and East European ethnic groups support the Visa Waiver Program but desire to see the program expanded to include their ancestral homelands. In the wake of September 11, such an expansion appears to be unlikely, as subsequent legislation has increased the requirements for countries to participate in the program.

13. While the United States supports economic and social development in Colombia, the vast majority of aid to Colombia is earmarked for narcotics control (Sullivan et al. 2007). US economic and social assistance to Colombia has declined (in terms of constant dollars) since 2004.

14. Economic and democratic aid to Croatia declined by 57.7 percent from 2003 to 2006.

15. The most active Cuban American organizations are very supportive of US policies toward Cuba. The Bush administration has taken a particularly hard line against Cuba, including initiating sting operations to halt individuals from smuggling hard currency into Cuba.

16. Since 2005, The American Friends of the Czech Republic has championed expanding the Visa Waiver Program to include the Czech Republic.

17. Eritrean American groups hope the United States will take a more hard line against Ethiopia in terms of the border dispute. While the United States states that it "fully supports the 'final and binding' decisions of the EEBC and has consistently called on both parties to cooperate with the EEBC," the United States believes blame for the continued dispute lies with both countries (Swan 2007). Further, the United States clearly believes Ethiopia has made much more progress toward political reforms than has Eritrea.

18. The United States believes Ethiopia is making strides toward democracy, and the State Department asserts that "under the present government, Ethiopians enjoy wider, albeit circumscribed, political freedom than ever before in Ethiopia's history." Ethiopian American groups argue the United States should apply greater pressure on the Ethiopian government to make democratic and humanitarian reforms.

19. Despite the jailing of opposition leaders and the fact that much of the independent media was shut down in 2005, the United States calls Ethiopia "a strategic partner . . . in the Global War on Terrorism" and asserts that "Ethiopia's political leaders have committed themselves to a new collaborative relationship for the good of the country" (Knight 2007; Swan 2007). Perhaps as a nod to critics, the United States does "encourage Ethiopia's leadership to insure that legitimate opposition enjoys access to media and the ability to campaign freely" (Knight 2007).

(continues)

Table D.1 continued

20. Filipinos who were inducted into the US Army during World War II were "promised U.S. citizenship and full veterans' benefits" (Lum and Niksch 2006). Although President Bush signed legislation in 2003 that extended Veterans Affairs health benefits to Filipino veterans, Filipino veterans do not receive full benefits.

21. Current law does not provide a path to citizenship for illegal immigrants, but the Immigration Reform and Control Act of 1986 provided a mechanism for legalization of illegal aliens who met certain requirements. Establishing a path to citizenship is also supported by President Bush.

22. US policy calls for a reunified Cyprus reached through negotiated agreement, but the United States refuses to call on Turkey to withdraw its troops.

23. Greek American organizations call for the United States to "develop a 'special relationship' with Greece" and "expand and deepen its relationship with Greece through a coordinated program in the political, military, commercial and cultural fields" (American Hellenic Institute 2002). According to US Department of State Background Notes, while the United States and Greece have good relations, the United States stopped providing military assistance to Greece in the 1990s, and the United States closed three of its four main Greek bases in the 1990s.

24. The US policy regarding the Aegean Sea boundary dispute is remarkably vague: US policy appears to support neither side in the dispute.

25. Many Hispanic American organizations opposed the passage of the Central American Free Trade Agreement (CAFTA) in 2005 and free trade pacts with Peru, Panama, and Colombia. Prior to the ratification of CAFTA, the status quo featured a history of free trade agreements (such as North American Free Trade Agreement [NAFTA]) and an administration that strongly supported free trade, but CAFTA itself represented a shift of the status quo. Therefore, prior to the ratification of CAFTA, Hispanic organizations supported the status quo. Congress ratified a free trade agreement with Peru in December 2007.

26. In November 2004, Congress passed legislation extending normal trade relations (NTR) with Laos despite opposition by Hmong American organizations that NTR status should not be granted until human rights conditions improved. Some Hmong Americans support regime change in Laos. According to the State Department, the "United States does not endorse or support violent activities carried out against the Lao Government," and in 2007 federal authorities arrested nine Hmong Americans on charges of conspiring to overthrow the government of Laos (Davey 2007).

27. Relations between the United States and India have been strained in the past, as India was allied with the Soviet Union, and India tested nuclear weapons in 1998. However, according to the State Department, the United States now recognizes India as "a key to strategic U.S. interests." In 2001 President Bush lifted the 1998 sanctions placed on India for its nuclear tests, and the United States and India began a dialogue on nonproliferation in 2001. The United States and India launched the Next Steps in Strategic Partnership in 2004, and the two countries announced the US-India Civilian Nuclear Agreement in 2005. According to the State Department, the United States desires for India to increase the pace of its economic reforms.

28. Indian American organizations strongly support the H-1B visa program. The number of aliens who may receive H-1B visas has been capped at 65,000 since fiscal year 2004 (the cap was raised temporarily to 195,000 from FY2001 to FY2003). Indian American organizations support increasing the cap to at least 95,000.

29. The United States views Iran as supporting international terrorism and promoting "harmful activities" in Lebanon, Iraq, and elsewhere. The United States has no formal diplomatic relations with Iran. Iranian Americans are not a united lobby, and some Iranian Americans support existing US policies.

30. The United States supports the 1998 Good Friday Agreement, which is based on the principle that a "change in the status of Northern Ireland can only come about with the consent of the majority of its people" (Donfried 2001). Although reunification is therefore a possibility, the United States appears to focus more on peace and reconciliation among Nationalists and Unionists. For example, according to the State Department, the "Northern Ireland Assembly must govern effectively in order to achieve economic growth and community reconciliation in Northern Ireland."

(continues)

Table D.1   continued

31. Based on testimony to Congress, US policy appears to be evenhanded toward both Nationalists and Unionists. The MacBride Principles, enacted in 1998, are designed to redress inequalities of employment opportunities. The enactment of the MacBride Principles represented a shift of US policy and is likely an example of how ethnic groups can change the status quo.

32. Irish American organizations have called for citizenship for illegal Irish immigrants, which would require a significant shift of US policy. On the other hand, Irish organizations support other immigration policies that allow greater numbers of Irish immigrants. For example, the Diversity Immigrant Visa Program is designed to encourage immigration from countries with "low rates of immigration to the United States." Despite the long history of Irish immigration, both Ireland and Northern Ireland are included in the program. In addition, the Visa Waiver Program allows nationals from Ireland and Northern Ireland to travel to the United States for ninety days without obtaining a visa.

33. Relations between the United States and Italy are very strong, and the State Department calls Italy "a leading partner in the war against terrorism."

34. The State Department asserts "the U.S.-Japan alliance is the cornerstone of U.S. security interests in Asia," and the United States supports Japan's efforts to gain a permanent seat on the UN Security Council.

35. The State Department asserts that "commitment to Israel's security and well being has been a cornerstone of U.S. policy in the Middle East since Israel's founding in 1948. . . . On a bilateral level, relations between the United States and Israel are continually strengthening in every field."

36. The United States imposes a number of sanctions upon Iran, including forbidding US trade and investment in Iran and sanctioning entities that assist Iran's proliferation efforts. Jewish American organizations support these sanctions, but some call for greater levels of international sanctions against Iran.

37. According to the State Department, "the United States believes that the question of peace and security on the Korean Peninsula is, first and foremost, a matter for the Korean people to decide." Although the United States supports reunification of Korea, critics charge that the United States neither wants nor foresees reunification in the short term. The National Association of Korean Americans (2004) asserts that the United States should engage in direct talks with North Korea, a tactic that the Bush administration opposes.

38. While the United States acknowledges the use of "comfort women" as deplorable, it does not support the resolution. According to Deputy Secretary of State John Negroponte (2007), the United States feels that "the trafficking in women that occurred during World War II was deplorable and that it was a grave human rights violation of enormous proportions . . . but we also feel that the Government of Japan has taken steps to address this issue."

39. Although the State Department acknowledges that the government of Turkey continues to "restrict expression by individuals sympathetic to . . . Kurdish nationalist or cultural viewpoints" (Bureau of Democracy, Human Rights, and Labor 2006), the United States agrees with Turkey that the Kurdistan Workers' Party (PKK) is a terrorist organization. As such, the United States supports Turkey's efforts to eliminate the PKK, while critics charge that Turkey's efforts are heavy-handed toward all Kurds.

40. According to the State Department, the United States "seeks to maintain its traditionally close ties with Lebanon," and the United States has given Lebanon at least $35 million in aid annually since 2001. Lebanese American organizations seek stronger relations. For example, Secretary of State Condoleezza Rice declined to meet with Lebanese president Émile Lahoud during her 2006 trip to Lebanon (Prados 2006). The American Task Force for Lebanon would like the United States to develop a "just solution to the Palestinian refugee issue in Lebanon" and to strengthen the military relationship between the United States and Lebanon.

41. In July 2006 the American Task Force for Lebanon called for the United States to pressure Israel to act with restraint in its war with Hezbollah. Although the United States stated that it wished to see an end to the violence, the United States sided strongly with Israel in the conflict and viewed Israel's response to the Hezbollah attacks as a "legitimate right to self-defense." For example, US ambassador to the UN John Bolton (2006) stated that Hezbollah operated "in Southern Lebanon with impunity," and Lebanon should have exercised its full authority over

(continues)

Table D.1 continued

Lebanese territory: "If that were done, then Israel would not be subject to terrorist attacks, [and] the people of Lebanon would not be subject to the reign of terror that Hezbollah inflicts."

42. According to the Congressional Research Service, the administration of Ronald Reagan suspended shipments of "so-called cluster bombs after allegations that Israel violated" the agreement to use the munitions only for defensive purposes (Mark 2005). The American Task Force for Lebanon indicates the ban is no longer in effect and the United States should pressure Israel to provide the coordinates for cluster bomb strikes against Lebanon to the UN to expedite demining operations.

43. See endnotes 9 and 10.

44. While the United States has expressed strong support for Pakistan since the 2001 terrorist attacks, the United States has declined to adopt the position of Pakistan and Pakistani Americans regarding Kashmir.

45. Serbian Americans opposed the UN Mission in Kosovo (UNMIK), while the United States supported the UN mission. Serbian Americans desired a "negotiated settlement" to the question of Kosovo, which involved "broad autonomy solutions" but would not involve granting the province independence. Serbian Americans did not appear to support US efforts to accelerate a decision regarding Kosovo, almost certainly because such efforts could result in granting Kosovo independence. US policy toward Kosovo shifted during the study: US policy in 2004 supported autonomy but not independence, and the United States opposed reaching an immediate decision on Kosovo. However, in 2005 the United States pressed for an accelerated time frame for reaching a resolution, and by 2007 the United States supported independence for the province. The coding is based on the status quo in 2005.

46. Somali American organizations advocate that the United States should develop a "more balanced and fair" policy toward the Horn of Africa, and a more active role in the humanitarian crisis in Somalia. However, while the United States supports achieving stability and peace in Somalia, it believes the best way to do so is by working "through the United Nations and NGO partners to improve governance in southern and central Somalia" (Knight 2007). In addition, some Somali American organizations seek the removal of Ethiopian troops from Somalia. The United States does not appear to believe Ethiopian troops should withdraw from Somalia until Somali stakeholders reconcile their differences and achieve a politically stable situation.

47. Although it is characterized as "nuanced and complex," official US policy states that "there is only one China and that Taiwan is a part of it" (Dumbaugh 2006). However, the Taiwan Relations Act provides for the sale of "defense articles and services" to Taiwan for its defense, and President Bush was quoted in 2001 as saying the United States would do "whatever it took" to defend Taiwan.

48. Taiwanese leaders face significant travel restrictions when visiting the United States, although the Bush administration allowed Taiwan president Chen Shui-bian to visit New York City in 2001 and 2003, and other Taiwanese officials were allowed to visit in 2002. This is a situation where the status quo has shifted slightly, and an ethnic group may have influenced the policymaking process.

49. US relations with Turkey are generally strong. The United States views Turkey to be of significant, perhaps critical, strategic importance. Since 2001, US military and security assistance to Turkey has increased, and Turkey received $200 million in economic support funds in 2002 to offset costs of Turkey's involvement in the International Security Assistance Force in Afghanistan (Migdalovitz 2002). The State Department has judged Turkey's human rights record as improving, but notes that serious problems remain.

50. Turkish American organizations would prefer that the issue of the Armenian genocide be removed from policy debates and that members of Congress cease their annual introduction of resolutions that acknowledge the genocide.

51. Ukrainian groups are most interested in providing "support for Ukraine's newly developing democracy" and securing aid for Ukrainians. The United States supports both these goals, although foreign aid for Ukraine peaked in fiscal year 2002 and has declined substantially since. The United States supported the "Orange Revolution" of 2004–2005, but the United States did not take significant actions against former president Viktor Yanukovych at the time (Woehrel 2006b).

Bibliography

Abraham, Yvonne. 2006. "Armenians Try to Stall Appointment of US Envoy." *Boston Globe* (August 30): B4.

Abramowitz, Alan. 1995. "It's Abortion, Stupid: Policy Voting in the 1992 Presidential Election." *Journal of Politics* 57: 176–186.

Adelman, Jonathan. 2000. "Condoleezza Rice Reflects a Changing of the Guard." *Rocky Mountain News* (Denver, December 19): 47A.

Adler, Emanuel, and Peter Haas. 1992. "Conclusion: Epistemic Communities, World Order, and the Creation of a Reflective Research Program." *International Organizations* 46: 367–390.

Agence France-Presse. 2004. "US Says World Court Barrier Ruling Would Undermine Peace Process." International News Section (February 23). Accessed from Lexis-Nexis.

Ahrari, Mohammed E. 1987. "Conclusions." In *Ethnic Groups and U.S. Foreign Policy,* ed. Mohammed E. Ahrari. Westport, CT: Greenwood Press.

Ainsworth, Scott H. 2002. *Analyzing Interest Groups: Group Influence on People and Policies.* New York: W. W. Norton & Co.

Albanian American Civic League. 2007. "About the Albanian American Civic League." http://aacl.com/about.shtml2.htm (accessed February 5, 2007).

Albert, Bruce. 2001. "Lobbying Work Pays Off for Livingston; Ex-Congressman Uses Old Ties to Help Clients." *Times-Picayune* (February 26): 1.

Almond, Gabriel A. 1960. *The American People and Foreign Policy.* New York: Praeger.

Ambrosio, Thomas. 2002a. "Congressional Perceptions of Ethnic Cleansing: Reactions to the Nagorno-Karabagh War and the Influence of Ethnic Interest Groups." *Review of International Affairs* 2: 24–45.

———. 2002b. "Entangling Alliances: The Turkish-Israeli Lobbying Partnership and Its Unintended Consequences." In *Ethnic Identity Groups and U.S. Foreign Policy,* ed. Thomas Ambrosio. Westport, CT: Praeger.

———. 2002c. "Legitimate Influence or Parochial Capture? Conclusions on Ethnic Identity Groups and the Formulation of U.S. Foreign Policy," in *Ethnic Identity Groups and U.S. Foreign Policy,* ed. Thomas Ambrosio. Westport, CT: Praeger.

Ament, Jonathon. 2004. *Jewish Immigrants in the United States.* New York: United Jewish Communities.

———. 2005. *Israel Connections and American Jews.* New York: United Jewish Communities.

American-Arab Anti Discrimination Committee. 2007. "Government Affairs: Get Active!" www.adc.org/index.php?id=2225 (accessed July 20, 2007).

American Hellenic Institute. 2002. "2002 Greek American Policy Statements." www.ahiworld.org/policystatement.html (accessed September 16, 2004).

———. 2007. "2007 Greek American Policy Statements." www.ahiworld.org/2007_policy_statements.html#1 (accessed August 14, 2007).

American Task Force for Lebanon. 2006. "Urgent Appeal—Must Lebanon be Destroyed?" www.atfl.org/cgi/print_announcement.cgi?&id=4857 (accessed August 13, 2007).

Anderson, Walter. 2006. "N-deal: The Turnaround of the US Congress." *The Indian Express* (July 11). www.indianexpress.com/story/8261.html.

Arab American Institute. 2006. "Talking Points on Middle East Crisis." www.aaiusa.org/issues/2274/talking-points-mideastcrisis (accessed August 14, 2007).

Armenia Assembly of America. 2007. "Vision and Mission." www.aaainc.org/index.php?id=86 (accessed August 8, 2007).

Armenian National Committee of America. 2005. "Armenian American Campaign Contributions Hit All-Time High." www.anca.org/press_releases/press_releases.php?prid=693 (accessed March 17, 2006).

Arsu, Sebnem, and Brian Knowlton. 2007. "Planned House Vote on Armenian Massacre Angers Turks." *New York Times* (March 30): A3.

Auerbach, Jon. 1995. "Scattered, a Community Bonds: A Vibrant Culture Melds a Tragic Past with a Bright Future." *Boston Globe* (April 23): 1.

Axtman, Kris. 2003. "Why Spanish Is the Favored New Language of Politics." *Christian Science Monitor* (August 20): 2.

Babcock, Charles R. 1991. "Israel's Backers Maximize Political Clout: Study Finds Supporters of Jewish State Give Directly to Candidates as Well as Related PACs." *Washington Post* (September 26): A21.

Bachrach, Peter, and Morton S. Baratz. 1962. "Two Faces of Power." *American Political Science Review* 56: 947–952.

Bachrack, Stanley D. 1976. *The Committee of One Million: "China Lobby" Politics, 1953–1971.* New York: Columbia University Press.

Bahrampour, Tara. 2006. "Reveling in Eritrea's Independence." *Washington Post* (May 30): B1.

Banerjee, Neela. 2006. "Muslims' Plight in Sudan Resonates with Jews in U.S." *New York Times* (April 30): A21.

Baradat, Leon P. 2000. *Political Ideologies: Their Origins and Impact,* 7th ed. Upper Saddle River, NJ: Prentice Hall.

Bard, Mitchell Geoffrey. 1991. *The Water's Edge and Beyond: Defining the Limits of Domestic Influence on United States Middle East Policy.* New Brunswick, NJ: Transaction Publishers.

Barilleaux, Ryan J. 1985. *The President and Foreign Affairs: Evaluation, Performance, and Power.* New York: Praeger.

Bauer, Raymond A., Ithiel de Sola Pool, and Lewis Anthony Dexter. 1963. *American Business and Public Policy: The Politics of Foreign Trade.* New York: Atherton Press.

Berry, Jeffery. 1997. *The Interest Group Society,* 3rd ed. New York: Longman.

Birnbaum, Jeffrey H. 2001. "Power 25 2001: Whose Party Is It?" *Fortune* (August 2).

———. 2005. "Hill a Steppingstone to K Street for Some; More Ex-Lawmakers Who Join Private Sector Are Becoming Lobbyists, Study Says." *Washington Post* (July 27): A19.

Bolton, John R. 2006. "Situation in the Middle East." USUN Press Release #179 (July 21). www.state.gov/p/io/rls/rm/69314.htm.

Boustany, Nora. 1990. "Arab-American Lobby Is Struggling: Internal Disputes, Money Problems Said to Limit Effectiveness." *Washington Post* (April 6): A10.

Brady, Henry E., Sidney Verba, and Kay Lehman Schlozman. 1995. "Beyond SES: A Resource Model of Political Participation." *American Political Science Review* 89: 271–294.

Brenner, Philip, and Saul Landau. 1990. "Passive Aggressive." *NACLA: Report on the Americas* 24 (3): 13–25.

Brown, Clifford W., Jr., Linda W. Powell, and Clyde Wilcox. 1995. *Serious Money: Fundraising and Contributing in Presidential Nomination Campaigns.* New York: Cambridge University Press.

Bureau of Democracy, Human Rights, and Labor. 2006. "Turkey: Country Reports on Human Rights Practices, 2005." www.state.gov/g/drl/rls/hrrpt/2005/61680.htm.

Burress, Charles. 1994. "Some Vietnamese Defend U.S. Embargo: Too Soon to Shift Policy, Bay Area Critics Say." *San Francisco Chronicle* (February 2): A11.

Carassava, Anthee. 2004. "U.S. to Recognize Ex-Yugoslav Republic as Macedonia." *New York Times* (November 5): A10.

Carroll, Joe. 1998. "US Funding for North Linked to Fair Employment Code: Congress Insists Recipients Stick to MacBride Principles." *The Irish Times* (October 22): 10.

Center for Responsive Politics. n.d. "The Cuban Connection: Cuban-American Money in U.S. Elections 1979–2000." www.opensecrets.org/pubs/cubareport/index.asp.

Challenor, Herschelle Sullivan. 1981. "The Influence of Black Americans on U.S. Foreign Policy Toward Africa." In *Ethnicity and U.S. Foreign Policy,* revised ed., ed. Abdul Aziz Said. New York: Praeger.

Chandrasekaran, Rajiv. 2007. "Kurds Cultivating Their Own Bonds with U.S." *Washington Post* (April 23): A1.

Chong, Dennis. 1991. *Collective Action and the Civil Rights Movement.* Chicago: University of Chicago Press.

Clough, Michael. 2001. "Grass-Roots Policymaking: Say Good-Bye to the 'Wise Men.'" *Foreign Affairs* 73 (1): 2–7.

Cody, Edward. 2006. "U.S. Aims to Improve Military Ties with China." *Washington Post* (May 16): A14.

Cohen, Bernard C. 1973. *The Public's Impact on Foreign Policy.* Boston: Little, Brown and Company.

Cohen, Eliot A. 2006. "Yes, It's Anti-Semitic." *Washington Post* (April 5): A23.

Coile, Zachary, and Robert Salladay. 2000. "Bush Picks Powell for State Dept., Aides Say; He'll Become First Black to Lead Diplomatic Corps." *San Francisco Chronicle* (December 16): A1.

Columbia Books and Information Services. 2004. *Washington Representatives.* Washington, DC: Columbia Books.

Conference of Presidents of Major American Jewish Organizations. 2008. "50 Years of Achievements." www.conferenceofpresidents.org/content.asp?id=52 (accessed March 5, 2008).

Congleton, Roger D. 1991. "Information, Special Interests, and Single-Issue Voting." *Public Choice* 69: 39–49.

Converse, Philip E. 1964. "The Nature of Belief Systems in the Mass Public." In *Ideology and Discontent,* ed. David E. Apter. New York: Free Press.

Cornwell, Rupert. 2006. "Row over US Ambassador's Armenia Genocide Remark." *The Independent* (London, March 23): 31.

Curry, Tom. 2006. "Gaffe Underscores Indian-American Clout: Sen. Allen's Blunder Puts Focus on Growing Group of Donors and Voters." MSNBC (posted on August 17). www.msnbc.msn.com/id/14395449/from/RS.2/ (accessed August 17, 2006).

Curtiss, Richard H. 1999. "Fallout from Ethnic Cleansing in Kosovo and Six Weeks of NATO Bombing of Serbia: 5 Lessons." *Washington Report on Middle East Affairs* 18 (4): 7.

———. 2000. "The Case for a Muslim- and Arab-American Bloc Vote in 2000." *Washington Report on Middle East Affairs* 19 (5): 22.

Dagne, Ted. 2005. *Sudan: Humanitarian Crisis, Peace Talks, Terrorism, and U.S. Policy.* CRS Issue Brief for Congress (June 9).

Dagne, Ted, and Bathsheaba Everett. 2004. *Sudan: The Darfur Crisis and the Status of the North-South Negotiations.* CRS Issue Brief for Congress (October 22).

Davey, Monica. 2007. "Leader's Arrest Uncovers Divide in Hmong-Americans." *New York Times* (June 14): A20.

DeConde, Alexander. 1992. *Ethnicity, Race, and American Foreign Policy: A History.* Boston: Northeastern Press.

Deutsch, Karl W. 1961. "Social Mobilization and Political Development." *American Political Science Review* 55 (3): 493–514.

Dillin, John. 2001. "The Price Taiwan Pays for US Vow of Assistance." *Christian Science Monitor* (April 30): 2.

Dobbs, Michael. 2001. "Foreign Aid Shrinks, but Not for All; With Clout in Congress, Armenia's Share Grows." *Washington Post* (January 24): A1.

Doherty, Carroll J. 1995a. "Appropriations: This Year, Aid Is a Weapon." *CQ Weekly* (June 17): 1763.

———. 1995b. "Bosnia: Bosnia's Weapon in the U.S." *CQ Weekly* (July 29): 2283.

———. 1995c. "House, Senate Remain at Odds over Family Planning Aid." *CQ Weekly* (November 4): 3387.

———. 1996a. "State Department: Conferees Agree on Bill to Abolish an Agency." *CQ Weekly* (March 9): 634.

———. 1996b. "Appropriations: House Curbs Aid to Turkey After Sharp Debate." *CQ Weekly* (June 8): 1610.

———. 1997. "Proliferation of Sanctions Creates a Tangle of Good Intentions." *CQ Weekly* (September 13): 2113.

Donfried, Karen. 2001. *Northern Ireland: Implementation of the Peace Agreement During the 106th Congress.* CRS Report for Congress (January 5).

Doyle, Michael. 2006. "Diplomatic Post Tangled in History: The U.S. Ambassadorship to Armenia Is Snagged on the Nominee's Refusal to Call the Slaughter of Armenians Genocide." *Star Tribune* (Minneapolis, August 6): 3A.

Dudden, Alexis. 2006. "US Congressional Resolution Calls on Japan to Accept Responsibility for Wartime Comfort Women." *Japan Focus* (posted on April 22, 2006). www.japanfocus.org/products/details/1908 (accessed February 7, 2007).

Dumbaugh, Kerry. 2006. *Taiwan-U.S. Political Relations: New Strains and Changes.* CRS Report for Congress (October 10).

Duncan, Philip D., and Brian Nutting, eds. 1999. *Congressional Quarterly's Politics in America: 2000, the 106rd Congress.* Washington, DC: CQ Press.

Edsall, Thomas. 2002. "GOP Eyes Jewish Vote with Bush Tack on Israel; President's Policy Has Community Leaders Questioning Democratic Allegiance." *Washington Post* (April 30): A7.

Enloe, Cynthia. 1986. *Ethnic Conflict and Political Development.* Lanham, MD: University Press of America.

Entman, Robert M. 2004. *Projections of Power: Framing News, Public Opinion, and U.S. Foreign Policy.* Chicago: University of Chicago Press.

Erikson, Robert S., and Kent L. Tedin. 2005. *American Public Opinion: Its Origins, Content, and Impact,* 7th ed. New York: Longman.

Esman, Milton J. 1994. *Ethnic Politics.* Ithaca: Cornell University Press.

Espiritu, Yen Le. 1992. *Asian American Pan-ethnicity: Bridging Institutions and Identities.* Philadelphia: Temple University Press.

Fears, Darryl. 2006. "IRS Ends 2-Year Probe of NAACP's Tax Status; Leader's Criticism of Bush in 2004 Did Not Violate Law, Agency Decides." *Washington Post* (September 1): A3.

Federal Election Commission. 1999. *Federal Elections 98: Election Results for the U.S. Senate and the U.S. House of Representatives.* April. Washington, DC.

———. 2001. *Federal Elections 2000: Election Results for the U.S. President, the U.S. Senate and the U.S. House of Representatives.* Washington, DC.

———. 2003. *Federal Elections 2002: Election Results for the U.S. Senate and the U.S. House of Representatives.* June. Washington, DC.

Federation of Korean Associations USA. 2007. "Goals and Guides." www.korean fedus.org/eng/fka_goals.php (accessed February 8, 2007).

Felton, John. 1984a. "Foreign Relations' Percy: On Political Tightrope." *CQ Weekly* (October 20): 2687.

———. 1984b. "Major Recipients of Aid: Capitol Hill Provides a Forum for Turkish-Greek Differences," *CQ Weekly* (December 15): 3098.

Fitzgerald, Barbara. 2003. "After a Slow Climb, Hispanics Gather Power." *New York Times* (January 20, section 14NJ): 1.

Foreign Agents Registration Act. 1938. *US Code* 22, §611.

Forsythe, Michael, and Veena Trehan. 2006. "Friends in High Places Help India." *International Herald Tribune* (July 17). www.iht.com/articles/2006/07/17/bloomberg/sxrupee.php.

Frankel, Glenn. 2006. "A Beautiful Friendship? In Search of the Truth About the Israel Lobby's Influence on Washington." *Washington Post Magazine* (July 16): W13.

Frieden, Jeffry A. 1996. "Economic Integration and the Politics of Monetary Policy in the United States." In *Internationalization and Domestic Politics,* ed. Robert O. Keohane and Helen V. Milner. Cambridge: Cambridge University Press.

Friess, Steve. 2004. "Oy Vegas! Sin City Gets Kosher: Rising Jewish Population Feels at Home." *Boston Globe* (April 4): A14.

Frisby, Michael K. 1991. "Taking Out Territory: Pro-Israeli Lobby Groups Viewed as a Force in D.C." *Boston Globe* (September 20): 1.

Garrett, Stephen A. 1978. "Eastern European Ethnic Groups and American Foreign Policy." *Political Science Quarterly* 93: 301–323.

Gerber, Elisabeth R. 1999. *The Populist Paradox: Interest Group Influence and the Promise of Direct Legislation.* Princeton, NJ: Princeton University Press.

German American National Congress. n.d. "What Is DANK?" www.dank.org/what_is_dank_.htm (accessed September 23, 2004).

Geron, Kim, Enrique de la Cruz, Leland T. Saito, and Jaideep Singh. 2001. "Asian Pacific Americans' Social Movements and Interest Groups." *PS: Political Science & Politics* 34: 619–624.

Glastris, Paul, Kevin Whitelaw, Bruce Auster, and Barbra Murray. 1997. "Multicultural Foreign Policy in Washington." *U.S. News & World Report* (July 21): 30.

Glazer, Nathan, and Daniel P. Moynihan. 1963. *Beyond the Melting Pot.* Cambridge MA: M.I.T. Press and Harvard University Press.

———. 1975. *Ethnicity.* Cambridge, MA: Harvard University Press.

Goldberg, David Howard. 1990. *Foreign Policy and Ethnic Interest Groups: American and Canadian Jews Lobby for Israel.* Westport, CT: Greenwood Press.

Goldgeier, James M. 1999. *Not Whether but When: The U.S. Decision to Enlarge NATO.* Washington, DC: Brookings Institution Press.

Gonzalez, David, and Abby Goodnough. 2006. "Cubans in U.S. Feel the Tug of Two Homes." *New York Times* (August 3): A1.

Goodnough, Abby. 2005. "Florida's Zeal Against Castro Is Losing Heat." *New York Times* (July 6): A1.

———. 2006. "All in the Family, Brothers Wage War on Uncle Fidel." *New York Times* (March 8): A18.

Graham, Thomas W. 1994. "Public Opinion and U.S. Foreign Policy." In *The New Politics of American Foreign Policy,* ed. David E. Deese. New York: St. Martin's Press.

Greenhouse, Stephen. 1994. "State Dept. Criticizes White House on Macedonia Ties." *New York Times* (April 19): A6.

———. 1995. "Greece and Macedonia Ready to Settle Dispute, U.S. Says." *New York Times* (September 5): A9.

Greve, Frank. 1995. "Ethnic Lobby Powers Up." *The Armenian Reporter* 28 (50) (September 30): 16.

Gugliotta, Guy. 1998. "Hard-Liners Dig in on the Issue of Embargo; Cuban American Foundation Is Determined Not to Founder After Loss of Its Leader." *Washington Post* (January 21): A16.

Haas, Peter M. 1992. "Introduction: Epistemic Communities and International Policy Coordination." *International Organization* 46 (1): 1–35.

Hackett, Clifford. 1981. "Ethnic Politics in Congress: The Turkish Embargo Experience." In *Ethnicity and U.S. Foreign Policy,* revised ed., ed. Abdul Aziz Said. New York: Praeger.

Hall, Richard L., and Frank W. Wayman. 1990. "Buying Time: Moneyed Interests and the Mobilization of Bias in Congressional Committees." *The American Political Science Review* 84 (3): 797–820.

Haney, Patrick J., and Walt Vanderbush. 1999. "The Role of Ethnic Interest Groups in U.S. Foreign Policy: The Case of the Cuban American National Foundation." *International Studies Quarterly* 43: 341–361.

Harris, John F. 1997. "Tape Catches Choice Words About Clinton," *Washington Post* (July 10): A24.

Hastedt, Glenn P. 2006. *American Foreign Policy: Past, Present, Future,* 6th ed. Upper Saddle River, NJ: Pearson Prentice Hall.

Hawkings, David, and Brian Nutting, eds. 2003. *Congressional Quarterly's Politics in America: 2004, the 108rd Congress.* Washington, DC: CQ Press.

Hayes, Michael T. 1992. *Incrementalism and Public Policy.* New York: Longman.

Hebrew Immigrant Aid Society. n.d. "Emergency Appeals." www.hias.org/get involved/eappeals.php#Chad (accessed September 6, 2007).

Herrmann, Richard K., Philip E. Tetlock, and Penny S. Visser. 1999. "Mass Public Decisions to Go to War: A Cognitive-Interactionist Framework." *American Political Science Review* 93: 553–573.

Herrnson, Paul S. 2005. "Interest Groups and Campaigns: The Electoral Connection." *The Interest Group Connection: Electioneering, Lobbying, and Policymaking in Washington,* 2nd ed., ed. Paul S. Herrnson, Ronald G. Shaiko, and Clyde Wilcox. Washington, DC: CQ Press.

———. 2008. *Congressional Elections: Campaigning at Home and in Washington,* 5th ed. Washington, DC: CQ Press.

Hicks, Sallie M., and Theodore A. Couloumbis. 1981. "The 'Greek Lobby': Illusion or Reality?" In *Ethnicity and U.S. Foreign Policy,* revised ed., ed. Abdul Aziz Said. New York: Praeger.

Hinkley, Barbara. 1994. *Less Than Meets the Eye: Congress, the President, and Foreign Policy.* Chicago: University of Chicago Press.

Hirsch, Herbert. 1995. *Genocide and the Politics of Memory.* Chapel Hill: University of North Carolina Press.

Holder, Kelly. 2006. *Voting and Registration in the Election of November 2004.* U.S. Department of Commerce. www.census.gov/prod/2006pubs/p20-556.pdf.

Holsti, Ole R. 2004. *Public Opinion and American Foreign Policy,* revised ed. Ann Arbor: University of Michigan Press.

Holzer, Jessica. 2005. "Hispanic Alliance Pushes for Trade Pact; Pro-CAFTA Latinos Needed a Voice, Group Says." *Houston Chronicle* (July 27): Business 4.

Hrebenar, Ronald J., and Clive S. Thomas. 1995. "The Japanese Lobby in Washington: How Different Is It?" In *Interest Group Politics,* 4th ed., ed. Allan J. Cigler and Burdett A. Loomis. Washington, DC: CQ Press.

Hula, Kevin. 1995. "Rounding Up the Usual Suspects: Forging Interest Group Coalitions in Washington." In *Interest Group Politics,* 4th ed., ed. Allan J. Cigler and Burdett A. Loomis. Washington, DC: CQ Press.

Huntington, Samuel P. 1997. "The Erosion of American National Interests." *Foreign Affairs* (September/October).

Idelson, Holly. 1996. "Ethnic Groups Add Voices to Critics of GOP Plans." *CQ Weekly* (January 13): 92.

Iritani, Evelyn. 2006. "Hopes for a Vietnam Trade Shift: A Proposal to Normalize Relations Would Benefit U.S. Importers." *Los Angeles Times* (July 24): C1.

Jacobs, Lawrence R., and Benjamin I. Page. 2005. "Who Influences U.S. Foreign Policy?" *American Political Science Review* 99 (1): 107–124.

Jentleson, Bruce W. 1992. "The Pretty Prudent Public: Post Post-Vietnam American Opinion on the Use of Military Force." *International Studies Quarterly* 36: 49–74.

Jentleson, Bruce W., and Rebecca L. Britton. 1998. "Still Pretty Prudent: Post–Cold War American Public Opinion on the Use of Military Force." *Journal of Conflict Resolution* 42: 395–417.

Johnson, Paul. 1997. "A Sieve Model of Interest Group Recruitment." Presented at the Meetings of the American Political Science Association, Washington, DC, August 1997.

Joint Baltic American National Committee. 2007. "U.S. Must Support Estonia and Other Targets of Russian Aggression." www.jbanc.org/paper23.html (accessed August 17, 2007).

Jones, Dale E., Sherri Doty, James E. Horsch, Richard Houseal, Ma Lynn, John P. Marcum, Kenneth M. Sanchagrin, and Richard H. Taylor. 2002. *Religious Congregations and Membership in the United States 2000: An Enumeration by Region, State, and County Based on Data Reported by 149 Religious Bodies.* Nashville, TN: Glenmary Research Center.

Jones-Correa, Michael. 2002. "Latinos and Latin America: A Unified Agenda?" In *Ethnic Identity Groups and U.S. Foreign Policy,* ed. Thomas Ambrosio. Westport, CT: Praeger.

Jubilee USA. 2007. "The Jubilee Act." www.jubileeusa.org/jubilee-act.html (accessed September 28, 2007).

Kahneman, Daniel, and Amos Tversky. 1979. "Prospect Theory: An Analysis of Decisions Under Risk." *Econometrica* 47: 263–291.

Kamen, Al. 1991. "Immigration 'Sweepstakes': Odds Will Favor the Irish; Program Earmarks 40% of Available Visas." *Washington Post* (July 28): A1.

Kegley, Charles W., Jr., and Eugene R. Wittkopf. 1999. *World Politics: Trend and Transformation,* 7th ed. New York: Worth Publishers.

Kemp, George. 1999. "Presidential Management of the Executive Bureaucracy." In *The Domestic Sources of American Foreign Policy: Insights and Evidence,* 3rd ed., ed. Eugene R. Wittkopf and James M. McCormick. Lanham, MD: Rowman & Littlefield.

Kennan, George Frost. 1977. *The Cloud of Danger: Current Realities of American Foreign Policy.* Boston: Little, Brown.

Kenworthy, Tom. 1990. "Unity Eludes Hill's Irish-Americans on Thorny Ulster Question." *Washington Post* (April 10): A4.

Keohane, Robert O. 1984. *After Hegemony: Cooperation and Discord in the World Political Economy.* Princeton, NJ: Princeton University Press.

Knight, James. 2007. "U.S. Policy in the Horn of Africa." Remarks from the Conference Working Toward a Lasting Peace in the Ogaden. University of San Diego, CA, December 7. www.state.gov/p/af/rls/rm/97261.htm.

Koh, Harold Hongju. 1988. "Why the President (Almost) Always Wins in Foreign Affairs: Lessons of the Iran-Contra Affair." *Yale Law Journal* 97: 1255–1342.

Kollman, Ken. 1998. *Outside Lobbying: Public Opinion & Interest Group Strategies.* Princeton, NJ: Princeton University Press.

Korean American Coalition. 2007a. "Justice for Comfort Women" (September 26, 2006). www.kacla.org/News_and_Events/Breaking_News/83.html (accessed February 8, 2007).

———. 2007b. "Mission Statement." www.kacla.org/About_KAC/About_KAC_pages/2.html (accessed February 8, 2007).

Koszczuk, Jackie, and H. Amy Stern, eds. 2005. *Congressional Quarterly's Politics in America: 2006, the 109th Congress.* Washington, DC: CQ Press.

Krosnick, Jon A. 1990. "Government Policy and Citizen Passion: A Study of Issue Publics in Contemporary America." *Political Behavior* 12: 59–92.

Lampman, Jane. 2004. "Mixing Prophecy and Politics." *Christian Science Monitor* (July 7): 15.

Lancaster, John. 1999. "Activism Boosts India's Fortunes; Politically Vocal Immigrants Help Tilt Policy in Washington." *Washington Post* (October 9): A1.

———. 2000. "Compromising Positions: Susan and Daniel Cohen Feel Twice Victimized." *Washington Post Magazine* (June 25): W10.

Landler, Mark. 2001. "A Visit Caught Between the Passions of International Rivalries." *New York Times* (May 21): B9.

Lindblom, Charles E. 1977. *Politics and Markets: The World's Political-Economic Systems.* New York: Basic Books.

Lindsay, James M. 1994. *Congress and the Politics of U.S. Foreign Policy.* Baltimore: Johns Hopkins University Press.

Lippmann, Walter. 1955. *Essays in Public Philosophy.* Boston: Little, Brown.

Longworth, R. C. 1998. "One Nation, Many Voices: As Members of Congress Exert More Leadership, Special Interests Find They Can Have Exceptional Influence." *Chicago Tribune* (April 13): 1.

Lowi, Theodore J. 1969. *The End of Liberalism.* New York: W. W. Norton & Company.

Lukes, Steven. 1974. *Power: A Radical View.* London: Macmillan.

Lum, Thomas, and Larry A. Niksch. 2006. *The Republic of the Philippines: Background and U.S. Relations.* CRS Report for Congress (January 10).

MacFarquhar, Neil. 2006. "Exiles in 'Tehrangeles' Are Split on Iran." *New York Times* (May 9): A1.

————. 2007. "In Arab Capital of U.S., Ethnic Divide Remains." *New York Times* (January 23): A12.

Madison, James. 1787. *The Federalist No. 10.*

Manning, Bayless. 1977. "The Congress, the Executive, and Intermestic Affairs: Three Proposals." *Foreign Affairs* (January): 306–324.

Mark, Clyde. 2004. *Palestinians and Middle East Peace: Issues for the United States.* CRS Issue Brief for Congress (July 8).

————. 2005. *Israel: U.S. Foreign Assistance.* CRS Issue Brief for Congress (April 25).

Mayhew, David R. 1974. *Congress: The Electoral Connection.* New Haven, CT: Yale University Press.

McCarthy, John D., and Mayer N. Zald. 1977. "Resource Mobilization and Social Movements: A Partial Theory." *American Journal of Sociology* 82: 1212–1241.

McIntire, Mike. 2006. "Indian-Americans Test Their Clout on Atom Pact." *New York Times* (June 5): A1.

McMahon, Janet. 2004. "If You've Got It, Flaunt It (or Maybe Not): An AIPAC Primer." *Washington Report on Middle East Affairs* (November). www.wrmea .com/archives/November_2004/0411024.html.

Mearsheimer, John J., and Stephen M. Walt. 2007. *The Israel Lobby and U.S. Foreign Policy.* New York: Farrar, Straus and Giroux.

Melanson, Richard A. 2005. *American Foreign Policy Since the Vietnam War: The Search for Consensus from Richard Nixon to George W. Bush,* 4th ed. Armonk, NY: M. E. Sharpe.

Melvin, Don, and Keith Graham. 2000. "Here and Abroad." *Atlanta Journal and Constitution* (June 8): 17A.

Menendez, Robert. 2006. "Menendez Blocks Bush Nominee for Ambassador to Armenia." Press release issued September 12, 2006. http://menendez.senate.gov/ newsroom/record.cfm?id=262886.

Mexican American Legal Defense and Education Fund. 2007. "About Us." www .maldef.org/about/index.htm (accessed February 14, 2007).

Migdalovitz, Carol. 2002. *Turkey: Issues for U.S. Policy.* CRS Report for Congress (May 22).

Milbrath, Lester W. 1967. "Interest Groups and Foreign Policy." In *Domestic Sources of Foreign Policy* ed. James N. Rosenau. New York: The Free Press.

Moe, Terry. 1980. *The Organization of Interests.* Chicago: University of Chicago Press.

————. 1981. "Toward a Broader View of Interest Groups." *Journal of Politics* 43: 531–543.

Moller, Jan. 2003. "Pakistani-Americans Back Blanco in Runoff; Jindal's Indian Roots Make Some Uneasy." *Times-Picayune* (November 7): 2.

Moon, Chung-In. 1988. "Complex Interdependence and Transnational Lobbying: South Korea in the United States." *International Studies Quarterly* 32: 67–89.

Morgan, Dan, and Kevin Merida. 1997. "South Asia Rivals Had Money on South Dakota Senate Race; Ethnic Donors Play Powerful Role in U.S. Politics." *Washington Post* (March 24): A01.

Mufson, Steven. 2000. "Local Politics Is Global as Hill Turns to Armenia." *Washington Post* (October 9): A1.

NAACP. 2004. "Legislative Priorities for the 108th Congress" (PDF file).

National Action Committee (NACPAC). 2007. Home Page. www.nacpac.org (accessed March 15, 2007).

National Albanian American Council. 2004. "NAAC Condemns the Violence in Kosovo, Calls for Recognition of Independence." www.naac.org/pr/2004/03-19-04.html (accessed September 14, 2004).

————. 2007. "The Albanian-American Voice in Washington." www.naac.org/index
.php?cid=1,2 (accessed February 5, 2007).

National Association of Korean Americans. 2003. "Call for New U.S.–North Korea
Relations." www.naka.org/news/news.asp?prmid=7 (accessed August 14, 2007).

National Council of Asian Pacific Americans. 2004. *Call to Action: Platform for
Asian Pacific National Policy Priorities.* http://ncapaonline.org/2004_Call_to_
Action.pdf.

Navarro, Mireya. 2004. "Blacks and Latinos Try to Find Balance in Touchy New
Math." *New York Times* (January 17): A1.

NCSJ. 2007. "About NCSJ." www.ncsj.org/about.shtml (accessed March 19, 2007).

Negroponte, John. 2007. "Remarks at Press Conference in Tokyo" (August 3). www
.state.gov/s/d/2007/90077.htm.

Newhouse, John. 1992. "Reporter at Large: Socialism or Death." *New Yorker* (April
27): 52–83.

NORPAC. 2007. "Welcome to NORPAC." www.norpac.net/ (accessed March 15, 2007).

Nownes, Anthony J. 2006. *Total Lobbying: What Lobbyists Want (and How They
Try to Get It).* New York: Cambridge University Press.

Nutting, Brian, and H. Amy Stern, eds. 2001. *Congressional Quarterly's Politics in
America: 2002, the 107th Congress.* Washington, DC: CQ Press.

O'Brien, Keith. 2007. "Armenian Campaign Aided by New Forces Recognition of
Genocide Grows." *Boston Globe* (August 26): A1.

Oliver, Pamela. 1984. "If You Don't Do It, Nobody Else Will." *American Sociological Review* 49: 601–610.

Olson, Mancur. 1965. *The Logic of Collective Action.* Cambridge: Harvard University Press.

Omestad, Thomas. 1988. "Dateline Taiwan: A Dynasty Ends." *Foreign Policy:*
176–198.

Onishi, Norimitsu. 1995. "Japanese in America Looking Beyond Past to Shape
Future." *New York Times* (December 25): A1.

Order Sons of Italy in America. 2007. "Legislation, Public Policy and Government
Affairs." www.osia.org/public/legislative/legislative_intro.asp (accessed June
27, 2007).

Ottaway, David B., and Dan Morgan. 1999. "Jewish-Armenian Split Spreads on the
Hill; Strategic Issues Put Onetime Lobbying Allies at Odds." *Washington Post*
(February 9): A15.

Page, Benjamin I., and Robert Y. Shapiro. 1983. "Effects of Public Opinion on Policy." *American Political Science Review* 77 (1): 175–190.

Paul, David M., and Rachel Anderson Paul. 2005. "Assessing the Power of Ethnic-
American Lobbies." Presented at the 2005 Annual Meeting of the Midwest
Political Science Association, Chicago, IL, April 7–10.

Paul, Rachel Anderson. 1999. *Mobilizing Diasporas: A Comparative Study of the
Political Mobilization of Ethnic Interest Groups in the United States.* Unpub-
lished dissertation.

————. 2000. "Grassroots Mobilization and Diaspora Politics: Armenian Interest
Groups and the Role of Collective Memory." *Nationalism and Ethnic Politics*
6: 24–47.

————. 2002. "Serbian-American Mobilization and Lobbying: The Relevance of
Jasenovac and Kosovo to Contemporary Grassroots Efforts in the United States."
In *Ethnic Identity Groups and U.S. Foreign Policy,* ed. Thomas Ambrosio. West-
port, CT: Praeger.

Pomper, Miles A., with Sumana Chatterjee. 2000. "Congress Embraces India as
Pakistan's Influence Fades." *CQ Weekly* (May 18).

Powlick, Philip J. 1991. "The Attitudinal Bases for Responsiveness to Public Opinion Among American Policy Officials." *The Journal of Conflict Resolution* 35: 611–641.

———. 1995. "The Sources of Public Opinion for American Foreign Policy Officials." *International Studies Quarterly* 39: 427–451.

Prados, Alfred B. 2006. *Lebanon*. CRS Issue Brief for Congress (June 8).

Pressman, Steven. 1985. "Maturing Arab Lobby Gears Up Against Israel." *CQ Weekly* (May 4): 859.

Rauch, Jonathan. 1994. *Demosclerosis: The Silent Killer of American Government*. New York: Times Books.

Reynolds, Maura. 2007. "Genocide Question Hits Home; Use of the Term by the Former U.S. Ambassador to Armenia Sets Up a Battle in Congress." *Los Angeles Times* (January 7): A20.

Rogers, Barbara, ed. 2005. *Congressional Quarterly's The Almanac of Federal PACs: 2006–2007*. Washington, DC: CQ Press.

Rogers, Elizabeth S. 1993. "The Conflicting Roles of American Ethnic and Business Interests in the U.S. Economic Sanctions Policy: The Case of South Africa." In *The Limits of State Autonomy: Societal Groups and Foreign Policy Formulation*, ed. David Skidmore and Valerie M. Hudson. Boulder, CO: Westview Press.

Rosenthal, Andrew. 1991. "Aides Say Bush Is Shifting Focus to Relations Among the Republics." *New York Times* (November 30): 1.

Ross, Robert S. 2006. "Taiwan's Fading Independence Movement." *Foreign Affairs* 85: 141–148.

Rothschild, Joseph. 1981. *Ethnopolitics: A Conceptual Framework*. New York: Columbia University Press.

Rothstein, Kevin. 2006. "Expert Says Slaughter Fits Bill, Despite Turks' Denial." *Boston Herald* (April 19): 4.

Rozell, Mark J., and Clyde Wilcox. 1999. *Interest Groups in American Campaigns*. Washington, DC: CQ Press.

Salisbury, Robert H. 1969. "An Exchange Theory of Interest Groups." *Midwest Journal of Political Science* 13: 1–32.

———. 1984. "Interest Representation: The Dominance of Institutions." *American Political Science Review* 78: 64–76.

Sammon, Richard. 1995. "Appropriations: McConnell: Get Tough on Myanmar." *CQ Weekly* (September 16): 2823.

Schattschneider, E. E. 1960. *The Semi-Sovereign People*. New York: Holt, Rinehart, and Winston.

Schlesinger, James R. 1997. "Fragmentation and Hubris: A Shaky Basis for American Leadership." *National Interest* 49: 3–9.

Schlozman, Kay Lehman, and John T. Tierney. 1986. *Organized Interests and American Democracy*. New York: HarperCollins.

Schmitt, Eric. 2000. "Republican's Unusual Gift: A Vote on the House Floor." *New York Times* (October 7): A11.

Scott, Fran, and Abdulah Osman. 2002. "Identity, African-Americans, and U.S. Foreign Policy: Differing Reactions to South African Apartheid and the Rwanda Genocide." In *Ethnic Identity Groups and U.S. Foreign Policy*, ed. Thomas Ambrosio. Westport, CT: Praeger.

Scroggins, Deborah. 1994. "Vietnamese in Atlanta Split over Lifting Curbs." *Atlanta Journal and Constitution* (February 3): A17.

Semerdjian, Elyse. 1997. "Diplomatic Doings: Azerbaijani President's Visit Makes Waves in Washington." *Washington Report on Middle East Affairs* (October/November): 64–65.

Serbian Unity Congress. 2007. "House Resolution 445: Help Support This Resolution." http://serbianunity.net/projects/Information/support_for_hres_445.doc (accessed August 13, 2007).

Shaiko, Ronald G. 2005. "Making the Connection: Organized Interest, Political Representation, and the Changing Rules of the Game in Washington Politics." In *The Interest Group Connection,* 2nd ed., ed. Paul. S. Herrnson, Ronald G. Shaiko, and Clyde Wilcox. Washington, DC: CQ Press.

Shain, Yossi. 1994. "Ethnic Diasporas and U.S. Foreign Policy." *Political Science Quarterly* 109: 811–841.

———. 1995. "Multicultural Foreign Policy." *Foreign Policy* 100: 69–87.

———. 1999. "The Mexican-American Diaspora's Impact on Mexico." *Political Science Quarterly* 114: 661–691.

Shapiro, Robert Y., and Benjamin I. Page. 1988. "Foreign Policy and the Rational Public." *Journal of Conflict Resolution* 32: 211–247.

Sheskin, Ira M. 2007a. *The 2005 Jewish Community Study of Southern Nevada,* Main Report Volume 1. United Jewish Community: Jewish Federation of Las Vegas. www.jewishdatabank.org.

———. 2007b. "Changes in American Jewish Demography: Political Implications." Presented at International Conference on U.S.-Israel Relations at the Begin-Sadat Center for Strategic Studies.

Sheskin, Ira M., and Arnold Dashefsky. 2006. "Jewish Population in the United States, 2006." In *The American Jewish Yearbook,* ed. David Singer and Lawrence Grossman, 133–193. New York: American Jewish Committee.

Siddiqui, Habib. 2006. "Israel's Latest Invasion of Lebanon and Western Culpability." www.aaiusa.org/press-room/2356/aainews080106.

Smith, Tony. 2000. *Foreign Attachments: The Power of Ethnic Groups in the Making of American Foreign Policy.* Cambridge, MA: Harvard University Press.

Smucker, Bob. 1999. *The Nonprofit Lobbying Guide,* 2nd ed. Washington, DC: The Independent Sector. www.independentsector.org/programs/gr/lobbyguide.html.

Snyder, Jim. 2006. "Ethiopian-American Group Tries to Raise Profile on Capitol Hill." *The Hill* (Washington, DC, September 21).

Solis, Dianna. 1993. "U.S. Hispanics Flex Political Muscles as Mexico Lobbies for Nafta Support." *Wall Street Journal* (March 3): 10.

Stanfield, Rochelle L. 1991. "Arab American Voices." *The National Journal* 23: 359.

Stern, Eric. 2004. "Iraq's Past and Future Assyrians Gather at Capitol Rally; Participants Praise U.S. Action and Call for a Stronger Role in Iraq." *Sacramento Bee* (March 20): A3.

Stolberg, Sheryl Gay. 2006. "Bush's Embrace of Israel Shows Gap with Father." *New York Times* (August 2): A1.

Sullivan, Mark P., Colleen W. Cook, J. F. Hornbeck, Clare M. Ribando, Maureen Taft-Morales, Connie Veillette, and M. Angeles Villarreal. 2007. *Latin America and the Caribbean: Issues for the 110th Congress.* CRS Report for Congress (January 23).

Surowiecki, James. 2004. *The Wisdom of Crowds: Why the Many Are Smarter Than the Few and How Collective Wisdom Shapes Business, Economics, Societies, and Nations.* New York: Doubleday.

Swan, James. 2007. "U.S. Policy in the Horn of Africa." Given at the 4th International Conference on Ethiopian Development Studies, Western Michigan University, Kalamazoo, MI (August 4). www.state.gov/p/af/rls/rm/90573.htm.

Sylvester, David A. 1994. "Clinton Move Upsets Some Bay Vietnamese." *San Francisco Chronicle* (February 4): A13.

Tarrow, Sidney. 1994. *Power in Movement.* Cambridge: University of Cambridge.

Tetreault, Steve. 2003. "Berkley Returns to Her Greek Roots." *Las Vegas Review-Journal* (May 31): 2B.

Thompson, Robert J., and Joseph R. Rudolph, Jr. 1987. "Irish-Americans in the American Foreign-Policy-Making Process." In *Ethnic Groups and U.S. Foreign Policy,* ed. Mohammed E. Ahrari. Westport, CT: Greenwood Press.

Tierney, John T. 1994. "Congressional Activism in Foreign Policy: Its Varied Forms and Stimuli." In *New Politics of American Foreign Policy.* ed. David A. Deese. New York: St. Martin's Press.

Tillotson, Kristin. 2004. "Immigrant Voters Shown How to Use New-Found Clout: Political Parties Are Courting New Communities." *Star Tribune* (November 1): 2B.

Tiron, Roxana. 2007. "'Comfort Women' Resolution to Reach Foreign Affairs Panel." *The Hill* (Washington, DC, June 20). http://thehill.com/business-lobby/comfort-women-resolution-to-reach-foreign-affairs-panel-2007-06-20.html.

Toner, Robin, and Katharine Q. Seelye. 2004. "Republicans Add Seats in South: Obama Wins." *New York Times* (November 3): A1.

TransAfrica Forum. 2007. "Our Mission." www.transafricaforum.org/mission.html (accessed March 19, 2007).

Trejos, Nancy. 2005. "An Old Social Tradition Produces Helping Hands; Somalis' Coffee Meetings Inspire an Association for Fellow Immigrants." *Washington Post, Prince George Extra* (October 6): T26.

Trice, Robert H. 1976. *Interest Groups and the Foreign Policy Process: U.S. Policy in the Middle East.* Beverly Hills: Sage Publications.

Truman, David B. 1951. *The Governmental Process.* New York: Knopf.

Uhlaner, Carole Jean. 1989. "Turnout in Recent American Presidential Elections." *Political Behavior* 11: 57–79.

Uhlaner, Carole J., Bruce E. Cain, and D. Roderick Kiewiet. 1989. "Political Participation of Ethnic Minorities in the 1980s." *Political Behavior* 11: 195–231.

United Jewish Communities. 2003. *The National Jewish Population Survey 2000–01: Strength, Challenge and Diversity in the American Jewish Population.* Available at www.ujc.org/local_includes/downloads/4606.pdf (accessed March 12, 2007).

US Census Bureau. 2000. Census 2000 Special Tabulations (STP-159). Table FBP-1. Profile of Selected Demographic and Social Characteristics: 2000. Population Universe: People Born in Eritrea.

USAID. 2007. "U.S. Overseas Loans and Grants." http://pdf.usaid.gov/pdf_docs/PNADF100.pdf (accessed March 14, 2007).

USINPAC. 2007a. "Issue Details: Terrorism and Homeland Security." www.usinpac.com/issue_details.asp?News_ID=3 (accessed August 13, 2007).

———. 2007b. "Mission Objective." www.usinpac.com/mission_objective.asp (accessed August 8, 2007).

Uslaner, Eric M. 1991. "A Tower of Babel on Foreign Policy?" In *Interest Group Politics,* 3rd ed., ed. Allan J. Cigler and Burdett A. Loomis. Washington, DC: CQ Press.

———. 2002. "Cracks in the Armor? Interest Groups and Foreign Policy." In *Interest Group Politics,* 6th ed., ed. Allan J. Cigler and Burdett A. Loomis. Washington, DC: CQ Press.

Verba, Sidney, Kay Lehman Schlozman, and Henry E. Brady. 1995. *Voice and Equality: Civic Voluntarism in American Politics.* Cambridge, MA: Harvard University Press.

Vitello, Paul. 2007. "Mayor Symbolizes Indian-Americans' Rise." *New York Times* (August 1): B1.

Walker, Jack. 1983. "The Origins and Maintenance of Interest Groups in America." *American Political Science Review* 77: 390–406.

Wallsten, Peter. 2000. "Rogan's Run: The GOP Fights for a Crucial Swing District." *CQ Weekly* (June 10): 1366.

Walt, Stephen M. 2005. *Taking American Power: The Global Response to U.S. Primacy.* New York: W. W. Norton.

Walters, Ronald W. 1987. "African-American Influence on U.S. Foreign Policy Toward South Africa." In *Ethnic Groups and U.S. Foreign Policy,* ed. Mohammed E. Ahrari. Westport, CT: Greenwood Press.

Washington PAC. 2007. "About the Washington PAC-Background." www.washington pac.com/The%20Pac.htm.

Watanabe, Paul Y. 1984. *Ethnic Groups, Congress, and American Foreign Policy: The Politics of the Turkish Arms Embargo.* Westport, CT: Greenwood Press.

———. 2002. "Asian-Americans and U.S.-Asia Relations." In *Ethnic Identity Groups and U.S. Foreign Policy,* ed. Thomas Ambrosio. Westport, CT: Praeger.

Weil, Martin. 1974. "Can the Blacks Do for Africa What the Jews Did for Israel?" *Foreign Policy* 15 (Summer 1974).

Weisman, Jonathan. 2005. "Administration Trying to Build CAFTA Majority Vote by Vote: Clash in House with Democrats Takes on Added Status." *Washington Post* (July 21): A4.

Weissman, Stephen R. 1995. *A Culture of Deference: Congress's Failure of Leadership in Foreign Policy.* New York: Basic Books.

Will, George F. 2001. "A War and Then a Wall." *Washington Post* (August 17): A23.

Williams, Sherri. 2006. "Somali, Latino Immigrants: Thousands of New Citizens Urged to Vote." *Columbus Dispatch* (October 2): 1A.

Wisby, Gary. 1994. "Viets Here Split on End of Embargo." *Chicago Sun-Times* (February 20): 28.

Woehrel, Steven. 2003. *Kosovo and U.S. Policy.* CRS Report for Congress (July 18).

———. 2006a. *Future of the Balkans and U.S. Policy Concerns.* CRS Report for Congress (January 18).

———. 2006b. *Ukraine: Current Issues and U.S. Policy.* CRS Report for Congress (August 23).

———. 2007. *Kosovo's Future Status and U.S. Policy.* CRS Report for Congress (July 12).

Woliver, Laura R. 1993. *From Outrage to Action.* Urbana: University of Illinois Press.

Wright, John R. 2003. *Interest Groups and Congress: Lobbying, Contributions, and Influence.* New York: Longman.

Index

grassroots organization, 157;
immigration, 20, 46, 117, 146–147,
187–188, 194; influence, 28–29, 138,
145–147, 173; political action
committees, 74, 85–86, 89;
population, 106–107, 109, 112;
resources, 120; trade, 19, 22, 146
Hispanic Democratic Organization PAC,
86
Hispanic PAC USA, 86
Hispanic Unity USA PAC, 74, 85
Hmong Americans, 38, 107, 115, 151,
194, 201
Hmong Veteran's Naturalization Act, 37
Hoagland, Richard, 144–145, 152–153,
209
Holocaust, 33, 114, 207
Honda, Rep. Mike, 117
Honduran Americans, 107, 188
Howard, James, 207
Human rights, 5, 18–19, 21, 188, 191
Human Rights Watch, 174
Hungarian-Americans, 34, 45
Hyde, Henry, 58 (n)

Immigration, 5, 7, 20, 22, 24, 117, 143,
146, 235; ethnic mobilization, 18
INC. *See* Irish National Caucus
India: Sikh minority, 18; tensions with
Pakistan, 114; US military ties, 19
Indian American Center for Political
Awareness, 57 (n)
Indian American Forum for Political
Education, 57 (n)
Indian American Friendship Council,
39
Indian Americans, 4, 20, 22, 37–38, 166,
184; assimilation, 130, 136; campaign
contributions, 19, 67–68, 149; foreign
policy, 17–18, 28–40, 149; Henry J.
Hyde US-India Peaceful Atomic
Energy Cooperation Act, 22, 39,
149–150; influence, 28, 39, 49, 138,
149–150, 198–199; issue salience,
113–115, 117–118, 155–156, 199;
military and security, 34, 188; political
action committees, 78, 86, 89;
population, 107, 111, 153; resources,
120, 122–123, 157; trade, 189
Individual rationality, 9
Inhofe, James, 208

Institutional organizations, 11–12;
influence, 183
Intermestic policies, 3–4, 6, 16, 21, 24
International Fund for Ireland, 58 (n)
International Monetary Fund, 173
International Red Cross, 174
Iran, 19–20, 236
Iranian Americans, 53, 118, 136
Iranian American PAC, 85, 90
Iran-Libya Sanctions Act of 1996, 196
Iraq, US war in, 53, 89, 156, 182, 185,
192, 201
Irish American Democrats, 42, 54, 74,
82, 157
Irish Americans, 16, 18, 20, 28, 209;
assimilation, 127; electoral strength,
142–143; foreign aid, 42, 58, 143;
immigration, 143, 146, 188; influence,
3, 49, 138, 142–143, 146, 152,
198–199, 210; issue salience, 117,
156, 199; MacBride Principles, 42,
143; Northern Ireland, 42–43, 127,
156; population, 103, 106–107, 109,
111, 153; reunification of Ireland, 42
Irish American Unity Conference, 42,
157
Irish National Caucus (INC), 42, 56, 97,
157, 201
Israeli American lobby, 8, 17–18,
20, 22, 28, 50, 136, 185; grassroots
organization, 157; influence, 3–4,
14–16, 136–141, 151, 192–194;
relation to Jewish American lobby,
48, 58 (n), 192, 207; political action
committees, 49, 67, 74, 78–80, 83,
89–93, 99
Israel-Lebanon conflict of 2006, 98, 118,
149, 236
Italian American Democratic Leadership
PAC, 74
Italian Americans, 35, 43, 128;
influence, 165–166; issue salience,
113, 156; population, 104, 106, 109,
111, 153

Japanese American Citizens League, 38,
55, 117
Japanese Americans, 38, 117–118, 127,
130, 166
JBANC. *See* Joint Baltic American
National Committee

About the Book

Dozens of ethnic groups work determinedly to achieve specific policy goals in Washington, but to what degree do they actually wield power? Which groups are the most influential, and why? David Paul and Rachel Anderson Paul consider the relative impact of thirty-eight ethnic lobbies to determine whether—and if so, how—they affect the course of US foreign policy.

Paul and Paul systematically examine the impact of ethnic group influence in six policy areas: aid, immigration, human rights, security, trade, and energy. They also compare the influence of ethnic lobbies with that of other actors, including business groups, the media, and foreign lobbyists. Challenging the conventional wisdom, the authors effectively draw on both qualitative and quantitative methods to shed needed light on this often heatedly contentious subject.

David M. Paul is the associate dean of student services and instruction at the Whidbey Island Campus of Skagit Valley College. **Rachel Anderson Paul** is visiting assistant professor at Western Washington University.